Contributions to Political Science

The book series offers an outlet for cutting-edge research in all areas of political science. Contributions to Political Science (CPS) welcomes theoretically sound and empirically robust monographs, edited volumes and handbooks from a variety of disciplines and approaches on topics such as political theory, comparative politics, democracy, European politics, electoral systems and voting behaviour, public policy and administration, political economy, and related fields.

All titles in this series are peer-reviewed. This book series is indexed in Scopus.

Ronald M. Glassman

The Great Global Transformation

Gender, Race, and Democracy in the Age of Capitalism

Springer

Ronald M. Glassman
New York, NY, USA

ISSN 2198-7289 ISSN 2198-7297 (electronic)
Contributions to Political Science
ISBN 978-3-031-90565-0 ISBN 978-3-031-90566-7 (eBook)
https://doi.org/10.1007/978-3-031-90566-7

This Springer imprint is published by the registered company Springer Nature Switzerland AG
The registered company address is: Gewerbestrasse 11, 6330 Cham, Switzerland

This book is dedicated to the millions of college-educated individuals, worldwide, who are creating a global culture based on national science and humanistic ethics.

Acknowledgments

This book, and all my books on Democracy, would never have seen the light of day without the support of Nico Stehr of Zeppelin University in Germany.

Nico encouraged my work, made learned suggestions for improving it, and helped to connect my work to Springer Publishers.

Nico did all this while publishing deep and meaningful works of his own.

I would also like to thank Niko Chtouris, editor at Springer, for recognizing the merit of my work and making useful suggestions to improve it.

And thank you to Karen Wilder, my editor, for her perfect organizing work and her masterful computer skills. Without her focused touches, there would be no books from me in this age of high technology publishing.

About the Book

Karl Polanyi's Vision: Free Market Capitalism and the Transformation of the World

In 1944, Karl Polanyi published his monumental work, *The Great Transformation*. Karl and his brother Michael were at the center of a remarkable group of intellectuals active in the organization called The Galileo Society, which met in Budapest. The group included Karl Mannheim, György Lukács, and other brilliant contributors.

However, the Polanyi brothers were not only Jewish, but also activist Marxists. They were forced to flee the Nazis in 1938. Karl took up residence in the United States, but he was persuaded by a group of British economic historians—including R.H. Tawney—to come to England and research the remarkable and unique emergence of capitalist market economics and industrial production that had occurred in England and Scotland before spreading to Western Europe, the United States, and the world.

Karl Polanyi emphasized the transformative power of the market, which he describes as altering the entire fabric of society as the various nation-states emerged into the modern world—the market, Polanyi emphasizes, did not just alter the economy, but also the culture of modern society.

The Fictional Commodities: Labor, Land, and Money

The transformation, according to Polanyi, was driven by three market factors. These three factors he calls the "fictional commodities" created by the market. The three fictional commodities are: labor, land, and money. All three altered dramatically by the market—labor from craft artisanship to alienated wage labor in machine-driven factories; land, from traditional feudal or village communal ownership, to private property bought, sold, and priced by market condition; and money from a medium of to exchange to "capital"—that is, the use of money to make more money through bank loans with interest charges and stock shares in large-scale business ventures.

In this treatise, we shall extend Polanyi's vision to the dramatic transformations occurring today. Polanyi was correct, however, to begin with the capitalist market, for it was the generator of transformations that would change the world.

Beyond Polanyi: The Modern Transformation of Gender, Sexuality, Race, and Religion

Polanyi was more than an economist. He believed that the capitalist market system had changed the very fabric of society. He was correct in this assessment. However, in 1944 it was not yet clear just how dramatic these changes would be.

What we will be focusing on in this treatise is, first, women's liberation—liberation from the family and then, the control over pregnancy. Then came the focus on female sexual pleasure. Then the main focus on women in the career world—in every profession from doctor to combat pilot in the military.

We will argue that women's liberation has had more of an effect in human society than the H-Bomb, which could wipe us out, of course, but has not been used as yet—though Putin keeps threatening to use nuclear weapons.

The family, marriage, the workplace, the bedroom—all have been dramatically changed by women's liberation. Of course, the effects vary from nation to nation, some nations changing, totally, others, changing far more slowly. We shall describe all of these.

With gay liberation becoming a world phenomenon, the very concept of "gender" has undergone a dramatic change—what is a man, what is a woman—how much is cultural, how much genetic?

LGBTQ rights have altered both social institutions and religious beliefs, forcing a re-definition of our basic institutions—such as marriage and family and traditional religion.

Again, we shall discuss the impact of LGBTQ rights and their variation from nation to nation. However, make no mistake about it, gay liberation is a world phenomenon.

Then there is race relations. The United States, of course, has had a Civil War. But that war to end slavery was overridden by the southern states' ability to overturn reconstruction, and re-impose a system of forced segregation. This segregation remained powerful in the South until the 1960s—one hundred years after the Civil War. And its influence spread to the North and Midwest as the frontier opened up the country and the capitalist-industrial revolution modernized the nation.

We shall discuss the United States in regard to race, of course, but, Africa and Asia and Latin America were opened up and became part of the world market economy, and the United Nations. So that after World War II, with colonialism declining and independent nations arising, racial issues emerged as problematical from south Africa to Mexico, and from Zimbabwe to Hong Kong, and from Algeria to France and more.

Race as a social, cultural, and biological phenomenon is now a world issue. The capitalist market opened up the world, and now the world's races and cultures have to deal with each other. Are biological factors significant in race, or is race a purely socially constructed phenomenon? What about mixed race individuals and mixed race societies?

We shall discuss "race" as we discuss "gender." That is, as a changing phenomenon, impacting world society.

And, along with race, "ethnicity" must be similarly analyzed in this new context of global awareness and global change.

Every cultural group is attached to its own ethnic culture. Ethnic intermarriage can be as contentious as racial intermarriage. And ethnic, cultural superiority and inferiority are a world issue.

So, the issue of ethnic culture, identity, and biology is similar to that of race, such that new and challenging ideas on "ethnicity" must be discussed as part of the great transformation of the global cultures.

Science and Religion: Beyond Economics Toward a New Worldview

In this treatise, we will analyze the ongoing changes in the modern belief systems, as the world's religions undergo the scrutiny of the new, college-educated, middle classes worldwide, and as comparative religion becomes part of the "Great Books" university sequence, which used to emphasize "Western Civilization" and the Judeo-Christian religion alone.

We shall also discuss science, as a new worldview, competing with the world's religions and clashing with them over certain ethical issues.

Both secular humanism and the rational-scientific worldview may form the basis for a new Hegelian zeitgeist, as human self-consciousness becomes ever heightened through social science and psychology and, as human self-actualization—"species being," as Marx called it—becomes more and more possible in this new world of work and achievement emerging with the advanced capitalist economies now grounded in computer technology, worldwide communications systems, automation, robotization, and artificial intelligence (AI).

Thus new economic systems are market based and capitalist in their financial structure, but they are science based on their technological development. And, it undergirds a massive alteration in every human social and political institution.

The Link Between Free Market Capitalism and Democracy: The Separation of the Economy from the Polity and Legal-Rational Legitimacy

Polanyi mentions in passing—barely mentions—that "popular government" arises from the capitalist market economy. Like most Marxists—and to the chagrin of his American hosts at Williams College and Columbia University—Polanyi clung to the Marxist vision of capitalist democracy being *oligarchy* in disguise. The rich capitalists rule, the workers have no power and no say, and the riches of society go to the capitalist class only.

Polanyi's American middle class hosts objected to this description and the rise of the new, expanding middle classes after World War II—worldwide—altered the picture in capitalist societies, such that the oligarchic over-influence within these societies was moderated enough so that these societies could be called democracies.

Of course, in today's world of the twenty-first century, the rise of tyranny and totalitarianism has become far more threatening to the existence of democracy than capitalist oligarchy.

In any case, and going far beyond Polanyi's weak comments on popular government, we shall analyze the modern transition to democracy—now existing in a "cyberworld," which we barely understand and cannot seem to control.

Are capitalism and democracy the "ends of history"? History never ends—unless we blow up the planet with nuclear weapons or destroy our atmosphere with carbon and other gaseous emissions.

Barring these catastrophes, we shall describe the link between free market capitalism and democracy, in terms of the rise of legal-rational authority, the separation of powers, and the encouragement of the rational-scientific worldview. The threats to democracy will also be discussed.

Contents

About the Author

Ronald M. Glassman has taught sociology at Queens College and Herbert Lehman College of the City University of New York, USA, Connecticut College, and William Paterson University of New Jersey, USA. He has also taught "great books" at New York University and Queens College. He holds a PhD in sociology from The New School for Social Research, New York, USA, where he studied under Arthur Vidich and Karl Meyer, an MA in psychology from Ohio State University, USA, and a BA from Queens College. Presently on hiatus from teaching, he continues writing scholarly books from his home in Manhattan's Upper West Side.

Part I
Karl Polanyi's Vision and Beyond

Chapter 1
Karl Polanyi's Vision: Free Market Capitalism and the Transformation of the World—Polanyi's Vision and its Shortcomings

In 1944, Karl Polanyi published his monumental work, *The Great Transformation*. Karl and his brother Michael were at the center of a remarkable group of intellectuals active in the organization called The Galileo Society, which met in Budapest. The group included Karl Mannheim, György Lukács, and other brilliant contributors.

However, the Polanyi brothers were not only Jewish but also activist Marxists. They were forced to flee the Nazis in 1938. Karl took up residence in the United States, but he was persuaded by a group of British economic historians—including R.H. Tawney—to come to England and research the remarkable and unique emergence of capitalist market economics and industrial production that had occurred in England and Scotland before spreading to Western Europe, the United States, and the world.

Karl Polanyi emphasized the transformative power of the market, which he describes as altering the entire fabric of society as the various nation-states emerged into the modern world—the market, Polanyi emphasizes, altered not just the economy but also the culture of modern society.

1.1 The Fictional Commodities: Labor, Land, and Money

The transformation, according to Polanyi, was driven by three market factors. He calls these three factors the "fictional commodities", which were created by the market. These three fictional commodities are labor, land, and money. All three were altered dramatically by the market—labor, from craft artisanship to alienated wage labor in machine-driven factories; land, from traditional feudal or village communal ownership to private property bought, sold, and priced by market conditions; and money, from a medium of to exchange to "capital"—that is, the use of

R. M. Glassman, *The Great Global Transformation*, Contributions to Political Science, https://doi.org/10.1007/978-3-031-90566-7_1

money to make more money through bank loans, with interest charges and stock shares in large-scale business ventures.

Let us look at labor, land and money more closely in order to understand why Polanyi believed they transformed the world when they were altered by market dynamics.

1.1.1 Labor as Wage Labor Connected with Machine-Factory Production

Trade capitalism had preceded industrial capitalism in Western Europe and Great Britain. Trade capitalism flourished as early as the Mesopotamian and Phoenician city-states approximately in 2000 BCE–500 BCE. Karl Polanyi would eventually edit a book on this early trade-capitalist phenomenon, entitled *Trade and Market in the Early Empires*.[1]

The market was not yet fully developed, and it was surrounded by the Great Empires of Egypt and Babylon, which often intervened economically and certainly dominated the city-states politically.

However, with the Greek city-states—600 BCE into the Roman era—a more fully developed trade-capitalist market emerged. The Greeks expanded coined money (derived from Lydia), established banking with set interest rates, and stepped up craft and cash-crop production to meet the growing demand.

But the Greeks had slaves, and they put their scientific technological energies into military development, not consumer production.

Similarly, centuries later, the Italian Renaissance city-states developed trade capitalism and banking and raised market dynamics to a higher level.

The Italians had no slaves, and the craftsman had organized into powerful guilds. The market was controlling more and more facets of economic life, but labor was still traditional—that is, labor was artisan labor—this work required great skill and expert training and was a source of great pride in the products produced. Labor was not alienated; labor was not a commodity yet.

The entire trade-capitalist system was transported to the German, Dutch, and Scandinavian city-states as Northern Europe experienced the Renaissance (and the Reformation).

In terms of labor, in Dutch and German city-states (the Hanseatic League and other leagues of city-states), the craft laborers were even more powerful than in Italy because the Dutch and German craft guilds were also the militias in their city-states. These craft-guild militias were well trained and fought heroically when called upon. There was no alienated labor in the Dutch and German city-states.

---

[1] Karl Polanyi, *Trade and Markets in the Early Empires*, New York, Free Press, 1952.

England and Scotland lacked a well-organized system of craft guilds. And the army of England was dominated by the monarchy—as in East Germany, France, and Spain.

When trade capitalism came to England and Scotland, it engendered a unique phenomenon called the enclosure movement. Lacking a strong craft industry, the English capitalists turned to the one product they had that Europe wanted—woolen clothing. To export woolen clothing production—still in craft mode—the financiers of London began buying up the land, evicting the peasants and keeping sheep. The conversion of land to sheep farming—the enclosure movement—destroyed the feudal peasant landholding system, evicting both the lords and the serfs from the land and converting the land to commercial use.

The evicted lords clustered at the King's Court in London and became quite decadent, losing the martial spirit of their knighthood forebears. As for the peasants, they became vagabonds and beggars, floating aimlessly in the countryside and gathering in lumpen proletariat slums in the cities.

Given the lack of craft guilds and the hordes of unemployed peasants, the emergence of machine-factory production with wage labor becomes possible. R.H. Tawney, in *Religion and the Rose of Capitalism*,[2] describes this in detail, and Friedrich Engels, before him, in *The Condition of the Working Class in England*,[3] bemoans the misery of the poorly paid factory workers. Max Weber writes in *The Protestant Ethic and the Spirit of Capitalism*[4] and Tawney dispute whether Calvinist Puritan Protestantism generated the capitalist industrial systems or was generated by it, but, Polanyi takes Tawney's description and updates it from the enclosure era into the modern world of industrial capitalism.

One fact is not controversial: labor did become a commodity—craft production and artisan skill, with pride in products, disappeared.

Wage labor became a commodity. The laborer could be replaced by a thousand others who needed a job—no skill required; they just needed to tend the machines as they showered forth the product. And the market dictated that the capitalist factory owner pay the laborer as little as he could to maximize his profit while barely paying enough to keep his factory laborers alive.

Of course, the union movement and the socialist and communist movements helped improve the condition of the factory laborers. But even today in 2020, giant capitalist corporations move their factory operations to those nations wherein labor is the cheapest and work ethic sufficient to prod them onto work while underpaid.

[RON ADD??]

Even with increasing automation, big corporations are moving to cheap labor. Automation may eliminate labor altogether—maybe—or create the need for new skilled labor—the "techi." This is occurring.

---

[2] R.H. Tawney, *Religion and the Rise of Capitalism*, London, Penguin Classics, 1955.

[3] Friedrich Engels, *The Condition of the Working Class in England*.

[4] Max Weber, *The Protestant Ethic and the Spirit of Capitalism*, NY, Random House, 1953.

1.1.2 Land as Private Property with Monetary Value

American Indians, as with most tribal people, had no conception of land alienation and land monetary value, or private property. When the Dutch, English, and French arrived in North America, they bought land, thinking the Indians were selling it. But the Indians had no conception of land as a commodity; they believed the Europeans were giving them gifts in return for temporary land usage.

Polanyi correctly describes how the traditional tribal, village, and monarchial view of land was dramatically altered by capitalist-market-oriented conceptions. In today's world, land in most regions is alienable and can be purchased for monetary value, determined by market dynamics—unless specifically designated as national park land or some other culturally and legally protected factor.

So land is now a commodity. Private property has replaced tribal, village, and monarchial community property. All across the globe, communal land has been converted into private property, whether for commercial use or personal use. This is a revolutionary transformation, as Polanyi emphasizes.

Today, as the market has spread worldwide, problems in land use have emerged due to the market orientation in land use. These include (1) the demand for land in big city centers and (2) the skyrocketing real estate prices due to the scarcity of land therein. Both residential real estate and commercial real estate in big cities have gone too high. The market—left to its own dynamics—has created a crisis in the world's big cities. The middle class and working class cannot afford housing, and small businesses cannot afford commercial space. Only giant corporations and the rich can afford urban land use.

From Tokyo to Paris to London to New York to San Francisco to Hong Kong, big-city real estate has become overpriced because of market dynamics. Therefore, in order to keep the middle classes and small businesses in cities—and this is necessary for a stable and vibrant society—rent control mechanisms of various sorts have become necessary. Pure capitalists oppose this, while democratic socialists demand this. The debate will continue into the latter part of the twenty-first century, but in any case, it is an issue emerging from the transformation of land into a commodity with monetary value, determined by supply and demand.

The second problem that has emerged worldwide, along with the real estate urban crisis, is that agricultural land use and production for the market have become problematic. Why? It is because—even with advanced mechanization of the farming process—fluctuations in climate (rainfall, insects, and plant diseases), fluctuations in demand, and global competition are so difficult to control or predict that farmers—even giant corporate farmers—must be subsidized by their national governments to survive. Market dynamics alone are not workable because farmers cannot be allowed to go out of business, or people will starve!

So worldwide nations—the EU, the USA, Russia, and China—subsidize their farmers; thus, globally, the market is supplemented by government subsidies.

However, agricultural land is being converted to private property throughout the world—small farmers and giant corporate farmers own land and use it to produce for the world and national markets.

1.1.3 Money as Capital

Money emerged as a medium of exchange: the means of exchange were, first, bars of precious metals, like gold, silver, and copper; then coins—invented in Lydia and later expanded by the Greeks—made of these same precious metals; then paper money, invented in China and then utilized in Europe; then checks; then plastic credit cards; and now digital forms of money.

But Polanyi emphasizes that with the emergence of capitalism in Great Britain and Western Europe, money became a commodity. That is, money was used to make more money; money became "capital"—something you could invest in order to make more money.

Money as capital goes all the way back to Mesopotamia, where the Sumerians and Babylonians established banking. The bankers made loans to merchant traders and charged interest. So the bankers did not just hold money safely, but they also made money on their loans. They could lose money as well.

In the Netherlands—first in Antwerp, which was Calvinist Protestant, and then in Amsterdam, when Antwerp was captured by Spanish-French monarchies and was forced back to Catholicism—the world's first stock market emerged. Individuals could buy shares in overseas trading ventures and make a share of the money if the venture was successful. Of course, they could also lose their money.

Polanyi emphasizes that through banking and the expansion of the stock market to all the world's capitals, the use of money to make more money has become a trillion-dollar industry in its own right. Banking and financial firms became heavily capitalized, and by investing in businesses, they not only make more money, but they sometimes control the direction of business expansion.

Thus, money as capital, not as a mere means of exchange, empowers the financial industry and is the foundation for industrial expansion and technological innovation—especially in the aggressive application of technological advances in the production process and in the products themselves.

Money as a medium of exchange may disappear into the cyberworld, wherein all transactions will be digitized. However, money as capital—which Polanyi calls a "fictitious" commodity—will continue to undergird the modern economy if it remains a market-driven economy. Of course, governments will intervene for nationalist reasons, but market-driven economies have proven to be more efficient and more innovative.

To sum up this topic, Polanyi correctly describes the prodigious transformation of the world due to market forces and their institutionalization in terms of labor, land, and money.

However, what Polanyi underemphasizes, in fact barely mentions and yet takes for granted, is that the Industrial Revolution—and the scientific and technological revolutions undergirding its possibility—transformed the world, along with the transformation of the capitalist market.

Like most Marxists and classical economists, Polanyi only links industrial production to capitalism because machine-factory production emerged under capitalist direction in England, Scotland, the USA, and the Netherlands.

However, they are not the same thing. Capitalism, as trade capitalism, existed long before the Industrial Revolution. And industrialism was generated in Russia and China without capitalism. The fact that Russian and Chinese industrialization was not efficient or innovative does not negate the fact that large-scale industrial production did occur without a capitalist component. Yes, capitalism makes industrial production more efficient and more innovative, but it also creates enormous disparities in wealth, and the development of scientific research can be independent of capitalist market forces as it is linked to universities and scientific organizations, which have become a global phenomenon.

So how is Polanyi's Great Transformation flawed?

First, it does not really describe the effects of industrialism in itself or the industrial advances through technological innovations. Second, it never discusses the role of science in creating possibilities for new technologies. And third, it barely discusses the form of government involved—assuming that a popular government somehow just emerges as part of market transformations.

Finally, Polanyi, writing in the 1940s and 1950s, could not foresee that the cultural transformations that the world would begin to go through extended beyond labor, land, and money and would encompass the family, marriage, race, and the culture of every nation in the world.

In this treatise, we shall extend Polanyi's vision to the dramatic transformations occurring today. Polanyi was correct, however, to begin with the capitalist market, for it was the generator of transformations that would change the world.

1.2 The Capitalist Revolution That Preceded the Industrial Revolution: The Invention of the Stock Market in Amsterdam in 1603

1.2.1 Max Weber, R.H. Tawney, and the Debate over the Causality of the Capitalist Revolution

Max Weber understood that a capitalist revolution occurred in the Calvinist-Protestant countries of the Netherlands, England, and Scotland—*before* the Industrial Revolution.

However, since in his book *The Protestant Ethic and the Spirit of Capitalism*[5] he emphasizes the influence of religion on capitalist development, the arguments become focused on whether religion “caused” the capitalist revolution or whether the capitalist revolution “caused” Calvinism to focus on moneymaking as a sign of heavenly grace.

R.H. Tawney, in his book *Religion and the Rise of Capitalism,*[6] favored economic causality, while Weber favored religious causality.

What was lost in this famous debate was the fact that a capitalist revolution had *preceded* the Industrial Revolution.

And while the Industrial Revolution occurred in England and Scotland in the 1700s, the capitalist revolution occurred in the Netherlands in the 1600s.

It was the invention of the stock exchange—the selling of shares in the Dutch East India Company—that generated a whole new level of capitalist development.

The stock exchange took capitalism beyond banks and interest-bearing loans to the generation of a whole set of financial institutions—from stock-offering companies to investment companies raising capital for new ventures.

These new financial institutions raised capitalism beyond the trade capitalism that preceded it.

The Italian city-states, especially Genoa, expanded and rationalized the banking system. But they never had a stock exchange. It was the stock exchange that took capitalism to a whole new level of financial expansion. Money, as capital, used for investment, now exploded in volume due to the selling of shares in expanding companies.

The stock market revolution first occurred in Amsterdam in 1603 and then spread to England, Scotland, and the USA.

Let us look more closely at the origins and expansion of the stock market.

1.2.2 The Origins of the Stock Market

In 2024, the stock exchange building in Copenhagen, Denmark, burned in an accidental fire.

The Danish Stock Exchange was established in 1625—very old!

But what was the earliest stock market?

The first actual stock exchange was established in Amsterdam in 1602. The Dutch East India Company needed money to finance its overseas venture to the Indonesian spice islands.

Trading in spices was exceedingly lucrative, but the Dutch Republic did not have the wealth of Spain or France to build the needed ships and pay the sailors and merchants involved in this new spice trade.

---

[5] Ibid.

[6] R.H. Tawney, *Religion and the Rise of Capitalism*, London, Penguin Classics, 1955.

So the Dutch East India Company was the first company to ever go public. They launched an initial public offering (IPO), where anybody could buy shares in the company.

The idea worked. Thousands of merchants, bankers, and guild masters bought shares in the company, and it successfully raised enough capital to fund its overseas ventures to the spice islands and beyond.

So successful was this idea of offering shares in the company to the public that other corporations followed suit. And the stock market became a major institution in the expanding trade capitalism of the Netherlands.

Dutch financiers crossed the Channel to London and helped the British establish a stock exchange there. Denmark followed suit, and between 1600 and 1700, many stock exchanges were established in Western Europe.

In 1792, a group of philanthropic financiers established the first American stock exchange. And then another group of financiers established what would become the world's largest and richest stock exchange: Wall Street in New York City, USA.

Now, just to keep the history accurate, it should be noted that in 1550, in the City of Antwerp, in what is now Belgium, there was a commodities exchange building called "The Bourse," in which commodities were priced, bought, and sold—especially craft goods and even diamonds.

The Bourse was not a stock exchange—no shares were offered to the public. But the idea of such a stock exchange was discussed by the Calvinist merchants of Antwerp.

However, before they could act on this, the Spanish invaded, took Antwerp under their control, reestablished Catholicism, and banned Calvinist Protestantism.

The result was that thousands of Dutch Calvinists and merchants fled Antwerp and went north to Amsterdam.

Thus, Amsterdam became the financial capital of the Low Countries and a model for England, Scotland, and Scandinavia. Eventually, even West Germany, in Frankfurt and Hamburg, began offering shares in their companies and trading ventures.

Max Weber made much of this, insisting that Calvinist Protestantism influenced the expansion of capitalism.[7]

Why? This was because the Calvinists believed that making money was a sign of heavenly grace—the more money you made, the more surely it was a sign that God was smiling on you.

This is a strange belief, but the Calvinists did believe it. Thus, they were motivated to make money in as creative way as they could.

So using money as capital to make more money was considered a brilliant idea. The Catholics frowned upon it and believed that money was corrupt and sinful. So they blocked capitalist development—Antwerp declined precipitously. But in Amsterdam, the Calvinists prevailed, flourished, and brought capitalism to a new level with the invention, and the institutionalization, of the stock exchange.

---

[7] Max Weber, *The Protestant Ethic and the Spirit of Capitalism*, NY, Random House, 1953.

And this brings us to our next point. Before the invention of the Industrial Revolution—machine-factory production—trade capitalism was raised to a new and revolutionary level.

The invention of the stock market and its institutionalization in the Netherlands, England, Scotland, Scandinavia, and West Germany lifted capitalism to a new level. It lifted capitalism beyond banking and bank loans at set interest rates and instituted capital markets with shares that could increase—or decrease—in value so that along with creating a dynamic new source of capital investment, it also introduced instability in capitalism.

Cycles of boom and bust, wild fluctuations in commodity prices, and fluctuations in the value of shares built uncertainty and instability into the system as never before.

There were always fluctuations in commodity value depending on trade successes or failures, but with the stock market came speculation and irrational exuberance, followed by panic and collapse.

The tulip crisis was the most famous of stock panics, wherein the price of tulips soared to enormous figures before collapsing to worthlessness.

Despite the boom and bust cycles, which the stock market introduced into capitalism, the use of a stock exchange to raise venture capitalism was so successful that the stock market became a central institution for capitalism as it developed into its modern form.

Let me emphasize that before the Industrial Revolution in England and Scotland in 1700–1800, a real capitalist revolution occurred in the Netherlands.

And just as the Dutch invented the "limited monarchy," which was then copied in England in 1688 by William of Orange—a Dutch Prince marrying Mary Tudor, heir to the British Throne—so did the Dutch invent the stock market, which was also copied in England (and later in America).

So capitalism is raised to a new level by stock market financing. Money was then used to make more money through the institutionalization of the stock exchange.

Having emphasized this capitalist revolution established by the institutionalization of the stock market, we shall go on to discuss the Industrial Revolution.

Polanyi links them together because in Great Britain, they did occur together. But actually, they are two different aspects of economic development.

So let us discuss industrialization further.

But first, let us add the expansion of the insurance industry as another important component of the financial revolution generated by the stock market.

1.2.3 The Expansion of the Insurance Industry as Part of the Capitalist Revolution

Along with the institutionalization of the stock exchange, the insurance industry exploded onto the financial scene. Again, as with the stock market, the modern form of the insurance industry took shape in Amsterdam in the 1600s and then spread to

England, where Lloyd's of London eventually became the world's leader in maritime insurance.

It was maritime insurance that first characterized the insurance industry as a whole. Then later in the 1800s, insurance expanded to cover factories, machines, and life. Life insurance would be the culmination of the insurance industry—expanding its reach to everyday citizens in capitalist industrial countries.

Now, maritime insurance (and caravan insurance) has been around since very ancient times. The cuneiform tablets of ancient Sumer and Babylon—dating back to over 2000 BC—explicitly describe both the rates and the risks of insuring trade-capitalist ventures.

Karl Polanyi, in his book *Trade and Markets in Early Empires*, touches upon this.[8] The Mesopotamians had the mathematics and the gold-based money supply to offer trade insurance, and they did so at a high premium—high because trading ventures were very risky.

As with so much else, the Greeks built upon the Mesopotamian calculations and offered their own maritime insurance. The Romans adapted the Greek calculus on trade insurance.

But it was definitely during the Italian Renaissance that the insurance industry was fully rationalized. In Genoa, where modern forms of banking had been established, modern forms of insurance were also pioneered.

The Genoese bankers and insurance brokers went north to the Netherlands and taught the Dutch both banking and insurance.

When the Dutch dramatically expanded their trade and established the Dutch East India Company and the Dutch West India Company and after they established the world's first stock exchange, they institutionalized maritime insurance on a large scale, following the Genoese model.

The British then copied the Dutch insurance companies, expanding insurance coverage to the industrial system, as well as a maritime trading system.

Eventually, the British insurance companies became the world's most famous companies. And in the nineteenth century, the Americans copied the British model, and a whole insurance industry emerged in the USA. New York, Philadelphia, and then Hartford became centers of the new insurance industry in the USA.

The insurance industry eventually raised so much capital that it became an integral part of the emerging financial industry, which paralleled the growth of industrial machine-factory productions.

So if we add the insurance capital to the capital raised by the stock market, we find an enormous capital market emerging. And this huge source could be used for an investment in new technology, advanced machinery, and expanded factories.

Thus, the financial institutions provided a massive source of investment capital to entrepreneurs seeking to upgrade their technology and produce more goods in a faster and more proficient way.

---

[8] Karl Polanyi, *Trade and Markets in the Early Empires*, New York, Free Press, 1952.

Karl Marx, in *Das Kapital*, emphasizes this fact and praises capitalism for its progressive improvement of technology and its expansion of scientific research in order to foster new technological advances.

Finally, Thorstein Veblen, in his *Theory of the Business Enterprise*[9] and *The Engineers and the Price System*, suggests that modern capitalism is driven by two groups of businessmen: "the captains of finance and the captains of industry."

Veblen mistakenly believed that the engineers could run modern industry without the captains of finance. He was wrong because the system needs financiers—not only to raise capital for investment but also to make sure that the industry runs efficiently and produces a profit. It turns out that factories run by the government became inefficient and unprofitable. We shall discuss this shortly.

To conclude, the invention of the stock market in Amsterdam in 1603 raised the capitalist revolution to a new level beyond "trade capitalism." And the expansion of the insurance industry created a financial sector of the modern economy that generated capital for investment at an unprecedented level.

1.2.4 Did Immigration Into Amsterdam Generate the Stock Market?

The debate between Weber and Tawney as to the origins of modern capitalism received an interesting update in 1972 with the publication of H.R. Trevor-Roper's book *Religion, the Reformation and Social Change*.[10]

Trevor-Roper postulated that mass immigration into Amsterdam after the Spanish-French Catholic invasion of the Low Country "caused" capitalism to surge to a new level. This new level included the invention and institutionalization of the stock market.

Trevor-Roper focused on four groups of immigrants: (1) Flemish Calvinists; (2) Portuguese and Spanish Jews; (3) Germans from Arzberg in South Germany; and (4) Italians from the northern Italian city-states.

Let us look at each of these groups.

Flemish Calvinists

Trade capitalism had reached a high level of development already in Flanders. Flanders was part of the Dutch coalitions of city-states that declared independence from French and Spanish incursions.

As mentioned, in Antwerp, trade capitalism and some glimmerings of a predecessor to the stock market had already occurred.

But before any further development of capitalism could occur in the many Flemish cities, the Spanish invaded. The Spanish King Philip, who was of Dutch

---

[9] Thorstein Veblen in his *Theory of the Business Enterprise.*

[10] H.R. Trevor-Roper, *Religion, the Reformation and Social Change*, 1972, London, Macmillan.

descent, was determined to re-Catholicize Flanders—wherein the Dutch Flemmings had converted to Calvinism in great numbers—and reassert his kingly control.

Though the Dutch coalition led by the Hollanders (generated by the Dutch Duke of Orange) won, the Flemish Dutch lost after a series of brutal battles.

With re-*Catholicization* carried out aggressively by the Spanish King Philip, thousands of Flemish Calvinists fled north to Amsterdam.

Now, there is no doubt that these thousands of new Dutch Calvinist immigrants had a profound effect on the development of capitalism in Amsterdam.

But here, Trevor-Roper is bolstering Weber's thesis. It was these fanatic Calvinists, already a majority in Amsterdam, who conceived the unique idea that making money was a sign of heavenly grace.

We have already discussed this strange theological phenomenon, which typifies Calvinism and is rejected by Catholicism, wherein moneymaking was considered gross and almost sinful—"Jesus pushed the moneychangers out of the Temple of Jerusalem!" In Calvinism, God rewards those who make money with heavenly grace.

So, yes, it was the immigrants from Flanders who helped generate the stock market because giving many people a "share" in the overseas trade gave them the potentiality of making money and going to heaven.

And I would add to the Calvinist origins of the stock market in Amsterdam the Dutch tribal holdovers, wherein gaining a share in overseas ventures was an extension of sharing in water projects, which allowed the Low Lands to utilize agriculture successfully.

So with the influence of the Flemish-Dutch Calvinists, who fled to Amsterdam by the thousands, I completely agree with Trevor-Roper that they were a critical factor in the origin of the stock market and the evolution of modern capitalism.

Portuguese and Spanish Jews: The Jews of Lisbon and Sevilla

His thesis was rejected by most scholars—and I shall explain why. However, Trevor-Roper revived the theory asserting that the Jews exerted a dramatic influence on the economy of Amsterdam.

Let us look at this.

In Iberia, the Jews—who had lived there for centuries—were caught between the Muslims and the Christians. Unable to own land or hold political positions, the Jews entered craft professions like glassmaking, jewelry making, and medicine, along with banking and finance.

Because the Spanish Catholics rejected money handling of any kind, and the Muslims also denigrated merchants and bankers, the Jews came to excel in banking, lending, and business transactions.

The Jews became prosperous in Iberia because the Catholics and Muslims forced them into finance and business.

Thus, though Queen Isabella allowed Columbus to sail to the New World, it was Luis de Santángel,[11] a Jewish banker, who actually funded Columbus' voyage.

---

[11] Luis de Santángel of Spain. Wikipedia: He convinced Queen Isabella to fund Christopher Columbus's expedition, and provided a large sum of money himself. He was a Valencian Banker

Once the Spanish Catholic reconquest of Spain was complete, with the battle of Granada in 1492 ending centuries of Muslim rule in Spain, not only did Columbus set sail, but situations of the Jews of Spain and Portugal also came into jeopardy.

Ferdinand and Isabella, along with the Portuguese King, united their countries by way of the Catholic Church. Catholicism, backed strongly by Rome, was the binding force in the otherwise fractious Iberian kingdoms.

All Iberians had to swear allegiance to the Roman Catholic Church or else die or be expelled.

The Inquisition—notorious for burning people alive—descended on the Jews. Either they converted, or they died—burned at the stake. Many converted, while others chose to die, but in the end, the Spaniards did not trust the Jews who converted, insisting that they secretly kept Jewish rituals and beliefs.

Thus, as Columbus sailed, the Jews of Spain and Portugal were expelled from Iberia en masse.

The Turkish King invited thousands of Jews to come to Istanbul and Thessaloniki, and there they were well received, which was ironic because the Turks did not trust the Greeks, who filled the positions that the Jews were to occupy. I shall have more to say about the Turkish Jews shortly.

Other Jews went—and this is really ironic—to Italy, especially Venice. Others went to Germany and France while some to North Africa, and a large community arrived in Amsterdam.

Now, we have pointed out that the Jews of Iberia were bankers, financiers, businessmen, and craftsmen. So they surely would fit in with the Calvinist Dutch, who were actively competing in the new capitalist processes.

And this they did. Of course, they used their banking and business skills in the expressly overseas trading economy of the Netherlands. And, of course, they brought their craft skills, especially glassmaking, diamond cutting, and jewelry making, to the Dutch economy.

Furthermore, they bought shares in the Dutch East India Company and in the Dutch West India Company. Jewish bankers and businessmen eventually joined the Dutch West India Company and went to the New World, living in the Dutch Islands of the Caribbean and in New Amsterdam.

Alexander Hamilton, the son of a Danish woman, had a Jewish stepfather in St. Croix, and he learned trade finance, banking practices, and the stock market share system under his stepfamily's tutelage.

The Calvinist Dutch of New Amsterdam brought with them a whole group of Spanish Jews. Peter Stuyvesant, the Governor of New Amsterdam, worked to expel the Jews, but the community stood up for them, and they stayed.

So is Trevor-Roper correct? Did the Jews of Lisbon and Sevilla help generate modern capitalism?

The answer is that the Iberian Jews expanded and enriched the emerging economy of the Dutch. They actively engaged in the banking and financing of overseas

---

of Jewish origin.

trade; they bought shares in Dutch trading companies, thus expanding their capital; and they improved capital production, especially in glass and jewelry making.

But the Jews did *not* innovate—they did not innovate the stock market; they did not invent the more modern banking and accounting systems.

How do we know this? It is because the Jews of Istanbul and Thessaloniki—with the same background and skills—did not introduce modern capitalism to Turkey. There was no stock market in Istanbul and no modern accounting methods.

Yes, there was an expansion of banking and craft production, but the Jews of Spain *alone* did not generate modern capitalism. Trevor-Roper is correct that the Jews participated in and expanded the modern capitalism that emerged in the Netherlands. But this still leaves the Dutch Calvinists as the main causal sequencers.

Italians from the Northern Italian City-States

I have mentioned that the Jews were bankers and financiers in Spain and Portugal, but they did not bring advanced banking and accounting techniques to Amsterdam. It was the Italians of the northern Italian city-states who generated new banking and accounting techniques, which would be incorporated into modern capitalism by the Dutch and English.

How do we know this? Again, it is because the Jews of Salonika and Istanbul did *not* innovate in the banking or accounting sphere. Furthermore, we know that the Italian immigrants to Amsterdam brought with them the new banking and accounting techniques. These new, more rationalized systems of banking and accounting were originally generated in Genoa and then copied in most of the northern Italian city-states.

These Italian-originated capitalist procedures were adopted by the Dutch and then later copied by the British. So not only did the British, English, and Scots adopt the stock market, but they also embraced the new banking and accounting systems. And it is important to assert that the English and the Scots also adopted Calvinism!

Thus, Trevor-Roper's notion that immigration generated modern capitalism and the stock market is correct but, in my view, also misleading. This is because even though the Jews and Italians contributed to the explosion of new ideas in the economic sphere, it was the Flemish and Hollander Dutch Calvinists who innovated the system of "shares," which generated the stock market.

Germans from Arzberg, South Germany

Trevor-Roper also mentions that after the "Peace of Arzberg," thousands of South German Calvinists fled to Amsterdam, as well as to England, because the Peace Treaty of Arzberg established that only Lutheranism and Catholicism would be recognized in Germany. Each local King decided which religion to establish, but Calvinism and Anabaptism were excluded completely.

The Anabaptists fled to Holland and England, and some ended up later on the frontiers of the USA. Many Calvinists fled to Amsterdam, where Calvinism was welcome and dominant as the Dutch religion.

The deep commitment to Calvinism by these immigrant Germans certainly expanded the theological influence of Calvinism in every sphere of life, including the economic sphere. Trevor-Roper therefore credits these Germans with having influenced the economic development of modern capitalism and the stock market. This also reinforces Weber's thesis on the centrality of Calvinism in the emergence of modern capitalism.

It seems to me, however, that the influence of the Calvinists from Flanders was more decisive. Why?

It is because the Flemish-Dutch-Calvinists were already innovating modern capitalist institutions in their city-states so that when they convened in Amsterdam, their Dutch innovations were quickly established and expanded upon.

Amsterdam replaced Antwerp as the new center of capitalist development, and the first stock exchange was soon invented, expanded, and eventually transplanted to England and New Amsterdam. When Alexander Hamilton established the First National Bank of the newly independent United States of America, there was already a stock exchange in New York, which, of course, was formerly New Amsterdam.

1.2.5 Max Weber's Commentary on the Stock Market

Max Weber understood that the institutionalization of the stock market was one of the key factors in the generation of modern capitalism. Remember, this occurred *before* the invention of the industrial factory system. As we have been describing, the stock market was invented in Amsterdam before the Industrial Revolution occurred in England and Scotland.

Weber's analysis of the stock market has been preserved for us by Walter Garrison Runciman in his edited book *Selections in Translation*.[12]

Here are some of Weber's insights.

To begin with, Weber emphasizes the fact that modern capitalism is part of a trend toward the "rationalization" of society. Weber focuses on the stock market's role in facilitating both large-scale investment and speculation.

Weber sees large-scale investment and speculation as part of the "spirit of capitalism"—and indeed, both these processes are characteristic of capitalism.

Weber views the stock market as a highly rationalized system, wherein decisions are based on calculated risk and economic analysis rather than personal recommendations or tradition.

Now, Weber is correct that both risk and analysis are carefully calculated and are rationally arrived at.

The problem with this analysis is that over the years, "irrational exuberance," a term popularized by Alan Greenspan[13] in twentieth-century America, characterized stock market transactions.

---

[12] W.G. Runciman, Editor, *Selections in Translation from Max Weber*, 1978. Translated by E. Mathews, Chapter 21, p. 370.

[13] Alan Greenspan was a federal reserve board chairman and influential Wall Street financier during and before the George W. Bush presidency. He popularized the phrase "irrational exuberance" after

Though Weber died before the Great Depression of 1929 and its massive stock market crash, he should have known that the stock market, since its inception in Amsterdam, has generated many cycles of boom and bust.

Weber must have known that the "tulip mania," wherein the price of tulips rose from a few pennies to thousands of dollars each, caused panic and a crash.

Thorstein Veblen, in *The Theory of Business Enterprise*[14] and *The Engineers and the Price System*,[15] described the economic process of boom and bust that was generated by the stock market's "irrational exuberance."

It seems that the rational process of long-term economic calculation is joined by the irrational process of getting caught up in the economically trendy activity of the moment.

So Weber is correct that the stock market does lead to rational calculation through risk and growth. But he is so wrong about ignoring irrational psychological human processes that destabilize the capitalist economy.

Modern capitalism is still characterized by both the rationalized processes and the irrational psychological processes of investment.

I must add here that from the 1980s onward, the control and correction and governmental bailouts of the crashed stock market are becoming better understood and undertaken. Thus, the crashes—the "busts" of the twentieth and twenty-first centuries—will be stabilized by intelligent government actions—as they were during the Obama administration—by a joint group of Republican and Democratic economic experts.

Still, the specter of boom and bust cycles haunts the stock market of the twenty-first century.

Now, let us look at one of Weber's worries about the stock market for it, too, still exists as a flaw in modern capitalism. We refer to uneven wealth distribution, which can lead to an *oligarchic* destabilization of democracy.

Weber noted that the social impact of the stock market could lead to "significant wealth concentrations and social inequality."

The stock market does lead to significant wealth concentrations because those with wealth invest it in long-term stock programs and bonds. Since the market grows over time—even with boom and bust destabilizations—the long-term effect is to increase the wealth of the wealthy.

A billionaire stratum emerges, and, of course, its political and social influences grow with its wealth.

Now, because of modern pension funds, such as 401 K in America, the middle class does benefit from the stock market. The upper middle class—worldwide—especially benefits from stock market pensions and stock market growth.

---

the stock market crash and the end of the W. Bush presidency. A successful bailout by the government at the beginning of the Obama administration put the American economy back on a stable footing.

[14] Thorstein Veblen, *The Theory of Business Enterprise, New Brunswick, New Jersey: Transaction Books, 1904.*

[15] Thorstein Veblen, *The Engineers and the Price System,* Benjamin W. Huebsch, Inc., 1921.

The problem is that the working class and the poor are not invested in the stock market. They gain nothing from it. Therefore, the working class, globally, feels left out of the economic growth cycles that beef up the wealth of the wealthy and the middle class.

The investment of union pensions into the stock market can help. But the emergence of a global billionaire class in all modern capitalist societies is problematic. At Donald Trump's inauguration in January of 2025, a group of tech billionaires sat in front of the Cabinet and Congress.

In fairness to Weber, seeing that capitalism was the most productive and innovative economy in the world and that it engendered a dangerous level of wealth concentration and social inequality, he said that the solution was to strongly back capitalism in the economy and to join with the social democrats in the polity in order to correct the excesses of capitalism in terms of inequality.

I will leave our analysis of the stock market with this advice from Max Weber.

1.3 The Industrial Revolution: Enmeshed with the Market yet Independent of the Market

The Industrial Revolution emerged in England and Scotland during the era of the commercialization of land—the enclosure movement—for sheep farming and woolen clothing production.

Lacking a strong artisan tradition and the powerful guilds that protected them, the labor force in England and Scotland was easily converted to wage labor—at very low wages. And the idea of producing goods with machines was not resisted by craft guilds—as it was in the Netherlands and West Germany.

Businessmen—the capitalist "gentry" of the woolen-producing countryside—invented machine-factory production early on, with Adam Smith describing the famous pin factory already in 1776 in *The Wealth of Nations*.[16]

Along with the pin factory, textile weaving machines were improved and adapted for the factory manufacturing of woolen cloth. With no craft guilds to impede them and with a few skilled craftsmen, the English and Scottish trade capitalists began applying machine technology to an expanding number of product lines. Even mining became mechanized as capitalist mineowners utilized steam engines to run up and down iron tracks to help extract coal and metal ore from the mines.

Max Weber has shown in his *Protestant Ethic and Spirit of Capitalism* that even though the Greeks and Chinese had invented the steam engine and had working models of it (because the Greeks had slaves—as war captives—and the Chinese had huge peasant conscript-labor teams), neither of them cared to utilize the steam engine for mining, manufacturing, or anything else fundamental to the economy.

---

[16]Adam Smith, *The Wealth of Nations*, NY, Amazon, 2012.

In Great Britain, where slavery was prohibited by Puritan Protestantism and the feudal peasantry had been displaced by the enclosure movement, the use of machines for mining and economic production became a possibility. And, of course, when it was discovered that machine-factory production could outproduce craft production, it was expanded to every aspect of the economy to which it could be adopted.

Machine-factory production became a sensation in England and Scotland, for, as Adam Smith had reported, the pin factory could produce one hundred times the amount of pins a craftsman could. And, as Adam Smith also described, the workers tasked with tending the machines in the factories could be paid low wages because the work was not skilled craftwork, and since thousands of British peasants had been displaced from their land, they would take any work they could to feed their families. In fact, the families—the women and children—were often also employed alongside the men—and paid even less.

Aside from the fact that conditions were terrible for the workers in these early factories (the air quality was dangerous, and the machines were dangerous to be near), the profit to be gained for capitalist factory owners were enormous—so enormous that these owners became like engineers or hired men with such technological skill, such that they kept inventing and applying newer and better machines to the factory system, thus increasing their productivity and, eventually after the initial investment was paid off, their profits.

In this way, the Industrial Revolution exploded onto the economic scene in Great Britain. It then spread to North American colonies and then to the Netherlands, Belgium, Germany, France, and northern Italy.

So the Industrial Revolution was intimately linked with capitalist market production as it emerged for the first time in Great Britain, the USA, and western Europe. Polanyi describes this well, as do Weber and Tawney, though the latter two disagree on the role that the Puritan Protestant religion played in the origins of industrial capitalism.

Industrialism, and I wish to emphasize this, also presupposes a highly developed system of scientific theorizing, experimentation, and expanding knowledge. The rational-scientific worldview and the industrial factory organizations had provided the basis for the technological innovations that supported the possibility for machine production.

When Galileo's notebooks were smuggled out of Italy, following Galileo's condemnation by the Roman Catholic Church, they became a sensation—first in Paris, where circles of scientists from all over Europe gathered to study them and debate on them, and then from Paris to the Dutch cities of Belgium and the Netherlands and then onto Germany and Great Britain.

French, Dutch, German, and British scientists expanded Galileo's groundbreaking work in astronomy, mathematics, and physics and then developed whole new scientific disciplines, such as chemistry, biology, and physiology. Breakthroughs in mathematics and all other scientific disciplines engendered a scientific revolution that is still ongoing and that has revolutionized human existence: we are traveling in space, flying around the globe, curing diseases, and making military weapons, so powerful that we are in danger of destroying ourselves, our atmosphere, and our planet itself.

1.3.1 Greek Science

The scientific revolution can be dated back to ancient Greece. Ancient Greek historians credit Thales of Miletus as the founder of rational-scientific thought.

Significantly, Thales is supposed to have traveled to Egypt, where he learned geometry, and then to Babylon, where he learned astronomy. Both civilizations also had creation myths, which differed but similarly involved water, air, earth, and fire.

For a history of Greek science, see John Burnet's *Early Greek Philosophy*.[17] Thales focused on water as the primary substance out of which all other matter is made, and he encouraged experimentation on water, including the formation of ice—a solid—and water vapor—a gas. He also encouraged his students to prove him wrong and to experiment with air, earth, and fire.

Eventually, the Milesian School of Science produced the theory that tiny particles—atoms—when grouped in different ways, were the primary substance. Leucippus of Miletus taught this atomic theory to Democritus, who resided in Athens, and Democritus expanded upon it and made it fundamental to scientific inquiry (as it emerged in the modern world).

After Thales, Pythagoras made mathematics the key to understanding the universe, and later in the Hellenistic era, Aristarchus and Ptolemy debated over the nature of the solar system—Aristarchus theorized that it was sun centered, while Ptolemy hypothesized it was earth centered. Centuries later, Copernicus and Galileo proved that Aristarchus had been correct.

In the same era as Ptolemy, Galen gathered the books of physiology from the Egyptian sources to the Greek improvements and wrote the definitive book on physiology which influenced medicine for centuries.

With the decline of the Roman Empire came the decline of the rational-scientific worldview. Christianity won the day, and though it added Judeo-Christian ethics to the Roman Empire—and thus morality was sorely needed—Christianity overrode the rational-scientific worldview and caused the schools of science and philosophy, which had existed throughout the Hellenic and Hellenistic eras, to close down.

It was not until the Arabic Golden Age that Greek science and philosophy were revived. Muslim thinkers, such as Avicenna and Averroes, and the Jewish Maimonides revived Aristotle, Galen, Ptolemy, Plato, and other Greek rational thinking.

[17] John Burnet, *Early Greek Philosophy*, Google Books, 2000.

1.3.2 The Arabic Golden Age and Renaissance Italy

From the Arabic Golden Age to the Italian Renaissance, Greek science and philosophy were revived. Thomas Aquinas and a circle of Roman Catholic thinkers—influenced by Averroes—deemed Aristotle and all other Greek scientists as acceptable to the Christian Church. From Aquinas to Copernicus and Galileo, the Roman Catholic Church was a friend to and sponsor of the revival of Greek and Roman science (and the incorporation of Arabic improvements in Mathematics—Indian numerals, algebra, and medical advances were incorporated into physiology).

In Galileo's old age, the Roman Catholic Church turned on science, rejecting Copernicus' and Galileo's work as heretical.

1.3.3 The Scientific Revolution and Machine Technology

This scientific revolution was necessary as a precondition for machine-factory production. Of course, as the Marxist and capitalist economists agree, the capitalists, because of their desire for profit, invented the Industrial Revolution—and it functioned on market principles in its inception and expansion. Ironically, Marx describes it best in *Capital*,[18] where he praises the capitalists for investing in new technologies, new machines, larger factories, and more productive enterprises. Of course, he curses the capitalists for their miserly wage payments and their selfish accumulation of profits.

The linking of industrial production to capitalist entrepreneurs—whom Veblen called "the captains of industry"[19]—was accepted by all economists of every ideological stripe. And this was correct until the Russian Revolution.

Since Russia had few entrepreneurs, Lenin and Communist Party intellectuals decided to create an Industrial Revolution using scientists, engineers, and factory managers directed by the Communist Party itself. The Russian communists knew that they would need scientists and engineers, as well as factory managers. Therefore, they created an excellent school system and university system based on the German model. Science and mathematics were emphasized. And even though communist propaganda held them back in some scientific fields, most were allowed free development.

The Russians succeeded in creating an excellent group of well-trained scientists and engineers. They attempted to run industrial factories not on the market principles of supply and demand, profit, pricing, banking, and stock shares but rather on government-directed demand principles. "The government" orders you to produce such an amount of guns, winter coats, tanks, can openers, or anything else.

---

[18] Karl Marx, *Capital*, International Publishers, 1948.

[19] Thorstein Veblen, *The Theory of Business Enterprise*, NY, Collier Books, 1949.

The factory systems directed by the Russian Communist Party did work. It produced everything the government wanted—but inefficiently and with little creative innovations. Further, military goods were made well, but consumer goods were made poorly.

The economy ran by the Russian Communist Party showed the world that industrial production could be accomplished without capitalism—no market, no banking, or no stock market financing. However, it also showed the world that government-run factories are inefficient and that all but military weaponry might be manufactured with poor quality.

When a similar set of productive events occurred in China, after the Communist Revolution there, the flaws in government-directed industrial production became evident.

Nevertheless, machine-factory production—industrialization—can exist without the capitalist market.

The reason I am emphasizing this fact is that in today's twenty-first century world, scientific and technological revolutions are expanding dramatically on their own. Yes, capitalist entrepreneurs are still applying technological advances to the productive process and the products produced—the new products are produced perfectly and efficiently. These capitalists are astonishing in their creativity in this technology-driven, advanced industrial economy, which is now a global phenomenon.

Because science and technology are developing so rapidly, we must look at them separately from the industrial system to see what transformations they are engendering in the new globally connected world.

Therefore, in this treatise, we will analyze the industrial factory system as it is evolving—such innovations as automations, computerization, robotism, and artificial intelligence (AI) will be described. But, obviously, none of these processes could be applied to the industrial process if scientists and engineers have not invented them. Therefore, the science and engineering behind these changes should be separately analyzed. And it is my view that they are engendering a transformative effect on society in their own right, impacting our cultural values and social interactions beyond the economic sphere. I will make this explicit in the text of this treatise.

Chapter 2
Beyond Polanyi

2.1 The Modern Transformation of Gender, Sexuality, Race, and Religion

Polanyi was more than an economist. He believed that the capitalist market system had changed the very fabric of society. He was correct in this assessment. However, in 1944, it was not yet clear just how dramatic these changes would be.

It was during the 1960s and 1970s that basic core changes in the culture began to take hold. These changes had been prefigured earlier, especially from the 1890s to World War I. But the two world wars temporarily impeded the social changes or took our attention away from what was happening. The wars actually motivated women and blacks to demand change, but their demands were muted during the wars.

What we will be focusing on in this treatise is, first, women's liberation—liberation from the family and, then, control over pregnancy. Then comes the focus on female sexual pleasure, then the main focus on women in the career world—in every profession from doctor to combat pilot in the military.

We will argue that women's liberation has had more of an effect on human society than the H-bomb, which could wipe us out, of course, but has not been used as yet (though Putin keeps threatening to use nuclear weapons).

The family, marriage, the workplace, the bedroom—all have been dramatically changed by women's liberation. Of course, the effects vary from nation to nation, with some nations changing totally while others changing far more slowly. We shall describe all of these.

With gay liberation becoming a world phenomenon, the very concept of "gender" has undergone a dramatic change—what is a man; what is a woman? How much is cultural; how much is genetic?

R. M. Glassman, *The Great Global Transformation*, Contributions to Political Science, https://doi.org/10.1007/978-3-031-90566-7_2

LGBTQ rights have altered both social institutions and religious beliefs, forcing a redefinition of our basic institutions, such as marriage and family and traditional religion.

Again, we shall discuss the impact of LGBTQ rights and their variation from nation to nation. However, make no mistake about it—gay liberation is a world phenomenon.

Then there is race relations. The United States, of course, has had a Civil War. But that war to end slavery was overridden by the southern states' ability to overturn reconstruction and reimpose a system of forced segregation. This segregation remained powerful in the South until the 1960s—100 years after the Civil War. And its influence spread to the North and Midwest as the frontier opened up the country and the capitalist Industrial Revolution modernized the nation.

We shall discuss the United States in regard to race, of course, but Africa, Asia, and Latin America were opened up and became part of the world market economy and the United Nations, so that after World War II, with colonialism declining and independent nations arising, racial issues emerged as problematical, from South Africa to Mexico, from Zimbabwe to Hong Kong, from Algeria to France, and more.

Race as a social, cultural, and biological phenomenon is now a world issue. The capitalist market opened up the world, and now the world's races and cultures have to deal with each other. Are biological factors significant in race, or is race a purely socially constructed phenomenon? What about mixed-race individuals and mixed-race societies?

We shall discuss "race" as we discuss "gender"—that is, as a changing phenomenon impacting world society.

And along with race, "ethnicity" must be similarly analyzed in this new context of global awareness and global change.

Every cultural group is attached to its own ethnic culture. Ethnic intermarriage can be as contentious as racial intermarriage. And ethnic, cultural superiority and inferiority are world issues.

Hungary's would-be dictator, *Viktor Orban*, says about George Soros: one cannot be a Hungarian Jew; one is either a Hungarian or a Jew. He makes a forceful case for "Magyar"—Hungarian culture and genetics—as opposed to the Jews, who moved into Hungary from the Austrian Empire. And further, he distinguishes Magyars from Syrian "Arabs," who flooded across Hungary as they ran from Syria to try to gain entrance to Germany.

The Chinese in both Tibet and Uyghur province have attempted to stamp out not only the Tibetan or Uyghur cultures but also their religions—Buddhism and Islam. And biologically, they have moved "Han" Chinese into these regions in such great numbers as to eventually overwhelm the ethnic groups, biologically, as well as culturally and religiously.

So the issue of ethnic culture, identity, and biology is similar to that of race, such that new and challenging ideas on "ethnicity" must be discussed as part of the great transformation of global cultures.

2.2 Science and Religion: Beyond Economics Toward a New Worldview

Here, I invoke Hegel rather than Polanyi. Hegel, in his *Philosophy of History*,[1] saw the progressive development of humankind in the stages of religious sophistication and in the rise of rational science.

From the fear of nature and the worship of nature gods and goddesses to Judaism and Christianity, with their anthropomorphic god and ethnical code, to Greek rational science, Hegel saw a progressive development of humans—a growing self-consciousness, which led to great leaps of human development—to domination over nature rather than fear of nature.

Hegel's highest stage of development for humankind is modern science and German Protestantism, in which *rationality* in thought and individualism in self-fulfillment are emphasized. Hegel believed that modern science and the Protestant religion were the final and most progressive worldview—the new "zeitgeist" for modern man.

Of course, history never ends even though Hegel and his disciple Marx projected their hopeful views on humankind's future.

In this treatise, we will analyze the ongoing changes in modern belief systems as the world's religions undergo the scrutiny of new, college-educated, middle classes worldwide and as comparative religion becomes part of the "Great Books" university sequence, which used to emphasize "Western Civilization" and the Judeo-Christian religion alone.

We shall also discuss science as a new worldview, competing with the world's religions and clashing with them over certain ethical issues.

Both secular humanism and the rational-scientific worldview may form the basis for a new Hegelian zeitgeist as human self-consciousness becomes ever heightened through social science and psychology and as human self-actualization—"species being," as Marx called it—becomes more and more possible in this new world of work and achievement, emerging with the advanced capitalist economies now grounded in computer technology, worldwide communications systems, automation, robotization, and artificial intelligence (AI).

Thus, new economic systems are market based and capitalist in their financial structure, but they are science based in their technological development. And they undergird a massive alteration in every human social and political institution.

[1] George Hegel, *The Philosophy of History*, NY Amazon, 2011.

2.3 The Link Between Free Market Capitalism and Democracy: The Separation of the Economy from the Polity and Legal-Rational Legitimacy

Polanyi mentions in passing—or barely mentions—that a "popular government" arises from a capitalist market economy. Like most Marxists—and to the chagrin of his American hosts at Williams College and Columbia University—Polanyi clung to the Marxist vision of capitalist democracy being *oligarchy* in disguise. The rich capitalists rule, the workers have no power and no say, and the riches of society go to the capitalist class only.

Polanyi's American middle-class hosts objected to this description and to the rise of new expanding middle classes after World War II—worldwide—altered the picture in capitalist societies, such that the oligarchic overinfluence within these societies was moderated enough so these societies could be called democracies.

We shall analyze the class balance in various modern democracies and discuss the problem of oligarchy as well. Of course, in today's twenty-first century world, the rise of tyranny and totalitarianism has become far more threatening to the existence of democracy than capitalist oligarchy.

In any case, and going far beyond Polanyi's weak comments on a popular government, we shall analyze the modern transition to democracy—now existing in a "cyberworld," which we barely understand and cannot seem to control.

Are capitalism and democracy the "ends of history"? History never ends—unless we blow up the planet with nuclear weapons or destroy our atmosphere with carbon and other gaseous emissions.

Barring these catastrophes, we shall describe the link between free market capitalism and democracy in terms of the rise of legal-rational authority, the separation of powers, and the encouragement of the rational-scientific worldview. The threats to democracy will also be discussed.[2].

[2] Niklas Luhmann in his "Systems Theory" has an interesting take on the separation of powers. He calls it "the functional differentiation" between the legal system, the political system, and the economic system, wherein each operates within its own distinct code and boundaries." Luhmann goes on to describe how these different spheres interact—he describes this within his systems theory terminology. I, Ronald M. Glassman, prefer to refer the reader to James Madison—checks and balances in the American Constitution—and French philosopher Baron de Montesquieu, upon whose works Madison leaned.

Part II
The Economic Transformation to High Technology Industrial Capitalism

Chapter 3
The Economic Transformation to High-Technology Industrial Capitalism

3.1 Free Market Capitalism and Industrial Production as Two Separate Processes

The Industrial Revolution emerged within the context of market capitalism in England and Scotland in the 1700s. Already in 1776, Adam Smith was describing the productive advantages of a pin factory over the craft production of pins.

But it must be understood that market capitalism preexisted the Industrial Revolution in the ancient world of the Phoenicians, Greeks, and Sumerians and then in the Renaissance era of the Italian city-states and Hansa city-states.

It must also be understood that industrial production—machine-factory production—was successfully established without market capitalism in Russia and China after their Marxist-Leninist revolutions. And even though these communist-party-run industrial systems proved to be inefficient and their creativity inhibited by government bureaucracies, the Industrial Revolution was successfully initiated and sustained without capitalism.

Further yet, market-driven capitalism evolved separately from the Industrial Revolution, developing new financial institutions connected to a completely new capitalist institution—the stock market.

The selling of shares in overseas trade-capitalist ventures was initiated in the Netherlands—first in Antwerp, and then when the Spanish-French Catholic kingly military coalition captured Antwerp and reimposed Catholicism on Calvinist-Protestant Antwerp, the stock market was moved to Amsterdam, which was still independent and still Calvinist-Protestant.

From Amsterdam, a similar stock market was established in London, such that the selling of shares became an integral part of capitalism as it evolved in the modern context.

That is, along with banking, loans, and interest charges—which have existed as part of trade capitalism since ancient times—the stock market became a second

R. M. Glassman, *The Great Global Transformation*, Contributions to Political Science, https://doi.org/10.1007/978-3-031-90566-7_3

monetary institution through which money could be converted to "capital"—money was used to make more money rather than simply utilized as a medium of exchange.

So even though capitalism and industrial production became linked at their inception in England and Scotland, both capitalism and industrial production continued to evolve separately.

The market dynamics of supply and demand and pricing for profit remained intact. But banking and the stock market system continued to evolve in both sophistication and complexity. Capitalist banking and capitalist stock exchanges spread across the globe as trade capitalism expanded globally in the nineteenth century.

At the same time, industrial production evolved because of scientific, engineering, and technological improvements in the machine-factory system.

It must be emphasized that it was the capitalist entrepreneurs who applied new technologies to industrial systems—it was not the scientists. Factory owners, in order to increase their profits, hired engineers to install the latest technological improvements into industrial productive systems. The capitalists were not the inventors of the new technology nor the scientists upon whose work the new technology was based. But they were the ones who quickly applied the latest innovations in order to increase their productivity and profits.

Notice, however, that improvements in industrial production were—and are—dependent on scientific advancement and the application of engineering to technology. So scientific and technological advancements preexist the improvements in industrial production. And these technological improvements are then rapidly incorporated into the industrial production process in order to maximize profits.

Marx saw early on what Adam Smith did not see: that giant corporations were necessary in order to raise enough capital to build and deploy expensive new technologies in the industrial system. Small firms—favored by Smith—could not raise the capital necessary for technological investment in the factory system. Thus, giant corporations emerged in each industrial sector. And, yes, these giant corporations were dangerously close to monopolies, which could inhibit market competition and fix prices against market dynamics.

In this treatise, we wish to emphasize both the evolution of industrial production toward even greater technological advancement and the separate evolution of capitalist, banking, and stock exchange institutions—which are influenced by scientific breakthroughs that lead to remarkable technological achievements.

Thus, the economic transformation of the world includes both the establishment of industrial production and the institutionalization of capitalist, banking, and stock finance as linked to a world market.

Finally, it must be described that even though industrialism and capitalism had merged in Great Britain and were then copied in the USA and Germany, industrial capitalism emerged with a slightly different organizational system. And then when the Japanese copied industrial capitalism, a very different system emerged.

We shall describe these differences, for in today's world, different models of industrial capitalism are still existent, with the USA on the more purely capitalist end of the spectrum and Japan and South Korea on the more industrial end of the spectrum.

Lastly, the communist Marxist-Leninist model of industrialization, without capitalism and market dynamics, has been abandoned as a failed approach.

Today, in 2020, economists speak about the "fourth Industrial Revolution"—which is characterized by automation, robotization, computerization, and artificial intelligence (AI). The first Industrial Revolution was characterized by the use of steam engines and coal fire, the second by electricity and the assembly line, and the third by some measure of primitive computerization.

In actuality, there has been only one Industrial Revolution, but this productive revolution has been ongoing in its scientific, engineering, and technocratic improvements.

Machine-factory production, with unskilled and skilled labor tending it was the model, and still is the model for industrial production. This model is, and always was, characterized by the use of machines to mass-produce products that were previously made by human craftsmen.

Machine-factory production was, and is, dependent on science, engineering, and technocratic breakthroughs and the willingness of capitalist entrepreneurs to apply these scientifically based breakthroughs to the productive process. Of course, once invented and made operational, the machine-factory system could be—and was—copied by communist and fascist government-appointed managers rather than capitalist entrepreneurs.

But without market dynamics demanding efficiency and quality in production and products, the machine-factory system lacked creativity and cost controls. The government managers were also caught up in bureaucratic inefficiency and obstructionism. The communist industrial systems were worse than the fascists because the fascists—in Italy, Greece, and Germany—allowed the capitalists to run corporations rather than government bureaucrats, as occurred under communism.

The point I wish to emphasize here is that the Industrial Revolution is an ongoing process, and its improvement and evolution are dependent on continuing scientific, engineering, and technological breakthroughs, which were slowly developing in the nineteenth and early twentieth centuries but have sped up in the twenty-first century with the globalization of science and the competition among advanced nations for technological superiority.

Furthermore, once communism—Marxism-Leninism—collapsed because of inefficiency in production and the lack of scientific and technological creativity, market principles—"the capitalist road "as the Chinese, call it—became adopted worldwide, even when communist party dictatorships control the political apparatus, as in China.

I will discuss the ongoing development of the free market—including the computerization of the global stock exchange system and the digitization of money—but first, I wish to emphasize the scientific and technological side of high-technology, industrial capitalism.

3.1.1 Science, Engineering, Technology, and Machine-Factory Production

The ancient Greeks and the Chinese independently invented the steam engine. They also utilized gears for the various inventions they had, some of which we do not even understand now.

However, neither the Greeks nor the Chinese used steam engines or geared gadgets for the mass production of craft goods. This would not occur until the British applied the steam engine to factory production.

Once machines were utilized for production, the movement to improve them—in order to increase production—was unleashed.

As Thorstein Veblen put it, the "captains of industry"[1] were often—in the early years—also engineers. They combined engineering-savvy with capitalist, business skills. However, by the nineteenth century, engineering became linked to a more sophisticated scientific base, which was beyond the knowledge of the average capitalist. So, again, as Veblen pointed out, the capitalist captains of industry began hiring engineers to improve the factory system.

These engineers began improving machine technology dramatically—so much so that Veblen believed that the engineers were going to take over the industrial systems. In his *The Engineers and the Price System*,[2] Veblen advocated a takeover by engineers.

However, it was the capitalists who innovated the assembly line, and it was the capitalists who demanded efficiency in production. And it was also the capitalists—the "captains of industry"—who returned control of the machine-factory system. The engineers remained paid employees of the businessman. These engineers continued to innovate and improve the machines and the factories, but they never gained control.

Today, the businessmen still control giant corporations but as corporate managers, while the "engineers, "as technocrats, remain employees of the giant corporations. Only where the technocrats innovate a product and then become the corporate manager do they hold control. Bill Gates, Steve Jobs, and Jeff Bezos come to mind. However, once the corporation is established, the managers hire young technocrats, whom they dominate.

So the evolution of the industrial system is dependent on the scientific engineering and technological innovations that have been occurring with ever greater frequency. The Industrial Revolution is thus ongoing.

I will discuss the impact of science, in general, later on in the section on the transition to a new worldview. Here, I wish to emphasize two facts: (1) that the Industrial Revolution is ever evolving and (2) that it is evolving because of scientific

[1] Thorstein Veblen, *The Engineers and the Price System*, NY, Knopf, 1945.

[2] Ibid.

advancement, as well as the capitalist application of these advancements to the production process.

3.1.2 *The Factory of the Future: Full Automation with New Classes of Labor*

Can we completely eliminate labor with automation and robotization? No. Both skilled and unskilled labor will still be needed. However, with ongoing automation, the nature of the labor force may be changing in the long run. But in the short run, the world's giant corporations are still moving their operations to cheap labor nations. As capitalists, cheap labor is still enticing. So China, Mexico, Bangladesh, and the Philippines are still destination countries for advanced industrial production.

Automation could change this in the long run. The case of Philips Norelco of the Netherlands is a good example in this regard. Philips, at first, moved their electric shaver factories to Indonesia and China to gain cheap labor. But back in the Netherlands, they automated the factories. They discovered that they could manufacture electric shavers for about the same price as in Southeast Asia. So Philips moved the production of the shavers back to the Netherlands.

However, the nature of the labor force changed. The laborers needed to be technologically skilled in order to tend the automated, robotized, corporate-directed machine-factory system. The cheap unskilled labor of Asia was eliminated, but they did not return the old-fashioned blue-color laboring jobs in the Netherlands. The nature of labor had changed to a new kind of skilled labor demanding technocratic training and skill.

Dutch Technium colleges are excellent, and they will expand to meet the needs of the new high-tech industrial capitalist workforce. Such Technium colleges are-performing excellently in Germany, Scandinavia, France, and Italy and are expanding in all EU nations—as well as part of the "red brick" universities in the UK. The USA lags far behind in this regard, though 2-year colleges are attempting to fill this role.

Thus, skilled, technocratic labor will be increasingly needed as automation of the industrial productive process increases. However, unskilled labor will still be needed in many areas of modern industry.

Meatpacking and farm picking still need unskilled laborers willing to work for low wages.

And in the delivery system for all industries, unskilled labor is still needed. United Parcel, Federal Express, Amazon, Alibaba, and all online and in-store outlets need cheap labor to sort boxes and load them on trucks and deliver them. Thus, even though Amazon and UPS have state-of-the-art automated packaging factories, loading and delivery are still done by unskilled, poorly paid workers.

Worldwide, the nature of the labor force is bifurcated: skilled technocratic jobs expanding at the same time as unskilled factory and farming jobs.

Also, the new tech jobs are not quite "white-collar" jobs, nor are they "blue collar." They are sometimes hands-on in terms of supervising automated factory machines, and they are sometimes purely office work in setting computer programs, checking algorithms, and monitoring AI systems.

The factory managers are like civil engineers in this regard.

To sum up then, automation will eventually shift the labor force away from unskilled, low-paid labor toward skilled, technocratically trained labor. However, as I have made central, unskilled labor in the food industry, agriculture, and package delivery systems will continue to be needed. Just as plumbers and electricians remained essential along with factory workers, so too will technocrats be needed along with unskilled laborers.

3.2 Science and Technology Alter the Capitalist Financial System, While Market Forces Remain Constant

The market dynamics of supply and demand, market pricing, profit motivation in terms of efficiency of production, and low labor costs all remain constant.

At the same time, science, engineering, and technological breakthroughs completely alter the industrial systems. And though the market forces remain unchanged, the entire financial system connected to capitalism has undergone a spectacular technological change.

That is, the banking system and the stock exchange system have been fully computerized, and artificial intelligence is monitoring the algorithms put in place to control stock market boom and bust cycles.

3.2.1 The Computer-Controlled Stock Market

All stock market transactions can now be done by computers. No one needs to be at Wall Street headquarters or in London or in Hong Kong or anywhere else. All transactions can be done virtually. "Wall Street" is now a metaphor for stock market transactions rather than an actual place.

Furthermore, due to the wild swings in stock market activity, which have led to wild run-ups and then terrible crashes, algorithms have been created that trigger slowdowns or speedups automatically—in an effort to avert the boom and bust cycles.

However, the algorithms have failed. And, in fact, they seem to have added to the instability of the stock market rather than to have helped the situation.

Nonetheless, even though the algorithms have not been successful at stabilizing the market, they continue to be improved by programmers, and they are still being utilized.

In terms of stock trading and stock ownership, computerization may have a democratic effect—meaning that more and more individuals will come to own stock and to speculate on stocks.

Whether the increase in stock ownership and stock trading will have a stabilizing effect on the market or not is not yet determined.

However, with an increasing number of modern individuals accumulating pensions invested in the stock market—401 in America—pension fund managers have gained more and more power, along with more individuals being invested in the market.

This latter phenomenon—the pension funds being invested in the stock market—is good for the middle class as long as the market remains stable. If it crashes, the pension funds must be bailed out. This occurred in the USA in 2008. Giant financial firms were bailed out, but it took 3 years for the pension funds to recover. This is problematic for any pension system invested in the stock market.

Also, it is very dangerous for democracy because the power of financial firms, globally, has generated an oligarchic overinfluence in many of the world's democracies—including in the USA—which is dangerously destabilizing because it weakens the middle class, weakens labor unions, and draws too much of a nation's capital to the rich. I discuss this in an earlier book entitled *Can Democracy Survive in the twenty-first Century?*[3]

Here, in this treatise, I wish to emphasize that the computerization of the stock market is already having ramifications that were unintended. So we must watch carefully in order to discern what the long-term effects of this computerization will engender.

3.2.2 The Computerization of the Banking System and the Digitization of Money

As with Wall Street or the London Stock Exchange, in the future, there will be no bank buildings. Banking will be virtual. The computerization of the banking systems globally is moving at a rapid pace, eventuating in a system of banking in which all transactions are done on the computer—no one will have to go into a bank and deal with a live teller or manager.

The process of banking is still the same, however one applies for loans and then gets an interest charge on repayment. One deposits to a savings account and gains an interest increment. Savings and loans are still the same but accomplished virtually.

The nature of money, though, will undergo a dramatic change. Money as capital—using money to make more money—will remain unchanged. But money as a

[3] Ronald M. Glassman, *Can Democracy Survive in the twenty-first Century?*

medium of exchange has already changed and will change even more dramatically in the near future.

Mostly, money as a medium of exchange replaced barter in ancient Mesopotamia in the Sumerian city-states as overseas and caravan trade emerged there.

Money was at first invented by trade merchants as bars of precious metal—gold, silver, and copper. Some of the trade merchants became the world's first bankers, carefully hoarding and weighing the bars of metal and determining the percentage of gold, silver, and copper that had to be maintained to standardize this newly invented "money.".

These standardized bars of metal remained the medium of exchange (money) until the Lydians invented coined money—standardized by weight and purity but smaller, easier to handle, and stamped with engravings that designated the city or monarchy of origin.

The Greeks copied the Lydian coins and utilized coined money so energetically in their overseas trading that, eventually, coined money replaced the heavy, unwieldy bars.

Centuries later, originating in China and brought to Italy by Marco Polo, paper money was introduced.

It was not until the twentieth century that paper money replaced coined money as the major medium of exchange—and even then, it was backed up by gold reserves hoarded in various nations.

In the twentieth century, banks around the globe introduced checks, and they replaced paper money in many transactions. The checks were backed by paper money, which was still backed by gold reserves.

Then after World War II, credit cards—made of plastic—were introduced. And, alongside checks, more and more monetary transactions were done by credit cards. These cards were invented by banks in order to gain a capital advantage along with the medium of exchange—they are credit cards; you must pay back with interest what you use for monetary exchange.

Today, there are many different kinds of credit cards. Some charge very high interest rates—as high as 22%—and therefore these cards were capital producers, not just a medium of exchange. However, there are also credit cards with no interest charge if paid back by a certain date—although some, like the American Express Card, have an annual fee, so they are still capital producers, not just money.

Now, in the twenty-first century, the computerization of all banking transactions is leading to the computerization of money. Money will now be "digitized." No checks will be necessary; no credit card will be needed. Online services, like PayPal and Amazon Prime, already offer the digital transfer of funds from one party to another. The money goes into, or comes out of, an individual's bank account. No medium of exchange is needed. It is all done through computer transactions.

If a fee is charged for this kind of digital money, then the digitized money is capital, as well as a medium of exchange.

Strange phenomena, like that of "Bitcoin, "may confuse the digitization process. But no Bitcoin is needed because money exchange transactions can be done in purely arithmetic terms by computerized systems that debit and credit one's bank accounts and one's shopping transactions.

So the nature of money will change dramatically, but the use of money as a medium of exchange will still occur, except that money will no longer be something you can touch, or weigh, or be something backed by gold reserves. Banking will be virtual, and money exchanges will be backed by the strengths of national economies and global banking institutions. These latter institutions are difficult to calculate, and, therefore, global capitalist monitoring organizations, like the World Bank and the International Monetary Fund, will become more important in stabilizing money transactions in the world as money becomes a phenomenon of the cyber world.

Incredible difficulties have already arisen, such as the Mexican financial crisis, the Argentinian financial crisis, and the USA stock market crash of 2008, as well as the Japanese real estate bubble. In all of these (regional and world) crises, monetary institutions were stressed to stabilize these situations.

Global capitalism has not as yet created a financial oversight organization that can fully deal with regional and world financial crises. This global capitalist system is still slowly evolving, and, of course, Russia and China are not fully included in this process at this time in history.

In this treatise, I wish to emphasize that money—one of Carl Polanyi's "fictitious commodities," along with labor and land—is changing under the dynamic impact of the ongoing computerization revolution. The computerization of money affects both money as a means of exchange and money as capital. Gold, coins, paper, checks, and even plastic credit cards may no longer be needed. Money may no longer "change hands" because money will be a virtual phenomenon, with no existence beyond the computerized cyber world.

Labor, land, and money are all altered by the science- and technology-based computer revolution.

3.3 Land in the Era of the Computer Revolution

We have already discussed the alteration of the labor force due to automation, where a bifurcated labor force is needed—skilled technocrats and unskilled workers in package delivery and food production.

We have also discussed the alteration of money as now linked to the cyber world.

So what about "land, "one of Polanyi's three fictitious commodities?

3.3.1 Agricultural Land

Land was held communally by tribes, villages, feudal lords, and monarchies. Land became a commodity when capitalism emerged. Land could be bought and sold, and it was valued by the market. Land ownership became a prestigious phenomenon, and land use was commercially determined.

But a problem emerged with agricultural production and the commercialization of land. Even when agricultural production was mechanized during the Industrial Revolution, farm production remained very risky. Crop production depends on rainfall—droughts and floods ruin the crops. Insects can also destroy a crop, and plant diseases can ruin a crop.

Thus, market-determined farming could be very profitable or a total loss.

Further, capitalist farmers have to borrow money from banks in order to buy seeds, new machinery, additional land, irrigation systems, and more. If everything goes well, they can pay the banks back and still make a profit. However, things do not always go well, and farmers can fail and go bankrupt.

Food supply, however, must continue, or starvation will occur in the urban centers that the capitalist farms feed. Therefore, capitalist farms—mechanized and linked with market dynamics—have to be subsidized in most of the capitalist-industrial nations. Agricultural land cannot be left to purely market dynamics because failure is unacceptable where starvation would be the result.

Most of the advanced capitalist industrial nations subsidize their farmers to help them through market fluctuations and climate-related disasters. So this is not pure capitalist farming determined by the free market. It is capitalist farming stabilized by government subsidies in order to keep the food supply safely constant.

Thus, if communist-style state farms have proven unproductive and backward—which they have—capitalist farming, which is highly productive and industrially innovative, has had to be aided by government subsidy, such that free market farmers could depend on the government to prevent failure and ensure food supply.

Further, now that the world is linked in terms of trade and markets, competition between the farmers of one nation and those of another has had to be regulated by world trade treaties.

So French dairy farmers have to be protected from English dairy farmers, and trade in dairy products has to be carefully regulated. Similarly, USA dairy farmers have to be protected from Canadian dairy farmers, who undercut them in price.

Wheat, soybean, rice, and most grain farming has to be regulated by world trade treaties so that cheap labor nations will not undermine the farmers in more expensive markets. Countries cannot allow their farms to go under, or they would be at the mercy of the nations providing their food.

Finally, even though capitalist market farming is competitive and production and pricing are market driven, the careful global regulation of competing national farmers has stabilized an agricultural market that could have produced booms and busts in food production and created terrible hardships in the world's population.

Instead, the system of capitalist market, mechanized farming, as stabilized by global agricultural treaties, has produced the greatest super-abundance of food—and the greatest diversity of food—ever in the history of humankind.

Along with contraception, world population control, and fertility reductions, the super-abundance of food and the slowing of the population explosion have stopped Malthus'[4] terrible predictions. Populations may not outrun the food supply. In fact, in most of the advanced capitalist-industrial nations—and even in most of the developing nations—obesity is the problem, not starvation, especially where fast-food outlets feed the working class and the poor.

3.3.2 *Urban Real Estate*

The other problem with land as a market commodity is the soaring price of commercial and residential properties in big cities.

In Tokyo, New York, London, Paris, San Francisco, Los Angeles, Rio and more, the price of urban real estate is too high. It is too high for small businesses to survive—they cannot make a profit—it is too high for families needing two- or three-bedroom apartments, and it is too high for young people just beginning their careers.

And the suburban real estate in and around these great cities has also soared beyond the economic ability of the middle class.

So in all the great cities of the world, a real estate crisis has emerged. Big businesses sustain high rents, and billionaires drive up the cost of urban real estate. Corporations and billionaires buy up commercial and residential properties and drive up prices in the whole real estate market, leaving the middle class overextended and economically weakened.

For instance, when Mike Bloomberg became the Mayor of New York City, he needed tax revenue to sustain the city's growth. He altered zoning laws so that hugely high residential and commercial buildings could be built. They were built, and giant corporations and private billionaires bought up the real estate.

This provided New York City with a huge tax windfall, and Bloomberg—to his credit—used the money to clean up, beautify, and expand services in the city.

Tourism boomed, New York City flourished, and all seemed well until it became evident that "the rents were too damn high."

The middle class was priced out—middle-income apartments were converted to million-dollar condominiums. Small restaurants and boutiques went out of business in large numbers. Young people had to take three roommates or move back in with their parents. Suburban houses tripled in price, ruining the upward mobility of the next generation.

[4]Thomas Robert Malthus, *An Essay on the Principle of Population*, 1798, London, Penguin Classics, 1951.

This same process occurred in Tokyo, almost destroying Japanese economic stability. This is a global urban phenomenon—Hong Kong, Singapore, Seoul, São Paulo, and so many other urban centers are exhibiting these same problems generated by free market dynamics.

Therefore, as with capitalist agricultural land, it is probable that urban real estate—both commercial and residential—will have to be stabilized and subsidized by various governments involved.

Agriculture was stabilized and regulated quickly because starvation of a nation's population was a very real factor. But because there is no immediate threat, the regulation and stabilization of urban real estate have been slower to develop.

The model for such a program of stabilization and subsidy was established in the USA around World War II and in the EU after World War II.

In the USA, rent control and rent stabilization helped the middle class stay in the cities. And middle-class housing was subsidized in suburbia, both by the government and by banks.

All of this was established after the Great Depression and World War II. However, these programs were forced out in the 1980s, and now, the free market has overridden them and created a crisis.

In the USA, free market economists who dominate much of academia and Republican Party policy have prevented earlier successful urban-suburban stabilization programs from being initiated.

The EU has retained much of its post-World War II stabilization programs in terms of real estate but is now experiencing the same problematic rise as the USA. Japan is still struggling with the real estate issue in part because of overpopulation—but the Japanese know that this is a serious crisis, and they are attempting to maintain some market modulation.

Globally, the urban-suburban real estate crisis will continue. And some sort of regulation and subsidy in the real estate market will be necessary in most of the great urban areas.

However, something new and unexpected is happening—showing us, again, how a technological invention can create unintended effects.

3.3.3 The Zoom Computer Meeting Revolution and Its Effect on Real Estate

The Covid-19 pandemic forced corporations and schools to hold virtual meetings on the computer. Systems like Zoom, Skype, and Microsoft Teams allow people to meet and learn virtually—so they are separated and sitting at home, working via their computers.

One no longer has to go to an office in a giant glass building. One no longer has to go to a college campus. One can stay at home—wherever that is, be it a street or continent away—and still do business, learn, do psychotherapy, or see a doctor.

But will this remove the need for giant office buildings and urban apartments or suburban homes near a city?

It is possible that this computer virtual world will alter the residential and business patterns now existent.

Cities may continue as centers of culture, artistry, music, gourmet cuisine, and communal excitement or not. Maybe this phenomenon will become virtual in the future and the cyber world will become the real world.

It is too soon to tell, but the Covid-19 pandemic showed that so much could be done via computer and virtual meetings, such that after the pandemic, this kind of global interaction will continue and be further expanded. If virtual computer systems are expanded, it is possible that the nature of cities and suburbs will change. We shall find out in the near future—the next 10 years from 2020, when this is being written.

Chapter 4
The Rapid But Uneven Transition to High-Technology Industrial Capitalism

4.1 The First Industrial Revolution: Capitalist Entrepreneurs

The first Industrial Revolution was a purely capitalist-initiated and -directed event. The gentry businessmen of Great Britain, lacking a strong craft tradition for the production of goods and celebrating the scientific discoveries advanced beyond the Italian Renaissance, had the idea of improving production in Great Britain by applying machine technology to the productive process.

These gentry businessmen invented the machine-factory system, which successfully outperformed guild-craft production in the manufacture of consumer goods. From pins to textiles—especially woolen textiles—the British factories produced more goods at a lower cost than the craft system in the Netherlands, Germany, or Italy.

Given this success, the British entrepreneurs began applying machine technology to as many facets of the economy as they could. The steam engine was the driving force behind the factory system. Steam power drove the specialized machines invented for specific product production. And when it was discovered that coal increased the efficacy of the steam engine, that engine was harnessed to the carts pulling coal out of the mines—the carts were on rails, and the steam engines pulled them up and down. Metal gears—long known and used in the Netherlands—were applied to the machines in the factories and the carts at the mines.

Thus, better engines and better factory machines were invented.

The application of scientific knowledge to the machine-factory-technology production process became an exciting activity for the British businessman, such that the expansion of the factory productive process and the application of new technology to every aspect of economic life became a wildly exciting motivation for them.

Once this machine-factory productive process was proven successful, businessmen in other countries began to copy it: first, in the United States, then in the

R. M. Glassman, *The Great Global Transformation*, Contributions to Political Science, https://doi.org/10.1007/978-3-031-90566-7_4

Netherlands and Belgium, then in Western Germany and Scandinavia, and, finally, in France and Italy.

In the USA, which like Great Britain had no craft guilds and no artistic craft traditions, the "Industrial Revolution" was pursued with great energy and provided dramatically successful results in terms of the production of goods. In the Netherlands and Italy, with strong craft guild opposition, the Industrial Revolution was adopted, though more slowly—especially in Italy.

Germany, competitive with England politically and militarily, adopted the industrial factory system in order to compete with Great Britain, but industrialization was slow compared to the USA. Spain was overextended in its New World colonies and failed to industrialize. Italy industrialized in the northern region, but the craft guilds slowed progress even there, while southern Italy remained agrarian. As for France, the old aristocratic families focused on wine production, perfumes, and high-fashion clothing, while farming remained dominant in central and southern France. However, northern France, bordering Germany and Belgium, did industrialize—there were also coal fields in Alsace Lorraine, which both France and Germany claimed as their own.

The point I wish to emphasize here is that the Industrial Revolution was at first initiated and directed by capitalist entrepreneurs with little government involvement. It was truly a capitalist-Industrial Revolution. Yet capitalism and industrial production are two different phenomena. Capitalism, as trade capitalism, preceded the Industrial Revolution by thousands of years, dating back to the ancient Sumerians in Mesopotamia around 2000 BCE.

And the Industrial Revolution presupposed huge scientific breakthroughs—from Galileo to Newton and beyond—which facilitated the new machine technology. Thus, though the steam engine and metal gears were invented independently in ancient Greece and China, the iron steam engine and gears of the Industrial Revolution were far superior in design and function.

Yet these marvelously improved machines would not have been harnessed to the craft-production process unless the gentry capitalists of Great Britain had done so. After all, the Greeks used machines for warfare and the Chinese for toys to amuse the Emperor. And the craft guilds of Italy and the Netherlands opposed the use of machines for production.

So the link between the capitalist and the Industrial Revolution was critical—it was these British capitalists who first harnessed the steam engine to the production process.

Both Weber[1] and Tawney[2] agree on this, though they famously disagree on the role of the Calvinist Puritan Protestant religion as causal in this application of machines to consumer production. And Marx[3] described the Industrial Revolution as capitalist to the core.

---

[1] Max Weber, *The Protestant Ethic and The Spirit of Capitalism*, NY, Random House, 1953.

[2] R.H. Tawney, *Religion and the Rise of Capitalism*, London, Penguin Classics, 1955.

[3] Karl Marx, *Capital*, International Publishers, 1948.

4.2 The Second Wave of Industrialization: Fascism and Communism

Netherlands, Northern France, and Western Germany all industrialized in the first wave in the eighteenth and nineteenth centuries—following the British model of machine-factory production with capitalist banking, finance, and market dynamics.

However, Eastern Germany, Italy, and Spain fell far behind in industrial production and began to lose their political-military competitiveness.

Given this geopolitical competition, Germany, Italy, and Spain began searching for ways in which to catch up quickly with Great Britain, the USA, and the Low Countries.

The governments of these nations sought to intervene to speed up industrialization. Significantly, these governments did not attempt to take control of the economy. They sought instead to support and encourage their capitalist entrepreneurs in their attempt to establish and expand competitive industrial factories.

These governments did not manage the industrial factories; they left that to the capitalists. But they became very proactive in securing raw materials, expanding mining activities, and encouraging banks to lend money to help expanding industries.

Germany and northern Italy began to become industrialized. And the government business "partnership" helped speed up the industrial process.

By World War I (1914 to 1917), Germany had caught up to Great Britain and the United States, and Italy was also slowly industrializing. Spain was still distracted by its past glories and was slow to industrialize.

As is so well known, the loss of World War I and The Great Depression ruined Germany—politically and economically. Italy, too, was disgraced by its poor war effort and economic backwardness.

4.2.1 Fascism in Italy and Germany

Again, as is well known, the fascist movement arose in Italy, demanding rapid industrialization, militarization, and the unification of Italy.

Harking back to the Roman domination of the world, Mussolini roused the Italians to a new nationalism, promising rapid industrialization and powerful militarization. And, unfortunately, for the world, Mussolini revived Machiavelli's *Prince* and established a murderous dictatorship in place of the barely instituted Parliamentary democratic government in Rome.

Hitler copied Mussolini's program to the letter in Germany, adding racial hatred of the Jews (and Gypsies and Slavs) to Mussolini's fascist militarist murderous dictatorial program.

Franco, in Spain, copied Mussolini's fascism after the horrific Spanish Civil War brought him to power.

Here, in this treatise, I wish to emphasize that fascism provided a different model from the purely capitalist approach of Great Britain and the USA.

Under fascism in Italy, Germany, and Spain, the dictatorial government supported and encouraged industrialization. The fascists, however, did *not* take charge of the economy—they did *not* manage the economy. They just ordered banks to loan huge sums of money to businessmen so that they—the capitalists—could expand industrialization. Yes, military production was demanded, but even military production was supervised by the capitalists. These "captains of industry," as Veblen called them, did produce what the fascist governments wanted, but they produced these military goods efficiently while still relying on market dynamics to guide their production practices. And they continued to produce civilian consumer goods as well because the fascist governments wanted to look good to the people.

Thus, for instance, Hitler not only ordered auto companies to make tanks, but he also directed them to make a "peoples car"—Volkswagen—to enhance his public support.

The point I wish to emphasize here is that the second wave of industrialization—the fascist wave—included government involvement but with capitalist control of the economy still occurring.

Fascism (Nazism) in Italy, Germany, and Spain was horrific beyond Machiavelli's imagination. The murder, genocide, and totalitarianism were the worst nightmare that humankind had ever produced—far surpassing the horrors brought by the kings and conquerors of old.

But in terms of speeding up the industrial process in Italy, Germany, and Spain, fascism succeeded. And because the fascists left the capitalists with the managerial control of the factory system, it was efficient and innovative, and was rapidly regenerated after World War II.

No praise of fascism is intended here, but it did lead to an alternative model of industrialization. That is, today in the EU—and in Japan—a government-corporate partnership is still extolled as the best model of industrial production. The EU and Japan are capitalist industrial—market dynamics do prevail—but their governments play more of a role in the support of industrial systems than in the UK and the USA. (I will discuss Japan and South Korea soon.)

4.2.2 Communism: Industrial Production with No Capitalists and No Market Dynamics—Russia and China

The communist intellectuals of Russia were not stupid. They knew about German and British industrialization. But when they took power, there were no Russian businessmen to give loans to or to encourage. There were no scientists or engineers to fund. Russia was still feudal agrarian.

Once in power, the Russian communists had to create a school system, a university system, roads, and buildings, along with machine-factory production.

The Communist Party had to manage the industrial system, though they barely understood it as yet in the early 1920s.

Once industrialization was underway, however, Lenin, Trotsky, and other communist intellectuals realized that their government management system was inefficient.

They, therefore, initiated the New Economic Policy (NEP), wherein market dynamics began to be included in their decision-making process in order to engender greater efficiency and worker motivation.

We will never know if NEP would have been successful in taking the Russians to the "capitalist road," as the Chinese would later call it, for Stalin took over and murdered most of the communist intellectuals, replacing them with frightened sycophants. Stalin ended NEP, deported the agrarian and urban entrepreneurs to Siberia, and reestablished the government management of the industrial system.

Stalin only cared about power, politics, and military production. His aim was to prevent German expansion into Slavic Europe and to advance Russia's geopolitical power against England and Germany.

So Marxism-Leninism under Stalinist control became a model for rapid industrialization, focusing on military production almost exclusively and engendering a "communal economy" that produced huge quantities of military equipment and some consumer goods, but producing them inefficiently and placing quality controls only on military products. Consumer products were shoddy and primitive, while military equipment was state of the art.

This was the model that Mao Zedong copied after World War II and the Chinese Civil War.

Stalin armed and trained Mao and his Communist Party. They won the Civil War and, from 1948 to 1970, institutionalized Stalinist-communist industrialization.

During the 1970s and 1980s, when the Stalinist model failed to produce consumer goods or a rising middle-class lifestyle, the Russians, under Gorbachev, and then the Chinese, under Deng Xiaoping, attempted to add capitalism to their industrial communist economies. Market dynamics on price, profit, supply, and demand were incorporated into China even though the Communist Party remained in control of the polity and the military.

China had businessmen. China had an entrepreneurial tradition—at least on the coast and in Southeast Asia (where there were settlements of Chinese merchants).

Thus, first, in Hong Kong and its nearby coastal territories, Chinese factories were established and run along capitalist lines—for profit, for efficiency in production, and for excellence in the products themselves.

The Chinese were good at capitalism, and capitalist industrialism spread all across China. China now has the fastest-growing capitalist-industrial economy in the world.

But, but, but—the Communist Party still controls the military, the police, and the political apparatus.

Gorbachev's push for capitalist industrialism in Russia failed. And his push for democratic governance also failed. After decades of Stalinism, few Russian entrepreneurs existed. And the Stalinist managers of industry would not give up their control.

With the precipitous breakup of the Soviet Union and the splitting away of Eastern Europe, Russia went from one of the leading world powers to a laughingstock.

Enter Vladimir Putin.

Putin promised to restore Russian power in the world. He was elected democratically. Once elected, he revived the old Committee for State Security (KGB), of which he was an active member, and ordered military production to continue with advanced scientific technological weaponry as the main focus of industrial production. He invaded Georgia, Chechnya, Crimea, and the Ukraine.

Putin succeeded in reestablishing Russia as a formidable military power. He even regained a Russian foothold in the Middle East by controlling Syria. He also has a peculiar hold on the American presidency as Donald Trump overruled the Americans' foreign policy establishment with his pro-Russia policy and strange allegiance to Putin and all his policies. This was reversed, of course, when Trump lost to Biden.

Further, and this is central to this treatise, Russia has failed to establish an advanced high-tech capital economy. The Russians produce few consumer goods, but they still make great tanks, MiG Jets, and nuclear weapons. They even make excellent space rockets and help maintain the International Space Station. However, most consumer goods are bought from the EU.

The only thing that saves the Russian economy—and Putin's popularity—is that Russia is one of the world's largest suppliers of raw materials. Russia possesses oil and natural gas and minerals on a colossal scale.

So Russia has a Third World raw material economy. But because it is so rich in these commodities, Russia can use the money brought in to exchange for upscale consumer goods sold in fancy stores in big cities. Upscale restaurants and coffee shops also abound. Yet nothing is Russian made except the food, and even much of the food is imported.

Because of the inefficiency of the communist economy, the Stalinist-communist model of industrial production has fallen out of favor as a model to emulate.

4.3 Japan: Giant Conglomerates, American Efficiency, and Japanese Reverse Engineering

The Japanese case is unique, but I describe it because the South Koreans have emulated it with the same great success that Japan had.

Japan had a history of borrowing civilizational achievements and adapting them to Japanese culture. Most of their borrowing was from China. The Japanese learned pictographic writing from China, as well as painting, architecture, ironworking, silk production, and so much more. In each case, the Japanese borrowed the innovation, adapted it to Japanese culture, and often improved upon it—Japanese samurai swords, for instance, being of better quality than Chinese steel swords.

When the Portuguese, Spanish, and English arrived in Japan with guns and cannons, the Japanese knew they could be defeated militarily. The Spanish had taken the Philippines, and the English were making inroads into China.

After a period of resistance to European technology, the Japanese decided to try to produce it as they had produced Chinese technologies.

Japan was dominated by aristocratic families oriented toward warfare. These families, though competitive with each other, sent emissaries to Europe and the United States in order to learn the principles of machine-factory production. The Japanese had no businessmen to establish market capitalism, nor did they have a powerful centralized government. Therefore, it was up to the aristocratic families to initiate and institutionalize industrial production.

The aristocratic Japanese men, returning from abroad, developed the machine-factory system in Japan. They copied British, Dutch, and German machine production—especially being influenced by the German factory system because it was newer and better than the British system and because the Japanese liked the German pride in workmanship and the German military orientation.

Once the Japanese families had successfully established excellent machines, the Japanese learned capitalist market efficiency from the American "efficiency expert" Frederick Winslow Taylor.

Taylorist efficiency in factory production was institutionalized by the Japanese without real capitalism. In Japan, banks were controlled by aristocratic families—they lent to them whatever they requested. And no stock exchange existed as yet. So without capitalism, market efficiency in production was successfully copied from America and included in their German-style machine-factory system.

The Japanese were not innovative—all the new technological inventions came forth from the USA, Germany, and Great Britain. However, as soon as a new product was developed—such as a train, a car, a truck, a new fertilizer, a new clothing fabric, or a new military weapon—the Japanese copied it and produced it.

Furthermore, the Japanese are marvelous "reverse engineers"—that is, even though they are not innovative. The Japanese are very good at copying a new product and then improving it. They literally would take apart a new product to see how it was made and then improve upon it. Good examples of this were German cameras, American airplanes, and Italian bicycle gears. In every case, the Japanese improved upon the product and produced it more efficiently and cheaply.

So what are the giant conglomerates? They are called "Zaibatsu," and they emerged from the control of differing, aristocratic families. They are monopolistic, but because of the Japanese obsession with efficiency in production and excellence in products, the Japanese Zaibatsu do not act like monopolies. That is, they are linked to market forces because of the competition with European and American firms. They do attempt to gain market control and wipe out the competition—in a true monopolistic fashion. However, because of the international pressure against the Japanese, these giant conglomerates have stopped flooding the market and now adhere to more scripted international market-based competition.

How is a conglomerate different from a monopoly? The Japanese Zaibatsu include many industries under the same family management umbrella, not just cars, for instance, but also electronics, clothing, and steel. Family control has yielded to a meritocracy of young men (now some women) trained and educated at elite Japanese schools—copied from the German school system. These young men then became managers in the economic system and, often in adulthood, retire early and go into government—thus assuming that no rigidity or conservatism would be built in and that the government could work cooperatively with the Zaibatsu managers to ensure Japanese economic success.

The giant conglomerates stem from preindustrial aristocratic families but have now gained a modern meritocratic managerial system. Still, they are peculiar economic organizations because conglomerates must excel in many industries.

Whatever its peculiarities are, the Japanese system works. Industrial production is efficient, the products are excellent, the profits are good, and the distribution of income is more equal than in any of the capitalist-industrial countries.

Capitalism, though innovative and efficient, has two flaws: inequality in wealth is extreme, and the system is unstable with boom and bust cycles.

The Japanese system avoids these flaws, though it is not without its problems.

Let me repeat: the Japanese system is so unique that I would not have mentioned it except for the fact that South Korea successfully copied it.

Because South Korea so successfully copied the Japanese system, it must be seen as an alternative form of industrial capitalism, along with American and British pure capitalism and EU government corporate union partnerships.

The South Koreans call the Zaibatsu conglomerates "Chaeboel," but they are similar to the Japanese conglomerates. The Koreans copy the machine-factory system of Japan, its meritocratic management system, and even Japanese products.

However, the Koreans have also been influenced by the Americans—who, of course, have occupied South Korea since World War II and the Korean War era.

Thus, the South Koreans copy iPhones and iPads; they copy American fashion and American rock music. "K-rock" is now so popular that Americans are copying the Koreans.

4.4 Three Models of Industrial Capitalism and One Failed Model

With the demise of communism, the Marxist-Leninist model of industrial production has disappeared, except in North Korea, where its failings continue to be obvious—famines and no consumer goods—and its strengths still there in the military sphere.

The military sphere of North Korea is dangerously real, but the world's nations see the failures too clearly to copy North Korea (at the moment, at least).

The economic models that do exist and are successful range from the most purely free-market model of American industrial capitalism to the government-corporate-union partnership model of Germany, and some of the EU, to the Japanese and Korean models, which are barely capitalist at all but are absorbed into the world market system, such that market dynamics do affect the Japanese and Korean economies.

In terms of emulation, Singapore, Hong Kong, and Taiwan incorporated British banking, stock market, and contract law systems into their growing industrialization. And China, ironically—since it had been Marxist-Leninist—copied the American system of entrepreneurial control and capitalist innovation.

China has unlimited cheap labor—a billion people—and a tradition of business success in trade all over southeast Asia—Singapore best exemplifies this tradition.

4.4.1 The Four Tigers of Asia: Singapore, Hong Kong, Taiwan, and South Korea

Singapore and Hong Kong were, of course, British colonies. They inherited the British banking system and stock exchange. When they became independent, the banks and stock market became combined with the indigenous Chinese business culture, which in both Singapore and Hong Kong was very entrepreneurial. The Chinese in Southeast Asia were known for their excellence in business. This business expertise, combined with British banking, enabled Singapore and Hong Kong to become centers of seafaring trade. Singapore is one of the largest ports in the world, and Hong Kong is not far behind.

Singapore exploded with capitalist enterprises: businessmen provided the capital for expanding and modernizing ports into container ship supply systems, with Singapore as the favored stopover place for all shipping between Asia and Europe. Small businesses boomed, and big businesses expanded.

Fascinatingly, this capitalist haven then elected a government that embodied Swedish-style social welfare programs. Lee—the elected Prime Minister—copied the Swedish model of democratic socialism, and this, along with the booming business culture, gave Singapore extraordinary stability. Even racism against the Malayans, who originally lived on the island, and East Indians, who migrated there, was inhibited by the Lee government, which encouraged the majority of Chinese (Cantonese speaking) not to discriminate against the Malays and Indians.

Perhaps the Swedish social democracy was instituted because it is consonant with Confucian values. Confucius insisted on "benevolence"—the paternalistic caring for people by the Emperor and his Mandarin officials. The government was supposed to care for the people the way a family takes care of its children.

Benevolence also includes the Golden Rule—do not do to others what you do not want them to do to you—hence the lack of discrimination.

Singapore then combines the best of Chinese entrepreneurial capitalism with the best of Swedish-style democratic socialism. Add to this British banking and finance and the perfect seaport position and facilities, and Singapore has come roaring into the world of high-technology industrial-capitalist nations.

Singapore's democracy, however, has been roundly criticized for being authoritarian. One can be publicly flogged in Singapore for minor offenses. Lawful protections do exist, but the Constitution allows for too much harsh punishment and too much control over social activities.

So while the economic transition in Singapore has been a complete success, the political transition to legal democracy is not yet complete.

Hong Kong has a similar developmental pattern as Singapore. The British banking and financial system was well developed and retained after independence. The business entrepreneurial drive was there, as in Singapore. And the Hong Kong government has been equally "benevolent" in that the thousands of boat people and impoverished mainlanders who fled to Hong Kong after the Chinese Civil War and communist takeover (between 1950 and 1980) were given housing, their children were educated in good schools, and they were given jobs.

The remarkable success of the Hong Kong Chinese in absorbing the immigrants, the boat people, and the poor have paid off in producing a new generation of middle-class educated Chinese.

The port facilities are similar to Singapore—modernized and perfectly situated between China and Europe and the USA. Huge amounts of containerized shipping move in and out of Hong Kong.

Further, and this is critical for both Hong Kong and Mainland China, when China decided to take "the capitalist road" under Deng Xiaoping, they first experimented with capitalist industrial factories in the New Territories, just adjacent to Hong Kong and Kowloon (under Hong Kong control).

These new capitalist-industrial factories were established by Hong Kong business and banking leaders in coordination with American and European corporations and the Beijing government.

Importantly, Beijing stayed out of it long enough so that the Hong Kong-American-EU partnerships worked very smoothly. The capitalist-industrial factories have been a tremendous success. So successful have they been that the model established in the New Territories has been copied all over China—first in Shanghai, which has become very competitive with Hong Kong, then in many other regions of China.

Chinese-EU-American partnerships have produced the fastest-growing capitalist-industrial economy in the world. China is, therefore, making a rapid transition to high-technology industrial capitalism.

However, China is a giant country and has a billion people. Confucian benevolence is existent as a cultural phenomenon, but a billion people cannot be upgraded to middle-class status very quickly. So China still has poverty on a large scale, and parts of China are still quite underdeveloped.

And, of course, Xi Jinping surprised the world—and most Chinese intellectuals—by not becoming more legit-democratic but rather becoming dictatorial—and totalitarian.

Hong Kong, however, has returned to the legit-democratic traditions inherited from Great Britain. The British were racist and imperious, but they did establish law and parliament.

Hong Kong is trying desperately to maintain its legal democracy, while Xi Jinping and the Beijing Communist Party are trying to destroy it.

When Britain returned Hong Kong to China, the treaty stipulated that democracy was to be left intact—one country, two systems.

Given the spectacular success of the Hong Kong economy and its supervision of the even more successful industrial-capitalist factory economy in the New Territories, the Hong Kong Chinese believed Beijing would honor the treaty. But Beijing has not. Xi Jinping is a totalitarian. He cannot tolerate anything out of his control.

So this remarkably successful Asian Tiger may be overwhelmed by the huge Chinese Dragon.

As is well known, the island of Taiwan was separated from China politically after the American-backed Kuomintang, led by Chiang Kai-Shek, lost to the Chinese communists. Chang and his army fled to Taiwan and were protected by the US fleet, which blocked a Chinese invasion.

When Taiwan began to develop economically, US corporations came into Taiwan and partnered with Chinese businessmen, creating a factory system that is similar to that in the New Territories of Hong Kong. The factories were smaller, and the enterprises were more modest.

There was some Japanese influence in Taiwan because the Japanese had occupied Taiwan during World War II. And Japanese corporations came to Taiwan during the 1990s, establishing joint factories of their own.

So Taiwan has established a high-tech industrial-capitalist economy, but the island itself is not a wealthy place like Singapore or Hong Kong. It is not a major port or banking center, though indigenous businessmen have established some successful brands—such as specialized bicycles and giant mountain bikes—and the best microchip factory in the world!

Democracy has slowly taken root in Taiwan under strong American tutelage. It is functioning well. The question is, will China continue to threaten Taiwan's independence? The answer is, unfortunately, yes.

I have already described how South Korea has created a high-technology industrial-capitalist economy following the Japanese model of giant "Zaibatsu" conglomerates.

The reason that I mention South Korea again is to show that the road to a modern capitalist-industrial economy can be different.

Singapore and Hong Kong combine British finance with Chinese business expertise. Taiwan follows American-style capitalist industrialism, while South Korea's industrial system is very different and modeled on Japan.

Outside of Asia, there have been various roads to a modern economy as well.

Let us look at a few Latin American nations first.

4.4.2 *The Chinese Economic Model as Unique: American-Style Capitalism and Communist Party Control*

One cannot call the Chinese economic system a "model" for it is quite unique. That is, it emerged from two completely divergent historical processes, yet it has been spectacularly successful. As everyone knows, the Communists took control of China after the Civil War in 1948. Mao Zedong copied the Russian system of economic development. The Communists built the modern infrastructure of China: they constructed roads, installed electrification, established schools and universities, and focused their economic development on science and military mechanization.

Like the Soviet Union, they succeeded with their schools, universities, science, and military buildup. And like the Soviet Union, they failed in their attempt to create an efficient consumer economy.

State-run business enterprises became bureaucratic and inefficient. Military equipment, like guns and tanks, can be produced, but the price will be ridiculously high, and the process will not be acceptable in terms of efficiency and quality in production.

Noting the failure of the Soviet economy in regard to consumer products and an upscale lifestyle and seeing that the economies of the United States and the EU were spectacular in this regard, Mao decided to do something drastic.

At first, he tried to stay within the Communist system: he initiated "The Great Leap Forward," wherein he utilized "Corvée labor teams"—like in ancient China—to try to catch up.

When "The Great Leap Forward" failed, Mao went to extremes and initiated "The Cultural Revolution," which he believed would modernize the thought of the nation and facilitate economic growth.

When "The Cultural Revolution" failed, Mao retired to a Buddhist monastery and famously told Deng Xiaoping to "take the capitalist road."

Deng had been telling Mao that capitalism was the most efficient and innovative economic system and that China should go with "the capitalist road."

And so in one of the most remarkable changes of direction in history, the Communist Party dictatorship of China attempted to establish a capitalist economy.

The model for Chinese capitalism was right at their doorstep. That is, Singapore, Hong Kong, and Taiwan already had very successful capitalist economies—they were part of "the Four Tigers"—and entrepreneurs and financiers built modern, high-tech, efficient, innovative, and highly productive capitalist economies.

The success of the capitalist economies of Singapore, Hong Kong, and Taiwan showed that the Chinese could excel at capitalism. The Chinese had been known historically to be excellent entrepreneurs—they were legendary in Southeast Asia and Melanesia as small businessmen skilled in trade and craft production.

After Mao's death, Deng Xiaoping chose the most extreme model of capitalism rather than the more controlled capitalism of Japan and South Korea.

Thus, from the 1970s to the present, we have the remarkable phenomenon of a freewheeling, wide-open, flamboyant capitalist economy, with the Communist Party still in dictatorial control of China politically. This is a combination nobody predicted, but so far, it has worked economically.

The Communist Party not only controls the people politically, but they also help the economy overseas. The Communist government organizes the purchase of raw materials from foreign nations; it arranges diplomatic ties with foreign nations, including the building of port facilities and trade infrastructure to help Chinese capitalist companies abroad.

For instance, the Chinese government arranged to build a supermodern container port in Greece. The port of Athens—Piraeus—was old-fashioned and could not receive the huge container ships used in today's shipping. So the Greeks contracted Chinese corporations to build and service a brand-new container port at Piraeus.

The Chinese did this, and, it was so successful that new highways were connected to it—going north—to Europe and facilitating the flow of Chinese-made goods into Europe.

This Greek port was so successful, that Brazil, Peru, and other Latin American countries—including Panama at the Canal—contracting with the Chinese government to build new ports in their countries. This program then spread to Africa, where Chinese ports and infrastructure now facilitate the movement of raw materials for China and Chinese goods to Africa.

All of this capitalist success was originally directed from Hong Kong. In the so-called new territories on the mainland near Hong Kong, the first capitalist factories were built and operated. So successful were the factories in the new territories that they were copied all along coastal China—from Shanghai, North and West, and eventually to dozens of new urban complexes around much of China.

Now, the success of the Chinese capitalist economy led many Western observers to predict a liberalization in Chinese politics. I, myself, wrote a book entitled *China in Transition: Communism, Capitalism, Democracy*.

We hoped that with the growth of a college-educated middle class—which accompanies capitalist economic expansion—demands for a legal democratic state would emerge. This had occurred in Hong Kong, Singapore, and Taiwan. But in those Chinese nations, Great Britain and the USA had been in control, establishing legal democratic institutions as they left.

In China, the Communist Party was still in control. And with 1 billion people, it is easy for the Chinese Communist Party to recruit a loyal military and police force attached closely to their control. Poor peasants and workers chosen for the military and the police are given power and economic security. They are then turned against the new rising middle and upper middle classes.

Jealous of the success and affluence of the middle classes, the military and police dominate and control the middle classes supporting the Communist Party dictatorships loyalty and violence.

When Xi Jinping was chosen as Chairman of the Communist Party, college-educated middle classes and the business elite thought that he would liberalize China politically. Xi had been the Mayor of Shanghai during its capitalist expansion. He was excellent at facilitating capitalist growth and seemed liberal politically.

Unfortunately, for China and the world, once ensconced as Chair of the Communist Party, he became more dictatorial—more totalitarian—than any Chinese leader since Mao.

Xi has initiated a totalitarian system—Orwellian—with high-tech cameras and surveillance devices invading the privacy of its citizens. Each citizen is "graded" on social cooperation with the government. A low score means your children will not go to college, and your economic condition will be reduced.

Xi has the population terrorized and has declared his solidarity with the memory of Mao Zedong.

So we have in contemporary China a paradox of monumental proportions: a free market economy with innovative capitalists operating in American style—even with an American-style stock exchange—combined with an increasingly totalitarian Communist Party dictatorship.

Can democracy emerge in China?

Confucius vs. Xunzi

In ancient China, there were two schools of thought on politics. Both believed you needed an emperorship and a trained bureaucracy. But Xunzi insisted that the Emperor and bureaucracy must be repressive and must use violence against the people. Xunzi believed that the people were essentially wicked, and if you did not use force and violence against them, they would run wild, commit crimes, and create disorder. Xunzi has been called the Chinese Machiavelli.

Confucius, on the other hand, believed that if the Emperor and the bureaucrats acted morally and benevolently—being honest and caring and carrying out their government roles efficiently and fairly—then the people would see them as positive role models and would act politely, morally, and benevolently in return. Thus, political order could be maintained without resorting to violence and repression.

Throughout the centuries, China oscillated between these two extremes of political process. Some emperors were benevolent—encouraging their bureaucrats to act in a positive way toward the people—while other emperors were violent and repressive, murdering whole clans whom they thought were not differential enough.

Xi Jinping thinks he is harking back to Mao, and he is actually following the politics of Xunzi.

The hope is that the tradition of Confucius on benevolence and nonrepressive models of government process will arise again in China. The college-educated middle class is growing in China, and so is their desire for a lawful democracy. But how does one overthrow the Communist Party? The hope is that the next generation of

Communists will be college educated and affluent enough to prefer benevolent democracy to totalitarian repression.

In the meantime, the capitalist economy is growing dramatically, and the Communist Party is assisting capitalist development with its overseas policies on raw materials and trade.

4.4.3 Mexico, Brazil, Argentina, and Venezuela

The cases of Mexico and Brazil exhibit dramatically uneven economic modernization patterns. The cities are very modern and very high tech, while the countryside is still village agrarian or, in the Amazon, tribal.

Mexico City, Rio de Janeiro, and São Paulo—these are modern cities, where factories for the manufacture of cars, trucks, television sets, and more have been established. However, in the countryside, village agriculture and crafts still characterize these regions.

Mexico and Brazil are examples of nations with uneven development—in fact, dramatically uneven development. The cities are modern, the factories are high tech, the labor force is productive, big glass buildings spring up, traffic jams clog the city boulevards, and the villages hark back to the Stone Age.

The Mexican countryside is archeologically wonderful, in that Olmec, Toltec, Mayan, and Aztec pyramids, temples, and stone cities exist. But they are abandoned, and the former civilizational populations live in villages far below the level that they once had attained. They declined before the Spanish invasion, in most cases, but were reduced to servitude by the Spaniards in many areas.

As a labor force, the Mexicans are excellent—these are the laborers who built the pyramids and temples, after all, and they work hard as well in modern Mexican factories. Their family structure is strong, and extended families are intact.

The problem is that thousands of native American Mexicans are left out of the modern sector of the economy. And they are not passive. These are the ancestors of the Aztecs and Toltecs and Mayas, and they can become violent—in an organized way.

The drug cartels in Mexico organize the poor Mexicans into deadly gangs controlling marijuana, cocaine, opioids, and other drug compounds. These drugs are currently easy to sell in the USA for big money. The cartels are so prosperous that they are able to buy military weapons and outgun the Mexican police. They have speedboats that outrun the American Coast Guard as well as tunneling equipment that defies Trump's border wall.

The drug cartels are like an alternative nation for the poor—and for the native American Mexicans who feel dominated by Spanish American Mexicans, who run the government and the modern economy. The Native Americans feel at home among the cartels.

Mexico, therefore, is developing a high-tech industrial-capitalist economy and modern cities, but the countryside and the Native Americans feel left out and have established a counterculture of primitive villages with craft markets and indigenous foods—wonderful foods except for stomach amoebas—and an alternative power system dominated by drug cartels.

Brazil has a similar system. Rio de Janeiro and São Paulo are modern cities with huge machine-factory production centers. High-tech industrial capitalism flourishes—especially in São Paulo—with EU and American companies partnering with Brazilian companies to produce cars, television sets, computers, and all modern products.

The Brazilian labor force is a mixed race made up of Portuguese Europeans, Africans, Native Americans, and other European immigrants. Many Brazilians are of mixed race that the Brazilians call themselves the "cosmic race," and they do look like a blend of Portuguese-African-Indians— or Mulatto, Mestizo, and everything in between. The Brazilians pride themselves in this and are not racist, even though the upper class still looks European. Meanwhile, the middle and lower classes look mixed, and the poor are the darkest, left over from slavery.

The problem in Brazil is not the countryside (although this is a problem in the Amazon, and we shall discuss it) but urban slum poverty, broken families, and abandoned children.

Unfortunately, under Portuguese slavery, casual sex between Portuguese men and African women or Native American women led to the abandonment of the child—first by the father, who simply left and claimed no legitimate child, then by the mother, who, because of extreme poverty and no family system, abandoned the child at puberty.

These abandoned children became wild gang kids. They had no education, no family, no skills, and no morality—they turned to crime and violence.

Since Rio has a huge tourist industry and a large wealthy population of Brazilians, there were ample targets for theft, and theft sometimes led to murder.

So Brazil has a thriving high-tech industrial-capitalist economy, but it also has a dangerously high crime rate. And the crime rate is not only among the poor. Government officials are notoriously corrupt in Brazil—this is true in Mexico, too. They used to call it *mordida* in Mexico or "pay or die"—so, too, in Brazil.

In recent years, the younger generation of Brazilians—college educated and incorporated into the modern economy in Rio and São Paulo and Brasilia—have been trying to reform the political system. After all, Spain and Portugal successfully reformed during the 1980s, so why not Brazil and Mexico?

Brazil has begun an ambitious reform system—we shall see if it is successful. As for Mexico, it is too soon to tell.

4.4.4 What About the Amazon?

When the Portuguese first conquered Brazil, they believed they were cheated because the Spaniards had gained the great Indian empires of the Aztecs, the Maya, and the Incas—rich in gold, silver, and jewels and with a fabulously organized labor force—while they, the Portuguese, received a jungle filled with naked savages—hostile, unwilling, and unable to work and possessing nothing of value.

It was not until the modern era that the Amazon proved worth its weight in gold. Natural resources abound in the Amazon rainforest, including the incredible trees themselves. Lumber, oil, and plants for fuel, along with minerals and pharmaceuticals, have made the Amazon a veritable gold mine.

However, there is the environmental problem and the problem of Indigenous people.

Cutting down the trees of the Amazon rainforest could destroy the climate of the entire earth. The Amazon trees absorb more carbon dioxide and give off more oxygen than any other ecosystem on earth—it must be protected.

But the Brazilian loggers keep cutting down trees—this is a world crisis and a Brazilian economic crisis.

And the environment of the Indigenous people is being slowly eroded along with the trees. Of course, these tribes, which have developed a unique adaptation to survival in the difficult and dangerous Amazon jungle, cannot remain in their tribal condition forever. The modern world is intruding upon them.

How do the Brazilians preserve the tribes' way of life while slowly modernizing the Amazon region? It is not an easy process. Conflicts between the tribes and the loggers are ongoing—and both the tribes and the loggers are violent.

One of the great books of modern anthropology was written by Claude Levi-Strauss, a student of Emile Durkheim. Levi-Strauss called his study of the Amazonian tribes *Tristes Tropiques* (Sad Tropics) because life was so difficult in the Amazon jungle. It is even more difficult today than in the 1900s, when *Tristes Tropiques* was written.

Argentina is very different. It has a much smaller percentage of Native Americans, and its European majority is a mixture of Spanish, Italian, German, and Jewish Europeans. The Spanish culture and language predominates, as does the Catholic Church, but Argentina has something of a European "Melting Pot."

Argentina also has a more temperate climate than Brazil or Mexico—more like the USA.

Furthermore, like the USA, Argentina has great open plains, where cattle ranching is practiced, such that beef is a major component of the Argentinian diet and the export of beef is a major component of the Argentinian economy.

Argentina restaurants feature steak, liver, and heart—"beef broilings" in huge quantities. Compare this to Mexico, which had no indigenous game, except turkeys, before the Spaniards introduced small pigs. (In southern Brazil and Uruguay, they run cattle and serve beef broilings on skewers.)

Along with cattle, Argentina also grows grains on its great plains—again, similarly as in the USA. And the grain is used as both cattle feed and for bread.

As with beef, Argentina grows so much grain that it exports it successfully.

Given its export economy, Argentina was able to trade beef and grain for cars and other manufactured products, buying from Europe and selling to Europe. So Buenos Aires grew modern, prosperous, and beautiful—comparisons with Madrid were commonplace among tourists.

However, the Argentine economy was not a machine-factory industrial-factory capitalist economy. It was based on the export of beef and grain, small businesses, and middlemen creating enterprises and restaurants that abounded in and around Buenos Aires.

Unfortunately, when the European economies rebounded after World War II and Argentinian beef and grain were less in demand, the Argentinian economy collapsed. The Argentines kept buying cars and other manufactured goods through loans, but with European purchases declining, the loans could not be paid back.

The world banking system had to step in and attempt to stabilize the situation with long-term credits and some debt forgiveness. Eventually, the Argentine economy did come back as demand for its beef and grain increased again in a fully prosperous Europe and a growing China and Asian market.

Some factories have been moved to Argentina, similarly as they had been in Brazil, but the Argentine working class is not as poor, is more unionized, and demands higher wages. Therefore, Argentina is not a cheap labor destination for giant corporations.

Still, because of their abundance of beef and grain, selling to the Asian and European markets is lucrative, and Argentina is able to buy products of the high-tech industrial-capitalist economy, even though they are not manufacturing theirs locally.

Further, because Argentina does not have a large lower class of Native Americans and because most of their population is urban and somewhat educated, Argentina does not have a population explosion—Argentina does not have a poverty-crime-violence syndrome like Brazil and Mexico. But it does not have an industrial economy either.

So Argentina is modernizing in terms of consumption and lifestyle—it is a lovely place to visit, especially Buenos Aires and the plains of Patagonia. But the economy is shaky because it is dependent on agricultural exports, which are always variable and impacted by weather, insects, and supply and demand variability, with large variations and swings.

As for Argentina's politics, the Spanish, Italian, and German immigrants were executed by the fascist movement in Italy, Spain, and Germany. Peron, an army officer, took control and tried to emulate his hero, Benito Mussolini, in Argentina. Peron murdered opponents, arrested leftist leaders, empowered right-wing militias, and ruled with an iron fist.

But whereas Mussolini expanded industrial production in Italy, improved the railroads, and built public buildings, Peron did none of this.

Peron was a military dictator, but he was not a modernizer or industrializer. The only good thing that happened under his rule was that his wife, Eva Peron (Evita), built hospitals and schools for the poor working class of Buenos Aires. She became a beloved icon, while he became reviled. The only legacy he left was one of death and murder and the disappearance of hundreds of young leftist intellectuals.

So while Mussolini and Franco helped industrialize their countries, Peron did not.

Let me emphasize again, however, that Argentina is a country with fewer social problems than most Latin American countries, that Buenos Aires is one of the world's great cities, that the restaurants and cuisine in the country are outstanding, that the people are big and strong on their diet of beef and broilings (vegetarians and vegans will not like this, but it is true), and that Patagonia is awesome.

4.4.5 *Venezuela: Triumph and Tragedy*

I will discuss Venezuela's politics elsewhere. Here, I wish to emphasize that Venezuela discovered huge quantities of oil and used the export of oil the way Argentina used the export of beef and grain to gain manufactured goods in return.

Venezuela's oil was far greater in value than Argentina's beef. Oil extraction, however, required American oil companies' partnership and practical control. Venezuela's economy was de facto controlled by US oil companies. But decisions on the use of oil revenues were determined by the elected government of Venezuela.

After a period of dictatorship, the election of Rómulo Betancourt ushered in an era of democracy in which oil revenues were used to build Caracas into a modern city, modern port facilities were constructed, resort areas were built on the coast, roads were paved well, airports were upgraded, and Venezuela was brought into the modern high-tech world.

Venezuela did not manufacture anything but was able to trade oil and gain all the amenities of industrial capitalism. As long as oil flows and the world needs oil, Venezuela should continue to gain a favorable trade balance, especially with China now needing Venezuelan oil and helping expand port facilities.

Unlike Argentina, Venezuela had a large Native American population in the backcountry. With modernization, an unintended effect occurred. The introduction of modern medicine into the village societies of the backcountry created a population explosion. There had been a high birth rate and a high death rate—the infant mortality rate was very high. But the introduction of modern medicine lowered the death rate and reduced the infant mortality rate, while the birth rate remained high. So the population expanded dramatically.

Unable to remain on the native lands for lack of food—shades of Malthus, the population outran the food supply—millions moved to Caracas looking for work and food.

Huge Chavez organized them into a voting bloc and surprised the middle-class Venezuelans by winning elections with the new majority poor.

However, when Chavez diverted the oil revenue from the modernization program to handouts for the poor, he eventually bankrupted the economy.

So the transition to high-tech industrial-capitalist economics, which was occurring quite successfully through "substitution capitalism"—trading oil for modern products as the Argentinians trade beef—came to an end.

Chapter 5
Polanyi Again: The Effect of the Market on Human Social Interactions

5.1 The Commodification of Human Interactions

Polanyi, being a Marxist, was worried that market capitalism would put a price on everything in the social world. But just as land could be bought and sold and price valued, so too could humans be bought and sold and price valued. He was worried that just as every "thing" has a price, every individual would have a price too.

That is, people would be valued by their income rather than by their talents or skills. "If you're so smart, why ain't you rich?" as the apocryphal working class American is supposed to have said.

And we do value billionaires more than artists or playwrights. Billionaires have adopted an aristocratic lifestyle, with private jets and "McMansions" all over the world. These billionaires do have inordinate political influence and semi-legal economic privileges, such as tax shelters in the Cayman Islands or Switzerland (the Swiss have resentfully cracked down the tax shelters but have not eliminated them completely).

Further, corporate executives have been able to take huge incomes for themselves from major corporations while denying workers—both blue collar and white collar—a fair share of the corporate income. Only in Japan do cultural limitations inhibit corporate executives from "pillaging" their firm.

If Polanyi was correct about the market evaluation of individuals based on their wealth, he was not correct that "the market" would pervert all of social life.

In fact, given the decline of the extended family and the high divorce rate, which will be discussed, modern individuals are in search of "meaningful relationships." Modern young adults search for satisfying sexual relationships, love relationships, and close friendships. Modern marriage has become a "partnership marriage," wherein the pairing couple share sex, love, and many social activities.

R. M. Glassman, *The Great Global Transformation*, Contributions to Political Science, https://doi.org/10.1007/978-3-031-90566-7_5

Partnership marriage is a difficult relationship to maintain, and the divorce rate is high. But when such marriages are successful, they are deep—the relationships are not commodified.

So, too, at the workplace—work interactions push for team coordination. And productive success in this new white-collar and professional world is not alienating. In fact, many middle- and upper-middle-class workers find their jobs to be fulfilling and interesting.

Even blue-collar workers engaged in factory work find their jobs to be fulfilling—and the automation and robotization of new high-tech factories seem to create an atmosphere of interest and involvement with the productive process itself and with the products that emerge from the factories.

Unlike Charlie Chaplin's portrayal in his movie *Modern Times*,[1] where the factory worker is physically and mentally ruined from his job, in the twenty-first century, high-tech factory workers find their work interesting and want more overtime, not less.

So our personal lives and our work lives have not been so commodified that alienation sets in. Personal relationships in marriage and friendship, along with teamwork relationships in the corporate world, have inhibited the alienation that Marx and Polanyi predicted for societies dominated by market dynamics.

There is a ridiculously unequal distribution of wealth in capitalist societies—billionaires have so much wealth that they do not know what to do with it, while the middle and working classes are barely able to meet their monthly expenses. But the alienation from labor and the commodification of human interactions have not occurred in the high-tech capitalist world, even though the economy is linked with market dynamics and money is the measure of many aspects of modern life.

5.2 Marx's Notion of "Species Being" and Maslow's "Self-Actualization"

In fact, as I will describe, individual self-actualization—beyond one's career aspirations—characterizes modern life. The modern individual—male or female—has to work in order to obtain enough money to establish a middle-class lifestyle. But then, many individuals find their fulfillment in poetry groups, marathon running, novel writing, bodybuilding and the gym, and other fulfilling activities.

Marx's notion of "species being,"[2] wherein a person is a worker in the morning, a violinist in the afternoon, and a poet in the evening, has been pushed in market-driven high-tech capitalist societies, not in Stalinist-communist societies.

And it is the power of market dynamics—producing goods at a profit and making as much money as can be made—that leads to remarkable technological creativity

[1] Charlie Chaplin movie *Modern Times*, 1936.

[2] Karl Marx, *Species Being*—in Marx and Engels Collected Works.

and its immediate application to the productive process—and the products themselves.

Nonetheless, these market dynamics—supply, demand, price, and profit—also lead to an overemphasis on money, and they justify the selfish accumulation of wealth that—if carried to an extreme—can destabilize society, for remember that a stable society and a stable democracy depend on a society exhibiting a majority middle class.[3] The accumulation of too much wealth by the rich and too little by the poor, and a squeezed middle class barely making it month to month, leads to social and political instability.

Having established that Polanyi's predicted commodification of social life has not really occurred, let me now establish that there is an area of economic life that the market has disturbed.

That is, market dynamics press toward the overproduction of goods and then massive advertising to sell these goods. This leads to what Marx called "the fetish of commodities."[4]

5.3 Polanyi yet Again: "The Fetish of Commodities"

In *Das Kapital*, Marx describes how the capitalist businessman obsessively applied the latest technology to the productive process in order to gain a maximum profit. This engendered the most creative and productive economic process in all of history.

Machines, embodying the newest technology, produced a massive amount of goods of every kind.

Writing a century later, Thorstein Veblen, in his *Theory of Business Enterprise*,[5] described how the "captains of industry," with their constantly innovative technology, not only produced a massive amount of consumer goods but also "overproduced" such goods.

Having overproduced, they needed to sell all these goods, or they would take a loss in profits.

So they turned to the mass advertising of these goods.

Mass advertising began with newspapers and consumer catalogs (for mail order, as with the famous Sears, Roebuck and Co. mail-order catalog). Then mass advertising turned to radio and then television. Now, it extends to the Internet and social media platforms, such that buying online is overtaking buying at the mall.

Both Marx and Veblen praised mass production but then warned that the mass advertising of consumer goods creates what they called "the fetish of commodities."

---

[3] Ronald M. Glassman, *The Middle Class and Democracy in Socio-Historical Perspective*, Brill, the Netherlands, 1985, and *The New Middle Class and Democracy in Global Perspective,* 1997.

[4] Karl Marx, "The Fetish of Commodities," in Marx and Engels Collected Works, International Publishers, 1948.

[5] Thorstein Veblen, *The Theory of Business Enterprise*, NY, Collier Books, 1949.

That is, mass advertising—and technological innovations in new products—engendered an uncontrolled craving in the consumer, a craving for anything and everything that was new and different and advertised. The consumer simply has to have the new product, or they feel unsatisfied and unfulfilled. Yet—and this is why they call it a fetish—as soon as they get the new product, it becomes obsolete, and they crave the newer technologically superior product. Or they crave a completely different product that is newly advertised.

No matter how much the consumer buys, they are not satisfied. They always want the newer product, the technologically superior product, and the latest fashionable product, and the fashions are purposely changed every year to force the consumer to desire something new and different.

This overproduction leads to overconsumption, and the whole economic process is fueled by this cycle of overproducing and overbuying.

This is great for technological innovation, creativity, and economic advance. However, it creates an insatiable desire for new and fashionable goods that engender not "happiness" but rather a constant fueling of unfulfillment—I don't have the latest tech miracle product; I don't have the latest kind of blue jeans or dress or cosmetics. I don't have it, and I want it. Without the latest gadget, I feel agitated; with it, I like it only until I see the newer and better product or newer and more fashionable product.

The consumer is never satisfied, and the advertising media makes sure of that. The consumer must buy, buy, buy so that the companies can make a profit. But all this buying does not produce happiness; it produces a feeling of insecurity and agitation.

All this is great for economic growth but not for individual fulfillment. "Things" do not produce happiness. Relationships produce happiness; self-actualization produces happiness. The absence of the newest "thing" produces unhappiness, but the acquisition of the newest "things" only produces temporary happiness because then you will need the newer, more trendy "thing."

This is a "fetish"-like process, and both Marx and Veblen warned that this would create instability in individuals living within a market-oriented economic system.

Again, however, both economists admit that such a market-oriented system, because it applies the latest technology—in fact, it is obsessed with creating the latest technology—will be the most productive economy in history.

Take the even, take the odd…

5.4 Beyond Polanyi: Climate Change and the Need for New Energy Sources and a New Infrastructure

The climate on earth is always changing from natural causes. But now in the twenty-first century, the industrialization of the entire world has generated a change in our climate that is occurring so rapidly that the very survival of our species—and so many other species—is in jeopardy.

The Industrial Revolution—whether capitalist or communist in origin—has been fueled by carbon-based energy sources. Machines and engines of various kinds were driven by coal, then oil, then natural (methane) gas. All these energy sources, including wood and peat (when burned), produce carbon dioxide and other gases that pollute our fragile atmosphere.

The atmosphere that sustains life is made up of oxygen, nitrogen, and other gases. It also contains carbon dioxide, which plants and trees need to grow. These same plants give off oxygen, which supports animal life.

The atmosphere was in good balance for both plant and animal life until the twentieth century. From then on, the expanding industrialization generated too much carbon dioxide and methane, such that the atmosphere is going out of balance.

Both the gas composition and the temperature are changing at dangerous levels.

The increasing carbon dioxide and methane in the atmosphere engenders global warming. As the ice in the poles melts, the oceans and the whole planet warm. Last year was the hottest year on record since records were kept.

The pollution of the atmosphere and the heating up of the planet could wipe out life on earth. The crisis is upon us.

Scientists tell us that the process can be reversed—if we hurry—and that life can be saved.

To accomplish this rescue, we need to employ new energy sources and create a new infrastructure to accommodate these new energy sources.

5.4.1 Solar, Wind, and Water

The sun is the key to renewable energy. Solar panels are needed on every building, along with vast fields of solar panels in desert areas, on dry mountains, above coastal waters, and more.

This process is urgent: every glass tower in the world can have solar panels added to its frame—experiments with this have been successful, so our major cities and business centers can become solar-generated centers.

Suburban houses and condominiums worldwide can add roof tiles of solar panels or large solar panels.

In sunny areas of the world, such as in the Mediterranean Sea, Florida, and Southeast Asia, solar panels alone can generate enormous amounts of energy year-round. However, in cloudy areas, such as Northwest Europe, the Northeast and

Northwest of the USA and Canada, and other cloudy areas, battery packs are needed to store solar energy gleaned from the sunny days to use during the cloudy days (and at night).

Such battery packs are now available from Tesla Motors in the USA, from Mercedes Benz in Germany, and in China.

These solar solutions are happening—but not quickly enough.

Wind turbines—great windmills—are being put in place along the windy ocean fronts all across the world. Ocean wind farms have been pioneered in the North Sea by the Scandinavians and Germans. And they are appearing in the Pacific nations from Japan to Australia.

Windmills are also going up in windy, arid plain areas, such as Texas, Arizona, and California in the USA; on top of arid mountains in Greece and Italy; and in open plains in Spain.

Windmill technology is improving and could be utilized globally—on land and at sea. But, again, it is occurring too slowly.

Hydroelectric generation has been in use for centuries. Waterwheels are ancient. Hydroelectric plants, such as that at Niagara Falls, generate enormous amounts of energy. Such plants exist worldwide.

Now, tidal energy is being harnessed. In Japan and in Nova Scotia, Canada, tidal generations are being experimented on. They are not yet perfected, but they show great potential.

Since neither solar, wind, nor water power can generate enough electrical energy to run our high-tech global economy, it is absolutely essential that we build and operate many nuclear power plants.

5.4.2 Nuclear Power: The Hope and the Fear

France, Sweden, and Russia have pioneered the nuclear power plant industry. France has no oil and little coal, so France went nuclear. Sweden, too, has no oil or natural gas. Russia has oil and gas in unlimited supply, but it also specializes in nuclear weapon systems so that its scientists can innovate in the nuclear power plant field.

The disaster in northern Japan warned the world that earthquakes and tsunamis make nuclear power plants dangerous. No one can live in that part of Japan where the nuclear power plant melted down. And the contaminated water—radioactive—from the destroyed plant is still problematic. It is slowly being let out into the ocean.

So should we take the risk of building many nuclear power plants? We have to do it. We need enormous amounts of energy to replace carbon-based energy sources.

Will nuclear plants become safer? Possibly. The French insist they have created safer plants—plants that also use up the nuclear waste that is generated.

The climate is changing so dramatically and so quickly that we may have to install nuclear power plants wherever it seems safe to do so.

5.4.3 *Electric Cars and Nonpolluting Factories*

Elon Musk, though controversial for his foolish exploits as owner of X (f/k/a Twitter), has led the way with electric cars, the electric charging stations needed for such cars, and the battery packs needed for home solar panels.

Pollution from cars, trucks, and buses accounts for a high percentage of air pollution. Of course, there is also airplane and space rocket pollution. Still, if we could eliminate car, truck, and bus pollution, we would have come a long way to reducing the ill effects of climate change.

The changeover to electric vehicles is critical, and if this can be combined with alternative energy generation and power plants, then a carbon-neutral footprint could be established. This is not impossible, but it includes nuclear energy, along with solar, wind, and water power.

All of this implies a dramatic change in economic production and in the products produced themselves.

In nations with no coal, oil, or gas, this transition is more easily accomplished than in nations—such as the USA and Russia—where carbon-based fuels abound. US oil and gas companies have blocked the conversion to renewable energy sources, and in Russia, the sale of carbon-based energy is their main source of revenue.

5.4.4 *Can We Convert in Time?*

Can the world's nations come together and save the planet? Maybe.

Today, October 15, 2023, Xi Jinping has come to San Francisco to a meeting of the Asian Economic Development Association. President Joe Biden will meet with Xi and climate change is one of the issues they have agreed to work together on.

So we shall see whether the world's nations have the will and the intelligence to make the change from carbon-based fuels to renewable energy sources.

If we cannot make this change, all other changes will be irrelevant, for the human species will die out.

Part III
The Social and Cultural Transformations of the Twenty-first Century

Chapter 6
Global Culture vs. Tribal Identity

6.1 The Big Blue Marble That Is Planet Earth

From the International Space Station, the Earth looks like a big blue marble spinning in space. It looks small and fragile and wonderful.

And on the International Space Station, Russians, Americans, Japanese, British, men, women, Blacks, Whites, and Asians all work together scientifically to make the Space Station safe and operational.

Is the International Space Station the model for the future of humankind? Or is the militarization of space, which is also going on, the model for the future? There are spy satellites from the USA, Russia, and China; there are space weapons and military space forces on the ready from all competing powers.

Humans always have the potential for war—it is in our DNA; it is part of our animal and primate heritage. However, *Homo sapiens*, the creature that "knows," the creature that has conscious awareness of self and surroundings, and the creature that has language and the ability to be rational, logical, and moral—these are also in our unique DNA.

So *Homo sapiens* can go either way: we can work by cooperating together in scientific and technological endeavors and explore space, or we can compete in space and cause great difficulties for success in that already harsh, unforgiving environment.

Having viewed the Big Blue Marble from the International Space Station, let us now go back to Earth and see what is happening in terms of national competition, ethnic cultures, racial differences, gender differences, and other dramatically changing norms and values as the world's peoples become closer together through the Internet, cell phones, television, movies, and air travel.

Let us start with race because it is so contentious these days and also because its very definition is clouded by both biological and cultural conditions.

R. M. Glassman, *The Great Global Transformation*, Contributions to Political Science, https://doi.org/10.1007/978-3-031-90566-7_6

6.2 Race in the Twenty-First Century: The Transformation Toward Racial Equality and Racial Justice

6.2.1 Race, Ethnicity, and Tribal Identity

Race began as a biological category. Biologists were attempting to describe *Homo sapiens* as they would describe any other animal. So just as they distinguished African elephants from Indian elephants or black rhinos from white rhinos, they attempted to establish different categories for the different kinds of humans found across the globe.

Thus, the biologists differentiated the Caucasoid, Negroid, and Mongoloid races; then they added Indian Pakistani, Austrian Aborigine, African Bushmen, Polynesian, Micronesian, and other racial categories that were unique.

There was no value judgment intended by the biologists—one race was not considered better than another.

This, of course, changed rapidly in the nineteenth century.

As the Europeans—Caucasoids—came to dominate the world through scientific and technological advances, they began to believe fervently that they were racially superior to all the other races whom they were gaining dominance over.

Mongoloids, Negroids, Indians, Bushmen, and all the other races were considered inferior to the Caucasoids.

This was no longer biology, no longer science; this was pure ideology.

Once this domination ideology took hold, then the racial category was extended to differing ethnic groups. So in the British Isles, the Celtic peoples were considered inferior to the Germanic peoples—the Irish especially being singled out for an inferior status.

In Germany, the Jews were singled out as inferior, and then the Gypsies, and finally the Slavic peoples, who were identified as inferior to the "Aryan" German race.

In the British Empire, not only the Celtic Irish were identified as inferior, but so, too, the Indians and the Chinese. The British would barely associate with the Indians and Chinese, whom they forced into servitude.

In Africa, the situation was the same: the British, the Dutch, and the Belgians denigrated the Negroid peoples and forced them into hard labor. Earlier in history, the Portuguese had actively generated a slave trade that forcibly captured Negroid Africans and sold them into slavery in Brazil, much of South America, the Caribbean, and, of course, the American South.

The surprising rise of the Japanese to world industrial prominence and military prowess surprised the European racists. The spectacular contribution to science by the Jews of Austria, Germany, and Central Europe also confounded the European racists. And Jesse Owens' sprint wins at the 1936 Olympics in Berlin dealt a blow to "Aryan" German superiority.

After World War II, with the rise of Russia and China as world powers and the anti-colonial movements in India, Africa, the Middle East, and Southeast Asia, the whole question of race as a meaningful category came into question. Are any of the racial differences significant for *Homo sapiens*? Could ethnic groups like the Celts and Jews be considered racial categories? Should we drop the whole concept of racial categorization as so value-laden that no scientific studies could be valid?

Where are we today, and where will we go in the future in terms of the categorization of *Homo sapiens* into different racial groupings?

First, by and large, the old racial categories of *Homo sapiens* are still gathered in certain continents or regions: Europe is still majority Caucasoid, Africa majority Negroid, and Asia majority Mongoloid.

However, in the United States, Mexico, Brazil, the Caribbean Islands, and some of South American countries, there is considerable racial intermarriage. In these countries, large mixed-race populations exist.

In the USA South, because White plantation owners took advantage of their Black women slaves, the African American population is a mixed race to a large extent. Many of the Whites in the South are mixed race as well. There is also some Native American mixture among the Blacks of the South and the Whites of the Midwest and West.

In Mexico, there is a huge Mestizo (Spanish-Native American mix) population in most of the big cities. So, too, in Central America.

Brazilians boast that they have produced "the cosmic race"—a mix of Portuguese Whites, African Blacks, and Native Americans—plus German, Italian, and Jewish mixtures, to contribute to their already mixed-race population.

Mestizos make up a large proportion of the population in Venezuela, Columbia, and Uruguay as well.

The Caribbean Islands exhibit a mixed population of Black and White—Mulatto—and some Native American. Also, East Indians have intermarried into the Mulatto mix in the British Caribbean and French-African Mulattos in Haiti.

In Africa, the English and Dutch did not intermarry with the African Blacks, but the Portuguese did in Angola and Mozambique. So a Mulatto population exists in these former Portuguese colonies.

North Africa has had a mixed population of Arabs, Berbers, Black Africans, Romans, and Carthaginians (Phoenicians) for centuries. How do you categorize them?

The Middle East has some Black Africans mixed with a largely White Arabic or Persian majority. Egypt has a much larger Black-African mix in the South.

India and Pakistan are their own racial category, and since there are a billion or more of them, they will stay that way—although their many immigrants abroad may intermarry.

China, with a billion people, will remain a separate cluster with little intermarriage, although, again, China's immigrants to the USA and Europe will intermarry at a high rate with Whites, largely. Japan is also a separate cluster, with less outmigration than China by far.

Indonesia and the Philippines are, of course, Mongoloid, and they are overpopulated. So outmigration does occur, and they intermarry in the USA and the Netherlands and elsewhere. A substantial intermarriage rate with White Europeans and Americans has been occurring.

Southeast Asia is densely populated and, as of now, exhibits low outmigration. So like China, it will remain a cluster of Mongoloid peoples.

The Polynesians on the Pacific Islands lost so much of their population to diseases brought by the White Europeans, and if they had not intermarried, they might have disappeared. They did, however, intermarry, such that many mixed-race peoples do exist in the Polynesian Islands—Polynesians first intermarried with Whites from the USA, France, and Britain. But now, the Polynesians are intermarrying with the Chinese and Japanese immigrants to these islands.

By now, I have probably offended every reader because I have had the stupidity to discuss racial intermarriage as a biological phenomenon.

However, the reason I did so was to attempt to project a world of the future wherein Internet connections and air travel will have allowed greater movement of peoples around the globe than today.

Already, there is an enormous amount of travel and Internet contact. And racial and cultural differences become minimized when people get absorbed into the world culture of science, university education, music, movies, TV shows, newscasts, and social media like Facebook, Instagram, TikTok, X (formerly Twitter), etc.

As this new world culture emerges, racial and cultural differences become less important.

So what does science tell us about the races?

Science tells us that, firstly and most importantly, there are no intellectual differences between the races. The brain capacity of *Homo sapiens* is fully developed in all racial groups.

When the Romans first encountered the Germanic tribes, they denigrated them as savages who knew nothing. And, of course, it was hundreds of years before the Germanic tribes began to become educated. Even during the Italian Renaissance, the Germanic peoples were considered backward.

Likewise, the British in India and China looked down on their subjects as hopelessly locked into ideas and rituals of the past and unable to become "civilized."

Similarly in Africa, the Dutch Afrikaners in South Africa and the British in Rhodesia (Zimbabwe) established "apartheid" and denigrated the African Blacks, preventing them from gaining a modern education and then blaming them for not having an education.

The social Darwinist[1] doctrine of the superiority of the White race and the "survival of the fittest" doctrine generated terrible racist policies and atrocities worldwide. Herbert Spencer, not Darwin, pushed this racist doctrine.

Now, however, with science insisting that there is racial equality biologically, a movement toward racial justice has emerged.

Now, physical differences can be acknowledged—Blacks get sickle cell anemia, Jews get Tay-Sachs disease, the Chinese cannot digest milk, and Native Americans have no immunity to certain diseases. And these physical differences can be scientifically attended to without any racism.

[1] Herbert Spencer, *Social Darwinism*, 1857.

Finally, the differences in technological development have nothing to do with the biological category of face. The fight to attain racial justice throughout the world does not eliminate biology. As long as there is no racial bias, race can be used as a biological category. But this biological category is often overwhelmed with cultural prejudice. So let us look at the ethnic cultures now—and I am sure I will offend the readers again, as I have already done by having the *chutzpah* discuss race.

6.2.2 Race, Ethnicity, and Tribal Identity

When we come to ethnic groups, we are discussing a phenomenon that is largely cultural and purely human. There is a biological element to ethnic identity, but it is submerged in cultural perception—hence purely human.

For example, the Serbs and the Croats are biologically so like each other that an outsider could not tell a Serb from a Croat. However, they have different "tribal" histories that eventually produced two different ethnic identities: they speak the same language—Serbo-Croatian—but since the Serbs were "civilized" by the Greeks and the Croats by the Romans, they use two different alphabets to write Serbo-Croatian, and the Serbs are Greek Orthodox Christians, while the Croats are Roman Catholic Christians.

Historically, when the Turks invaded Europe in the early 1500s, they invaded Serbia, and the Serbs fought heroically against them, although they lost. The Serbs pleaded for help from the Croats, but the Croats did not fight. The Serbs never forgave the Croats for this, and when, once again during World War II, the Serbs joined the Russians and fought the Germans, the Croats not only did not fight the Germans but they also joined them.

After World War II, though Tito—a Croat—attempted to forge a union of all the South Slavs into a united Yugoslavia, the Serbs and Croats broke up the union after Tito's death, and a horrifying genocidal civil war between them, entailing terrible atrocities on both sides, eventuated in separated "tribal" nations: Serbia, Croatia, Slovenia, Bosnia-Herzegovina, and more.

So the ethnic identity of the Serbs and Croats had little to do with biology and everything to do with differing histories, religious identification, and tribal separatism.

No "racial" biological differences exist between the Serbs and Croats.

If we go over to Africa, Rwanda-Burundi exhibits the other terrible genocidal civil war between two different ethnic groups. In this case, as with the Serbs and Croats, there is no racial difference between the Tutsi and the Bantus—both are Negroid, just as the Serbs and Croats are both Caucasoid.

However, the Tutsi and the Bantus do look different: the Tutsi are very tall—famously tall—and their facial features are slender. The Bantus are average height—not short—and their facial features are broad.

The problem in Rwanda-Burundi is that the Tutsi had ruled the Bantus traditionally for centuries and put themselves forth as superior—physically and culturally—to the Bantu. They ruled uncontested for centuries.

However, the French, after World War II, introduced ideas of democracy. And the Bantus outnumbered the Tutsi and so could win a democratic election. Therefore, democracy reversed the centuries-long domination by the Tutsi and put the Bantus in control.

The Tutsi did not accept this and attempted to maintain their political domination.

This eventuated into a civil war where, like the Serbs and Croats, horrific atrocities were committed and genocide was attempted at different times by both sides.

Because the geography in Rwanda-Burundi makes complete segregation of the two ethnic groups difficult, as opposed to Yugoslavia, where separation already existed, some sort of healing between the two competing ethnic groups has become necessary. This healing has begun to take hold. But the different ethnic identities of the two groups still exist and will be part of the newly formed nation-states emerging from the post-civil war era.

In the case of the Tutsi and Bantus, biological differences do exist, but it is cultural differences that are still central—the fact that the Tutsi are tall was used by them to assert their superiority. But it was the cultural superiority—not the tallness—that led to the domination.

By contrast, the tall Gauls, when they invaded Rome back in 500 BCE, were looked down upon by the shorter Romans as savages—the tallness of the Gauls gave them no superiority in terms of their ethnic identity. Thus, it was not the Tutsis' tallness but their cultural superiority that allowed them to dominate the Bantus.

Ethnic identity thus sometimes has a biological component, but it is usually culturally determined.

What I want to emphasize is that ethnic identity is very powerful. Humans cling to ethnic identification as part of their self-image. Ethnic identification makes up a strong portion of self-identity—so strong that people are willing to fight to the death for it. Look at the terrible violence that occurred between the Serbs and Croats as well as the Tutsis and the Bantus.

The Greek word "ethnos" means "tribe," and tribes have been fighting each other since before human history was written.

Who could tell the difference between the Canaanites and the Israelites? Yet once the Israelites became committed to the new religion, similarities of language and culture became minimized, and the ethnic difference between those who followed the one true god and those who clung to their pantheon of gods and goddesses outweighed all other factors.

Ethnic differences can be defined by cultural, religious, linguistic, or historical factors. But once a group is self-defined as being different from all other groups, such ethnic differentiation takes hold, and self-identity and tribal identity become merged into a powerful in-group/out-group phenomenon.

This kind of powerful ethnic identity has reemerged as critical, even as the world moves toward a homogenized world culture. Multiculturalism—the acceptance of the equality of all cultures, the importance of all cultures, and the acceptance of all cultures—is a powerful global phenomenon—more so, as science and the Internet are actually creating a global culture that transcends all ethnic differences.

Here are some further examples of ethnic groups that could be illuminating.

The Hungarians are a perfect example of an ethnic group with, as usual, strong "tribal" identification.

The Magyars—which is their tribal name—split off from the Finns—"Laplanders"—sometime in prehistory. The two groups speak related languages, but the Finns went North from the Asian steppe lands, while the Hungarians went South to the Turkish-dominated steppe lands. The Finns eventually intermarried with the Swedes, retaining their language but merging their culture with that of the Swedes. The Finns, as an ethnic group, exhibit a blend of Lapp and Swedish culture—both biologically and culturally.

The Magyars moved into what is now Hungary after a sojourn in Turkish-held territory. The Magyars adopted the Turkish style of military action—horse cavalry with bows and arrows (similar to the Mongols but without their great population size).

The Magyars, at first, defeated the Germanic tribes on the Danube Plain and pushed them back into what is now Austria. And they pushed the Slavic tribes out of the Danube basin as well. The Germanic tribes regrouped and limited the Magyar expansion, while the Slavic tribes made peace with the Magyars and established trade relations with them.

The Magyars maintained a strong military position in the land, which is present even now. However, the Mongols defeated the Hungarians and killed so many of the Hungarian men that if the Magyar women had not intermarried with the neighboring Slavic men, the Magyars might have disappeared.

Intermarrying with the Slavs did occur enough so that in the next generation—with the Mongol's withdrawal to the Russian southern steppe, establishing the Golden Horde Kingdom—the Magyars regained their dominant position, making alliances with the Germanic tribes and continuing peaceful trade with the Slavic tribes.

The Magyars, even after the Mongol's defeat, were able to successfully reestablish their ethnic culture, unique language, and military organization. Biologically, the Hungarians—as they came to be called—exhibit both Magyar and Slavic physical characteristics. The Magyars are shorter, darker, and more squarely built than the tall, thin, blond, and blue-eyed Slavs. The Hungarians are a blend biologically.

Because of their near annihilation by the Mongols and their historical subservience to the Germanic tribes of the North, the Hungarians cling passionately to their Magyar tribal, ethnic identity—their language, their dances and music, and their cuisine are unique and recognized as such by the Germans and Slavs who surround them.

But, of course, every ethnic group clings ferociously to its cultural uniqueness. And every ethnic group fights hard to maintain its unique culture against the others. Even in the case of the Chinese with a billion population—the "Han" Chinese cling to their ethnic culture, forcing it on the conquered Tibetans and Uighurs ruthlessly—they still feel inferior to Americans and European culture in terms of scientific and technological development.

If the Chinese with a billion population feel ethnically insecure, imagine the insecurity of the Hungarians. This explains their desperate rejection of Syrian immigrants and their continuing rejection of the ghosts of their Jewish population. The vilification of George Soros, the billionaire financier who grew up in Hungary but was of Jewish descent, becomes understandable when viewed from the vantage point of Magyar tribal identity feelings.

When George Soros characterized himself as a Hungarian Jew, the dictator Viktor Orbán insisted that an individual could not be a Hungarian Jew—one had to be either Hungarian or Jewish but could not be both. And, of course, contemporary Jews cling to their ethnic uniqueness, whether they came from Eastern Europe or the Middle East. But this must be discussed separately.

Here, I wish to utilize the Hungarians as a good example of an ethnic group virulently clinging to their Magyar tribal identification in the face of competing ethnic groups around them, world immigration movements, and global citizen Internet homogenization.

I would like to conclude my examples of ethnic groups with, by far, the largest in the world—the Han Chinese—and one of the smallest—the Dinka of South Sudan.

There are a billion Han Chinese—by far the largest ethnic group on the globe.

Originally, there were two different ethnic groups speaking two different unintelligible dialects: the Cantonese speakers of South China and the coast and the Mandarin speakers of North and Inland China.

Peculiarly, and most importantly, because the Chinese developed a pictographic language, written Chinese unified the two ethnic groups into one group because they shared the same literature, Confucian ethics, cultural rituals, and history.

The Cantonese pronounced the written words differently, but they were the same words in meaning. So after centuries of shared ethical, ritual, and historical culture, the Cantonese and Mandarin speakers came to consider themselves as one ethnic group: Han Chinese.

Having become dominant in the region, both civilizationally and militarily, the Han Chinese developed a feeling of cultural superiority over the less civilized peoples surrounding them, such as the Mongols, Turkish speakers, and Tibetans to the North.

This sense of cultural superiority was so strong that even after the Mongol invasion, the Mongols were so successfully Sinofied—"Hanofied"—that the Chinese belief in their cultural superiority quickly returned.

It was not until the British invasion in near-modern times that this cultural superiority came into question.

In fact, before the British invasion back in the 1450s, when the Eunuch Admiral took the world's largest fleet around the world—from Southeast Asia to India to Africa—the Emperor decided that there was nothing that the Chinese could learn from the world, and he ordered the fleet to be burned and the Great Wall to be extended. Earlier in the 1200s, Marco Polo and his father and uncle were considered interesting barbarians who were amazed at the brilliance of Chinese culture and who had nothing to add to it.

Of course, Marco Polo brought back gunpowder to Italy, and the invention of steel cannons and guns would create a superiority that the Chinese could not ignore.

The British invasion in the late 1800s, for the first time, altered the conception of Han Chinese cultural superiority. It took a century, however, before the Chinese finally understood that science and other “Western” ideas made Chinese culture backward rather than superior.

This deeply hurt the pride of the Chinese. But with the Communist Revolution and then the success in fighting the Americans to a draw in Korea, Chinese pride began to return.

Once Dong Chou Ping was allowed by the dying Mau Tse-Tung to embark on “the capitalist road,” the Chinese began to engage in competition with the USA and the EU in terms of economic production and scientific and technological development.

Still feeling inferior to “the West” in technology and science, the Han Chinese are today reasserting their cultural superiority through geopolitical and military expansion, space ventures, and entrepreneurial capital enterprises.

Thus today in 2020, the Chinese as an ethnic group are expanding their power and influence. Elements of traditional Chinese culture and Confucian ethics still characterize modern China as it incorporates various strains of Western culture into its traditional basket of values.

Whether democracy and legal authority will eventually be absorbed into the Chinese culture—as they have been in Hong Kong and Singapore—will be discussed later in the section on political transition. Here, I wish to emphasize that even as China modernizes economically and scientifically, their conception of themselves as an ethnic group distinct from the West and the surrounding Asia cultures has been strengthened. The Han Chinese are attempting to *Sinofy* the Tibetans and Uyghurs as we write.

On the other hand, the millions of Chinese students studying in the United States and Europe are becoming Westernized and globalized such that they are less inclined to cling to their Han Chinese traditions. So both trends are occurring at the same time—as in most modernizing societies.

Having described the world’s largest ethnic group, now let us turn to one of the smallest.

I have chosen the Dinka of South Sudan because the rigidity of “tribal” identity is best exhibited by the two South Sudanese tribal ethnic groups.

The two tribal peoples of South Sudan were being raped and murdered by the North Sudanese, Arabic-speaking Muslim people who are more technologically modern than their South Sudanese subjects. This attempted genocide by the North Sudanese against the South Sudanese was stopped by the United Nations.

Once the attempted genocide was stopped, one would have thought that the South Sudanese would have celebrated their survival and newfound nationhood. Instead, the two distinct ethnic groups—the Dinka and the Nuer—began killing each other, just as genocidally as the Northerners.

The power of ethnic identification is so strong that as with the Croats and the Serbs, even when no biological racial disturbances exist and even where the cultures are similar, "tribal" identity takes over and tribal exclusiveness prevents cooperation from occurring and fosters conflict between competing ethnic groups.

There is temporary peace now in South Sudan, brokered by the United Nations. But as in the defunct Yugoslavia, South Sudan may never become one country.

Belgium and Canada—French and Dutch, French and English—both exhibit this ethnic "tribal" identification problem even with full technological modernization. So who knows if South Sudan, an underdeveloped region, will ever succeed as a nation-state?

Having seen the ongoing power of ethnic identification, let us now look at the modern concept of "multiculturalism."

6.2.3 Tribal Identification vs. Multiculturalism

Multiculturalism is a modern concept asserting that all cultures of the world are equally valuable—equally "good"—and that no culture is superior to another, just different. Technological superiority is real, but separating this off, all cultures are valuable and good, technological level notwithstanding.

This point of view is derived from Emile Durkheim[2] and his foundational school of modern anthropology.

Against the background of social Darwinism emanating from England and espoused also in Germany, wherein northern European culture was deemed superior and "the White man's burden" was to dominate India, Africa, and Asia and "civilize" the inferior peoples of the world, Durkheim and his school insisted that all the world's cultures should be studied and should not be judged negatively just because they were scientifically and technologically behind.

Social Darwinism[3]—the survival of the "fittest" culture—culminated in the Nazi attempt to genocidally eradicate the Jews and Gypsies and dominate the Slavs, bringing social Darwinism to its hideous peak. But when it ended in failure—the loss of World War II—the idea of "Aryan" cultural superiority was trashed, and Durkheim's counteridea of all cultures being valuable and "good" came to replace social Darwinist ideas.

Hence, multiculturalism is an idea now gaining strength globally as all cultures of the world meet on the Internet or mingle at the world's universities or meet through air travel or participate in science and adopt the latest technological advances.

[2] Emile Durkheim, *The Elementary Forms of Religious Life*, NY Free Press, 1952.

[3] Herbert Spencer, *Social Darwinism*, 1857.

The acceptance of differing cultural traditions as equally valid and the engagement of most of the world's people with modern technology have strengthened the idea of multiculturalism.

However, at the same time, there has been a powerful revival of "tribalism"—the notion that one's own culture is superior to all others and must be preserved at all costs against multicultural acceptance and also against the growing emergence of a world culture fostered by the Internet, mass media of entertainment, and university education.

Multiculturalism is rejected by tribalist fanatics, who want to assert their own cultural superiority or who are afraid that their culture will disappear. The tribalists do not accept that all cultures are equal and good; they insist that their culture is unique, wonderful, and superior to all others.

There is, thus, tension in the world between the multicultural liberals and the tribalist conservatives.

6.2.4 Tribalism vs. the Global Culture

There is a world culture emerging wherein through university education, world science, the Internet, mass media entertainment, and the spread of the English language, young people of the world find mutual cultural similarities with each other.

The young people of Hong Kong, Tokyo, Paris, Berlin, London, New York, Los Angeles, Melbourne, Toronto, Johannesburg, Nairobi, etc. have more in common with each other than with their own grandparents.

Yes, a world culture is emerging.

And in reaction to this, a renewed tribalist revival of ethnic cultures has also emerged, especially among non-college individuals in their own areas.

Should we move to a world cultural identity, or should we preserve our unique cultural heritages?

There is a terrible tension between these two phenomena. And, unfortunately, dictators and would-be dictators have used this tension to create xenophobic reactions to immigrants, multiculturalists, and globalists.

6.3 The Modern Global Transformation: Multiculturalism and World Culture

In terms of multiculturalism, all the world's cultures will be considered valued. The old "Western Civilization" great book courses have now been altered to include the great books of all the world's civilizations. Thus, along with Plato, Aristotle, and Cicero, the works of Confucius and Mencius have been added to the canon of great books. So, too, have the works of Avicenna, Averröes, and Maimonides—from the

Arabic Golden Age—been added. Furthermore, along with the Vedas and Upanishads of India, the art, music, architecture, astronomy, and even folklore from Central and South American civilizations have been added to the study of great works. Finally, the learning from Timbuktu in Africa and the rediscovery of the great architecture, geometry, medicine, and theology of ancient Egypt have added African civilizations to the canon.

As great works from cultures all over the world are rediscovered, a broad multicultural perspective has emerged worldwide.

Now, this is not to say that some cultural productions might not be more valuable in terms of the development of science, rational philosophy, technology, and human progress. It is a mistake made by the rigid "politically correct" intellectuals who are dominant in many of the American universities to deemphasize Greek, Roman, Italian Renaissance, and Enlightenment thinkers in favor of thinkers from non-Western civilizations.

Why is it a mistake? It is because Confucius—great as he is—never mentions democracy, equality, science, or law. So, yes, teach Confucius, but no, do not drop Thales or Herodotus. Yes, teach Averröes, but note that his work is an exploitation of Aristotle. And, yes, teach Xunzi, but note that Machiavelli wrote *The Discourses*—an explication of the separation of power and lawful government—along with *The Prince*—a handbook for tyranny. Xunzi's work parallels *The Prince*, but there are no discourses.

So what is my conclusion? The great works of all the world's cultures must be taught, such that knowledge becomes "global knowledge." However, the Western traditions of science, rational philosophy, democracy, and legal authority should not be eliminated under any circumstances.

Does this make the "great books" sequence longer? Yes. But what is education for?

Thus, "progress" in terms of science, technology, and democracy must not be minimized. And if these come from Western traditions, so what? They must be included if they are to be maintained in the global society that is emerging. All the world's nations will teach science and technology, for this gives them the power to compete in the geopolitical world. But democracy, legal authority, and humanistic enlightenment may not be taught and could be lost from the world.

Therefore, multiculturalism is a good thing—all the world's cultures have something to teach us, even tribal cultures. However, the cherished Western traditions should not be downplayed, or they will be lost. We do not want another "Age of Kings"—a dystopian world of tyranny amid high technology.

6.4 Global Culture Emerging

Although every culture is different, a world culture is emerging. The unique national cultures will remain strong, but due to the merging of these national cultures with different cultures, a world culture has been emerging.

The forces behind the new world culture are numerous: they include a university education, mass media entertainment on television and in the movies, and Internet computer websites and socially connective apps, along with air travel and world business connections and tourism.

Globally, more and more millions of students are being sent to universities. There, students study science, mathematics, medicine, and various technological sciences, like computer programming or artificial intelligence (AI) algorithms.

These subjects are the same in all the world's universities such that a global network of scientists, computer technologists, and engineers is rapidly emerging. Using English as the lingua franca—pardon the pun—these university graduates can and do talk to each other by way of research institutes, think tanks, and global scientific organizations and conferences.

Along with science and technology, world history is also taught. One can study the history of China or Greece or Germany or anywhere else. And history as a rational scientific discipline creates the same level of global interconnections between all the universities offering history as a modern discipline. So, too, with many social sciences. Anthropology, archaeology, sociology, psychology, and economics—these have all become internationally established disciplines, with students from all over the world sharing their findings and studies through international organizations and conferences.

Similarly with literature, art, history, and musicology—these are all worldwide disciplines now, studied multiculturally around the globe. Although there are national and cultural traditions, the study of all of these disciplines is now fairly universal.

So university students studying worldwide and in interchange programs are unwittingly sharing in a new world culture generated by the universities globally. The more university-educated students there are, the more easily will they relate to each other and share with each other the educational background that has now become ubiquitous in all the world's universities.

Beyond the high culture of universities, the pop culture of television, movies, and the Internet has also provided a link between the world's peoples as they share the same movie images and characters, sing the same pop songs, move to the same dances, and participate in shared social media outlets like Facebook, Instagram, TikTok, X (Twitter), and more.

If you look at a Filipino rapper or a Korean K-rock group, you can see the powerful influence of the mass media of entertainment on the world's population—especially the young.

I can still remember my amazement as a cousin of my wife visiting from Greece asked me to take him around New York City—not to the Statue of Liberty or the Empire State Building but to the sites where the movie *Ghostbusters* was filmed. He, like millions of teenage boys around the globe, had loved that movie.

The adolescent and college-age population is sharing a global culture of mass-mediated popular movies, TV shows, pop music, and dance. The young people share this similar cultural experience. They still retain their own ethnic culture but add the world culture to it. Thus, a Korean adolescent and an Italian adolescent are culturally different, but they share the mass-mediated pop culture, as well as a university education. Furthermore, they possess the same smartphone, tablet, computer, television set, automobile, and clothing styles, and even perhaps proficiency in the English language as their second language.

They are different because of their indigenous ethnic culture, but they are the same in terms of the mass-mediated world culture and university education. They share the same science and medicine, as well as the same pop music or TikTok videos.

The more ubiquitous the mass-mediated pop culture becomes and the more extensive and inclusive the university education becomes, the more indelible the world culture becomes.

I remember visiting Hong Kong just before it was returned to China. And I was delighted that I had more in common with the sociologists I met in Hong Kong than differences. Yes, my hosts drank tea, and I drank coffee, but we all spoke English and studied the same great socialists. I had more in common with the Hong Kong Chinese university-educated middle class than I did with the high-school-educated farmers in Ohio, where I spent a year gaining a master's degree.

The new world culture is powerful. It does not illuminate indigenous ethnic-cultural differences—these remain strong and create differences in people. However, the new world culture creates a bridge over which the world's ethnically diverse people can communicate successfully.

To sum up, science, medicine, university education, and the worldwide web of social media are creating a world culture that—though it does not unite the world's people geopolitically—can create the foundation for an eventual, non-utopian, universal world culture that will allow all the world's people to share at least some semblance of a universal, global identity.

The case of Assad of Syria is a warning against utopianizing this process. After Assad and his wife gained an Oxford education, they returned to Syria. When Assad's father died in office as a dictator of Syria, Assad did not allow British-style democracy and legal authority to emerge in Syria, for if he did, he would have lost the election because his base was a minority population of Alawite Shia and Christian Syrians. The Sunni Syrians had the majority.

Therefore, Oxford education be damned, Assad embarked on a murderous repression of the Sunni majority—with Russian military backing—and has remained the dictator of Syria.

We should not be overly pessimistic, however, because the world culture and university education have barely penetrated the Syrian countryside and interior cities. Syria was basically a village society, with some tribal areas still untouched by any modernization. And even the big cities were just becoming modernized.

So the world culture is emerging, and the world's people will be able to better communicate with each other. But this does not imply any utopian future for the "Big Blue Marble."

Up on the International Space Station, however, the astronauts and cosmonauts speak mostly English and join together in scientific cooperation—men, women, Blacks, Whites, Asians, Caucasians, and many other ethnicities from many nations.

Chapter 7
Women's Liberation in Historical Perspective

7.1 Ancient Greece

7.1.1 Sappho and Her School for Girls

The earliest-known glimmerings of a women's liberation movement began in ancient Greece. Sappho is the world's first proponent of women's liberation. She opened a school for girls—wealthy girls—on the Island of Lesbos, where she lived. The girls were taught poetry and dancing—typical for Greek women and not liberationist—but Sappho also taught the girls philosophy and history and Olympic-style athletics, including running, jumping, and wrestling—no boxing because that would have disfigured the girls' faces. And Sappho was also teaching the girls marriage etiquette—sexual and household management. Sappho was a marriage counselor as well as a sophist-style teacher of knowledge.

Sappho was bisexual. She loved her girls—physically—and she also loved men. This was typical of the Greek upper class men and women—men were loving boys sexually while in the warrior organization but marrying women at the age of 30 after their warrior days were almost over.

Sappho's poetry reflects her love for girls and men. The key here is that Sappho educated the girls in rational philosophy and Olympic athletics—this was revolutionary.

7.1.2 Aspasia: The Intellectual from Miletus

Later, at the height of the Greek Golden Age, an upper-class woman from Miletus (the city of scientific fame wherein science, as we know it, emerged from Thales and his students) named Aspasia traveled to Athens. In Athens, she founded a school

R. M. Glassman, *The Great Global Transformation*, Contributions to Political Science, https://doi.org/10.1007/978-3-031-90566-7_7

for girls—teaching philosophy, Pythagorean mathematics, and marriage counseling. Aspasia was the first person we know to teach "partnership marriage," wherein the husband and wife were both educated, both managed the household, and both participated in the political life of their city-state.

Importantly, Aspasia became the romantic partner of Pericles, the leader of Athenian democracy. She persuaded Pericles to invite many of the great scientific and philosophical thinkers of the Greek world to come to Athens. This was controversial, for many of these thinkers were considered subversive—some did not believe in the gods, some had strange theories about the primary substance of the universe, while all of them opened debates and dialogues on every aspect of social life and on every aspect of the conception of the universe and the gods.

Athens did become the center of Greek intellectual life, superseding Miletus. And, along with Aspasia, many other prominent, wealthy women entered into the intellectual discourses occurring in Athens.

7.1.3 Plato[1] vs. Aristotle[2] on Women

Plato's mother was probably a Pythagorean philosopher, advocating that mathematics was the key to understanding the universe and teaching Pythagoras' theory of the soul as living on beyond the body.

Plato, whose father had died young, was greatly influenced by his mother and the Pythagoreans. And it is he, Plato, who had written the first tract on complete women's liberation. In *The Republic*—Plato's ideal city-state—women would be fully liberated, not only gaining the same excellent education as men but also participating in the governance of city-states as members of the "guardian" elite if they succeeded educationally in the same way as their male counterparts.

Plato would have the women not only participate in the gymnasium training of their bodies alongside the men but also fight in the military alongside the men. Plato acknowledged the difference in strength between men and women but believed that—like a female guard dog—they could be militarily very useful.

Most importantly, Plato states unequivocally that "women are equal to men in one critical capacity: their intellect." Since women are equal to men in their intellect, they should get an equal education and participate economically in all the trades that men do and participate politically in the democratic assembly.

Importantly, recognizing the woman's central role in producing the next generation of humans and the need for women as nurturers and breast feeders, Plato, in his ideal city-state—would have state nurseries, run by women as one of their career lives, because if the need for breast feeding—these state nurseries would free up all

---

[1] Plato, *The Republic*, London, Penguin Classes, 1950.

[2] Aristotle, *Politics*, Barker Translation, Oxford University Press, London, 1960.

the other women to participate in all the economic, political and military activities alongside the men.

This was a remarkable insight of Plato's, for even today, with contraception and late marriage, child care is still a major issue facing liberated women and their spouses.

After Plato, Aristotle, his student, reversed all of Plato's ideas on the liberation of women. He believed that women were biologically specialized for child-rearing. Aristotle believed that because of this different biology, women were "emotional" and nonrational in their thinking. Therefore, they should stay within the family and not gain a philosophical or scientific education. Nor should they participate politically. Aristotle believed that because of women's emotionality, women were not as smart as men—they were inferior to men and should remain in their biologically designated nurturance role.

Aristotle's views prevailed for centuries, later being revived during the Italian Renaissance and into the Enlightenment era.

7.1.4 Aristophanes[3] Favors Women's Cause

However, in ancient Greece, the women's liberation movement continued to have its advocates.

Aristophanes, for instance, wrote two plays favoring women's liberation: *The Assemblywomen* and *Worshipping Women*.

In *The Assemblywomen*, the women of Athens meet together and decide that they should have the vote and participate in the Athenian Democratic Assembly. The Athenian women are in the majority over men because men die in battles between city-states. So dressed as men, the women sneak into the assembly, outvote the men, and pass legislation favorable to women. Aristophanes' play is a comedy, and it becomes a farce as it goes on. However, the idea of women participating in the Democratic Assembly is forcefully put forth at the beginning of the play.

Women never did gain entrance to the Democratic Assembly—it was, in its origins, the Warriors Assembly, and the women never did become warriors in Greece. Still, the issue was raised.

In *Worshipping Women*, Aristophanes has the women of Athens put Euripides on trial for defaming them in his play, *The Bacchae*.[4] Euripides has the women acting like murderous "furies" in the Dionysian festivals. But Aristophanes women tell Euripides during his trial that they, the women, run the religious festivals rationally and spiritually. No murderous rituals occur—these were mythical or primitive ideas, which the women and/or the contemporary populations no longer held onto.

[3] Aristophanes, *The Assemblywomen*, London, Penguin Classics, 1968.

[4] Euripides, *The Bacchae*.

The women show Euripides that they are rational and capable and that he knows full well that the religious festivals had become symbolic. The "mystery cults" involved death and resurrection and the ever-living soul, but no violence occurred anymore.

The women convict Euripides and then forgive him, having established their competence and moral virtue in organizing the religious festivals of Athens.

Among the upper class, at least, some vestige of a woman's liberation movement continued on in ancient Greece for centuries—through the Hellenistic period and into the Roman period.

7.1.5 *Hypatia*[5] *and the Library at Alexandria*

The last great woman of the Greek world was Hypatia of Alexandria. Her father was the head of the university and library of Alexandria. Alexandria had become the center of scientific and mathematical studies, including astronomy.

When her father died, Hypatia was supported as head of the university and library. She was the first woman to hold that position—and unfortunately, she would become the last.

She was a teacher of mathematics and astronomy. And she was very beautiful. This was problematic because her young male students sometimes fell in love with her. Once, such a student later became the bishop of North Africa when Rome became Christianized. That young man—spurned by Hypatia—went on many years later to lead a band of fanatical Christians, who murdered Hypatia and burned the great library.

Not only did the women's liberation movement end with Hypatia's death, but so, too, did scientific learning. The Christian mob would destroy the university and eventually disband the schools of science and philosophy—even ending the Olympic Games because they were done in the nude.

7.1.6 *Cleopatra:*[6] *the Last Pharaoh of Egypt*

Before Hypatia, one other woman asserted her liberation: Cleopatra, the last Pharaoh of Egypt. The reason I mention Cleopatra is that she is the perfect example of a great woman who was maligned by male historians—especially the Roman historians. In fact, if it were not for the works of a few Greek historians, such as Plutarch, we would be left with only the negative reports about Cleopatra.

---

[5] Hypatia of Alexandria and the Library and Science Center, Astronomy.

[6] Cleopatra, The Last Pharaoh of Egypt.

Cleopatra was far less ruthless than some of her predecessors—the Macedonian-Greek pharaohs. And because of her seduction of Julius Caesar, and then Mark Anthony, she was able to preserve Egypt's independence from Roman domination as long as she lived. Once she died, Rome dominated and ruthlessly exploited Egypt.

After the Roman Empire went Christian, there was no further women's movement, until the Italian Renaissance. And, even then, aside from Christine de Pizan,[7] there was little women's liberation. There were women artists and sculpturers, and Christine de Pizan, in *The Book of the City of Ladies*, defended the great women of history from vilification by male intellectuals. She defended Eve, Medea, Jezebel, and, yes, Cleopatra.

7.2 The French Enlightenment and Women's Liberation

But it was not until the French Enlightenment that women's liberation reached its modern form.

7.2.1 Marquis of Condorcet[8] and Mary Wollstonecraft[9]

The Marquis of Condorcet, assailed by the activist women of the French Revolution, wrote about including women in the voting process of the hoped-for new democracy in France. And Mary Wollstonecraft, visiting Paris from London, read Condorcet and wrote *The Vindication of the Rights of Women*, demanding not only the right to vote for Parliament but also the right to a university education, which women, including herself, were deprived of in England and France. Mary Wollstonecraft also wrote about "partnership marriage," wherein the husband and wife—both university educated—would jointly raise their children and jointly work in professional careers. The idea of partnership marriage was first presented by Aspasia, who was in a "partnership" relationship with Pericles in ancient Athens during the Golden Age of Greece. However, it had not been a topic of discussion for millennia, until Mary Wollstonecraft revived the idea.

Women did not get the vote after the French Revolution, but the idea that women should get the vote and that they should gain a university education did gain some ground. Abigail Adams,[10] for instance, encouraged her husband, John Adams, to

[7] Christine de Pizan, *The Book of the City of Ladies*, 1405.

[8] *Marquis of Condorcet.*

[9] Mary Wollstonecraft, *A Vindication of the Rights of Woman*, 1792.

[10] Abigail Adams, *Remember the Ladies*, Letter to John Adams asking him to include women in voting, March 31, 1776.

include women in the American Constitution. However, John Adams did not include women.

7.2.2 The American Suffragette Movement

It was not until after the Civil War in the 1890s that the American suffragette movement began. And even then, it took until after World War I for the women's movement to gain their goal. The women's suffragette movement succeeded in Great Britain as well and then much later in France. The rest of Europe was not yet democratic, or where it was democratic, as in the Netherlands, women's rights were not yet being discussed.

The women's movement had another ideological advocate, along with the democratic rights movement. The socialist movement and its most viral leader, Karl Marx, advocated complete women's liberation.

7.2.3 Karl Marx[11] and Women's Liberation

Marx, classically educated in Germany, was quite familiar with Plato's *Republic*. In it, Plato advocated, as mentioned, the complete liberation of women in every aspect of life—economic, political, and even military. And Plato praised women's intellect as being equal to men.

Marx, following Plato, advocated for equal university education, equal careers, political inclusion, and, like Plato, state-run nurseries where women could leave their children to pursue their economic, political, and educational fulfillment.

When the Soviet Union was established after the Russian Revolution, complete liberation of women was achieved—including the creation of state-run nursery schools. Whatever the failures of communism were, the liberation of women was more completely achieved there than anywhere else, until the 1970s women's liberation movement began the global campaign for acceptance. Stalin partially reversed the trend, but university education and professional careers for women and excellent nursery schools did continue into modern Russia and its Soviet republics.

---

[11] Karl Marx, *The Woman Question*, International Publishers, New York, 1952.

7.3 The Modern World: Two Technological Changes Liberate Women

In our modern world, it was two technological phenomena that liberated modern women more completely: (1) the shift from bluecolor factory and mining work to white-collar office and professional jobs and (2) the invention of the contraceptive pill.

7.3.1 White-Collar Work[12]

In terms of work, women were originally included in factory jobs. However, because early industrial factories had poor air quality and unsafe conditions, women were "protected" from such work, as were children.

It was sociologically significant that jobs in modern nations from the 1950s onward became white-collar office and professional work. Not only was there nothing to protect women from, but also women were better than men at routine office work.

Thus, after the destruction of World War II was overcome, by the 1970s, women's liberation burst forth as an American movement of this global phenomenon. Women gained a university education in all modern nations. And once educated, they began to break into male-dominated professions, such as medicine, law, accounting, and university professorships.

Women's political participation also increased, culminating in their ascension to prime ministerships in England, Germany, Israel, Denmark, Norway, New Zealand, and India.

Women athletes became equally included in all Olympic sports, and now, in the twenty-first century, women are included in the military—something Plato advocated and for which he was satirized.

Giant corporations, including "tech" firms, have been the slowest to absorb women into top management positions, but even this "glass ceiling" is being shattered.

7.3.2 The Contraceptive Pill and Baby Formula

What of the pill?

Women—as Aristotle forcefully argued in contradistinction to his mentor, Pluto—were linked by their biology to pregnancy, breastfeeding, and child care. Aristotle saw this as women's strength, emphasizing their "emotionality" as a good

[12] C. Wright Mills, *White Collar*, NY Free Press, 1951.

thing for child care but a bad thing for politics or careers. According to Aristotle, women's heightened emotionality ruined their ability to be rational minded. And one needed to be rational to be political or managerial.

Aristophanes has the spokeswoman for women's political rights counteract Aristotle's views by establishing that the women of Athens managed the household while the men were away at endless and irrational wars.

However, Aristotle's views dominated discourse until modern times. Women were trapped in their own biology as long as they would be pregnant throughout their early adult life.

Therefore, late marriage and reduced pregnancies could only be established as normative when women could take control of contraception. Condoms helped, but men controlled their use, and men do not get pregnant.

It was the pill that put contraceptive control into women's hands, and the results have altered modern society dramatically.

The average age of marriage for women went from 17 in the 1940s and 1950s to 28 in 2021.

Marriage has become "partnership marriage" for university-educated couples, while child-rearing, cooking, shopping, and cleaning have become shared activities among couples in partnership marriages.

The reduction in the fertility rate is welcome news in an overpopulated world, and even in Third World nations, women have begun to utilize contraception to reduce the number of children they will have.

Of course, people are living longer—into their 90 s—and so, then, global problems regarding the care for the elderly are occurring.

Now, along with the positive aspects of women's liberation, which have catapulted women into positions of power, wealth, and high status, there have also been some negative effects. If women are ascending, are men descending from their dominant status and power?

7.3.3 Men's Backlash Against Women's Liberation

To the above question, the answer is "no," men are retaining their positions in the economy, the professions, the polity, and universities. But "yes," men in general are feeling threatened by women's success.

Especially threatened are working-class men who, lacking a university education, are watching women pass them by into positions of power, wealth, and prestige.

These men (and this is a global phenomenon) have been absorbed into "populist" movements, asserting male dominance and old-fashioned masculinity—macho seduction of women, muscular dominance in sports, military heroism, and more.

These populist movements have generated strong support for dictatorships, such as that of Putin in Russia, Orbán in Hungary, Ferdinand "Bongbong" Romualdez Marcos Jr. in the Philippines, Erdoğan in Turkey, and others.

These dictators assert their masculinity very directly: they kill their opponents; they show off their bodily strength—like Putin working out with weights at his regular gymnasium sessions and riding shirtless on a horse.

Power, murder, military expansion, and male dominance over women—all these phenomena characterize populist dictators, all following in Mussolini's footsteps and following Machiavelli's assertions of Roman "virtue": military assertiveness, murder of rivals, and seduction and domination over women. All of this was *partially* generated from the backlash against women's liberation and women's success in the career and political worlds and in family power relationships.

As the women's movement continues to expand its reach globally—even in super-male-dominant countries such as Japan and Argentina—the backlash among non-college-educated men will also occur.

Men are working out at the gyms, as are women. But men want to look like Arnold Schwarzenegger—overly muscular and super strong. Women do not usually like this overly muscular look, but men idolize it as a last bastion of muscular superiority.

7.3.4 Women's Liberation Continues in All Fields of Life

So we have two global trends: one, women excelling at every aspect of human life—going into space as astronauts, competing in the Olympics, going into military combat, and gaining political office and professional success—and, two, a continuing backlash against women's success among less successful men.

However, though both trends are continuing, the long-term transformation toward women's equality with men will continue because women's biology is not an issue in the new white-collar and professional world of work, nor in modern sexuality, which has been decoupled from pregnancy. Modern women are, at least, partially liberated from their own biology.

As of the twenty-first century, women have proven that they can be rational-minded political leaders. But can men be emotionally connected child-care partners? Probably, but we have not gotten to the liberation of men as yet.

One last phenomenon: women's liberation is spreading unevenly in different regions.

7.4 The Uneven Speed of Women's Liberation

In the USA, the UK, and Germanic northwestern Europe, women's liberation is expanding rapidly.

However, in Mediterranean nations—France, Italy, Spain, and Greece—it is expanding quite slowly. In these latter countries, women are gaining a university education and becoming medical professionals, but in much of the economic and political spheres, male dominance continues. Importantly, the Mediterranean countries exhibit a "Don Juan" and "Casanova" culture. The seduction of women is culturally demanded. Furthermore, men have been encouraged to have both a wife and a mistress. And women have been taught to participate in this "macho" culture. So women's liberation is occurring but much slower.

Similarly, in Slavic countries and Russia, women, because of utopian Marxism, have gained a university education and have excelled in the fields of medicine and hard sciences. However, recently, in the twenty-first century, there has been a backlash against Marxist idealism. This backlash is also against liberal democracy and the political correctness (PC) movement—especially against gay liberation but also against women's liberation.

The Russian Orthodox Church has been enlisted in this backlash battle to reaffirm "old-fashioned" family values and roles. Male-dominant gender role modeling is characterized by Putin and his copiers, such as Orban of Hungary and the new Polish leadership.

So women in Slavic countries and Russia are well educated, professionally oriented, and athletic (as Olympic champions and tennis players), yet they have been encouraged to be femininely sexual figures as well as mothering figures. Putin recently jokingly boasted that Russian prostitutes are the best prostitutes—and he meant it as a compliment. Along these lines, Russian, Polish, and Yugoslavian (formerly) women have been emigrating and using their sexuality to gain upper-middle-class husbands in Greece, Italy, France, and the USA. This is assertive, but it is not what the feminists would call "liberated" behavior.

Latin America also has this Mediterranean macho culture, and therefore, women's liberation has also expanded slowly there. Recently (2021), Argentinian men have been reassessing their macho culture and opening doors to women. Whether this will continue is too soon to tell, but no such reassessment is presently occurring in Brazil, Mexico, Peru, or anywhere else in Latin America. The problem of the absorption of the Indigenous peoples is so overwhelming in most of Latin America that women's issues have not yet been confronted.

Similarly, Africans are concerned with economic and political modernization such that women's issues are not a priority. However, the traditional cultures of much of the African peoples already had a high status for women.

West African culture especially exhibits a traditionally high status for its women. West African women have been prominent in economics, professionally, and even politically. So women's liberation may make rapid progress in West African nations.

East Africa is different. The "cattle complex" of much of East Africa and South Africa is very male dominant, even to the point where female circumcision has become an issue in terms of vaginal mutilation—in the same way as foot binding was in China. The women's movement—through the United Nations and civil society organizations—has had an impact on East and South Africa. And as of the twenty-first century, the women's movement has made advances, such that East African women are not only refusing circumcision but also gaining an education and opening small businesses in the markets of emerging cities.

In the Muslim Middle East and North Africa, women had been heavily subjugated. Covered from head to toe and not allowed to go out without a male escort, the women of Muslim countries—especially Arabic-speaking countries—had no voice in society at all.

This is not true for Persian, Kurdish, or Pakistani women. In these countries, women have gained enormously. They are well educated, they enter the professions, and they have gained political leadership positions. The ayatollahs have prevented women from holding political office in Iran, but Iranian women are among the world's best educated, and they do gain professional status economically. Kurdish Women even fight—side by side with men—in the military. Benazir Bhutto was the Prime Minister of Pakistan—yes, she was assassinated, but so was her father.

The women's movement in Arabic countries is gaining some traction. Women in Saudi Arabia have gained the right to drive a car and go out—in groups—without a male escort. It will be a long slow fight, but Arabic women will make progress as the Arab nations slowly modernize. Christian Arab women have already made progress along these lines—and they no longer wear the traditional head coverings.

Indian women have already gained access to the excellent British-style educational system in India. Women hold professional positions, and, of course, Indira Gandhi—Nehru's daughter—did become Prime Minister. She, too, was assassinated by her own Sihk guards, but she did rule for many years and gained world prestige as India's leader.

Today, Modi and his Hindu Nationalist Party are attempting to hold back the gains of women. They, like the Slavic "populists," want to return to traditional societal values and norms—this includes the subjugation of women.

The genie, however, is out of the bottle, and the women of India are making great progress educationally, professionally, and economically. As to the family, it is too soon to tell.

As we turn to Asia, there are three different societal areas of interest: China, Japan, and Southeast Asia (and we will discuss Korea).

China is a fascinating case because the traditional "Confucian" culture was very male dominant. Baby girls were sometimes left out to die, and even today, with the "one child" mandate, Chinese couples will abort if the ultrasound tells them it is a girl.

The extreme of women's subjugation came with the tying of the feet of girls, such that they could hardly walk. And in that era, girls were sold as concubines to wealthy men.

What is interesting is that under Mao's communism, women were liberated and gender roles obliterated in a Marxian utopian equalization plan. Men and women had the same hairdo—the rice bowl hairdo—and wore the same clothes—blue or khaki "pajamas."

Where is China today with its monumentally successful capitalist economy and its tragically totalitarian polity?

Women's fashions—high end and cheap copies—flourish in China. Chinese women are super fashionable, well dressed, and attractive sexually. However,

Chinese women do gain a university education and can become professionals in all fields, especially the sciences and medical fields.

Women had been prominent during the revolutionary era of the 1950s and the 1960s, but now, men dominate the political realm once again. However, with the one-child policy, women have time to excel educationally and professionally—and they are doing so. Political quality will probably have to wait for political democracy—this could be a long wait, although there are some prominent women in the Communist Party.

Japan was pressed into democracy by General Douglas MacArthur and the American State Department. Having been defeated and humiliated (remember, the atomic bomb was dropped on Hiroshima and Nagasaki), the Japanese adopted American-mandated democracy—and baseball.

But no culture remained more traditional than the Japanese—neither democracy nor industrial capitalism impacted Japanese culture as Japan rebuilt its dominance in the manufacturing and engineering fields.

This meant that Japanese men controlled politics, economics, and the family. Japanese men could, and did, visit geisha houses rather than go home to their wives and children.

The women's movement was slow to gain any traction in Japan, even as Japanese women began to gain a university education. Men's control seemed impenetrable in all spheres of society—even in the family, where women were often relegated to another room when male guests came to dinner.

Even today, women are not found in the ranks of the economic and political elite. As Japanese women gain more education and professional study, they may gain entrance into the male-dominated patriarchy. As of today, 2021, Japanese women are gaining some status advance but have been reticent to really challenge their male dominant society.

Southeast Asia is different because women held high status in the traditional cultures of many Southeast Asian nations, especially in Malaysia, Thailand, and the Philippines.

Women in these societies were known as sexually aggressive and dominant within the family. This did not extend to the political realm. There, male-dominant monarchy prevailed. But the households were matriarchal, even though political power was in the hands of men.

Given the cultured traditions, women have become prominent politically as these nations transition from monarchy to democracy.

In Southeast Asia, women run shops in the markets, and they run entertainment clubs, theaters, and sex industries as well. From restaurants to exotic dance clubs, women are prominent. And they are attaining university degrees and professional status and gaining political office where there are elections.

But just a mention of Korea. Korean women have the reputation of being very aggressive—as opposed to Japanese or Chinese women. This is a traditional phenomenon.

Aggressive or not, outside of the family, Korean women were not prominent. Today, in South Korea, so many women are gaining a university education that—along with their traditional strong status—they have begun to enter the political and economic spheres.

South Korean women are making rapid games in terms of acceptance in all spheres of social life. North Korea, on the other hand, never implemented any Marxian idealistic programs and remains a dynastic caricature of a communist totalitarian regime.

To sum up then, one must study each region of the world in order to follow the progress—or lack of progress—of women's liberation. However, the global transformation of gender equality is a world phenomenon and will continue to gain traction as the world's nations modernize technologically.

The new technology creates a gender-neutral labor situation. And as women become better educated in the sciences, mathematics, medicine, and other fields, women's equality will become a greater and greater reality.

Just a few years ago, it was thought that women could not run a marathon nor perform a pole vault. Now, they excel in these, and both of these are Olympic events.

Therefore, with the world's peoples recognizing the need for population control through late marriage and contraception, women will be liberated from their biologically given gender roles. However, the raising of children will be problematical—even with excellent nursery schools. And women will be more burdened than men in terms of combining career roles with their child-rearing role. Nevertheless, women's liberation will proceed, and the long-term global transformation of gender, family, economic, and political roles will continue.

Chapter 8
Some Unintended Effects of Women's Liberation

8.1 Introduction and Overview

Women's liberation is, of course, a major social change. And its effect on human society has been monumental.

Contraception has liberated women from the kind of continuous pregnancies that locked women into the child-producing role that was necessary for human survival in premodern eras.

And baby formula released women from the breast nurturance role that was also necessary for human survival. Though many modern women choose to breastfeed their babies—because breast milk is still the healthiest form of milk—others choose not to or use baby formula or allow pumped breast milk to be used by another person to feed the baby: a husband, a nanny, a grandparent, or some chosen child-care person.

In any case, baby formula provides the potential to liberate a mother from years of breastfeeding, such that she can turn her attention to some other activity beyond child nurturance.

So, biologically, women have been liberated from a life of continuous pregnancy and child nurturance—if they choose to be liberated from it.

Once the biological limitations to women's liberation were removed, then the socialized limitations had to be addressed.

What is the role of wives and mothers in modern society? Does the modern woman still have to accept the bulk of the responsibility for child care?

What is the role of the husband in a marriage in which the woman is liberated such that she has a career and an equal income to her husband?

If women are liberated into the career world, should they also be liberated into the political, military, and athletic worlds?

Of course, in most modern societies, women have been liberated into all spheres of civic life, including the military and athletics.

R. M. Glassman, *The Great Global Transformation*, Contributions to Political Science, https://doi.org/10.1007/978-3-031-90566-7_8

Here, in this section, I wish to assess both the remarkable achievements and the unintended effects that have occurred because of women's liberation. Some of the unintended effects are positive in terms of human society, and some are problematical. Let us look at both sets of unintended effects.

The concept of the "unintended effects" of a social phenomenon was made famous by Max Weber, found in Hans Gerth and C. Wright Mills, *From Max Weber: Essays in Sociology*[1] or in Guenther Roth and Claus Wittich, *Economy and Society: The Works of Max Weber*.[2]

I would like to discuss the phenomenon of the unintended effects of women's liberation, beginning with the high divorce rate and the low fertility rate.

8.2 The High Divorce Rate in Modern Society Is an Unintended Effect of Women's Liberation

It is not that marriages were better before women's liberation. Traditional marriages were not better; however, they were based on role integration. That is, the husband made money, and the wife managed the household. The husband was grateful that the wife cooked the food, cared for the children, and managed household affairs. And the wife was grateful that the husband sustained the household economically.

The couple was not expected to be madly in love with each other, just compatible in their interlocking roles. The couple did not have to have a great sex life, just a functional sex life that produced babies. And the couple was not expected to have an intellectual camaraderie; rather, men talked to other men, and women talked to other women, and the genders generally discussed different things: the men, politics and sports; the women, child care and relationships.

These traditional marriages were tolerated by the couple because their interlocking roles benefited them both. As for fulfillment, love, sex, and interested friendships, these things were either considered fantasies that were unattainable or allowed for in extramarital affairs and friendships.

Producing children and keeping up the family name were the goals of traditional marriage.

---

[1] Hans Gerth and C. Wright Mills, *From Max Weber: Essays in Sociology*, and Guenther Roth and Claus Wittich, *Economy and Society: The Works of Max Weber*. See also Max Weber, *The Methodology of the Social Sciences*.

[2] Bella Vivante, *Daughters of Gaia*, University of Oklahoma Press, 2008.

8.2.1 *Partnership Marriage: Wonderful but Difficult*

Recently, after the second Gulf War (under George W. Bush), a woman whose husband had been killed in the war said, "He wasn't, just my husband, he was my best friend."

Modern marriage is like a partnership: both husband and wife work full-time careers, both take care of household chores, both take turns cooking and cleaning, both do the laundry, and they do everything together—they socialize, work out, travel, and talk together.

Unlike their traditional marital roles, modern husbands and wives discuss everything with each other—they have friends, but their marital partner is their main friend.

This kind of partnership marriage, wherein there are no role distinctions—no husband role, no wife role, and both do all things together—was actually prefigured and taught by Aspasia, Pericles' love partner, during the Golden Age of ancient Greece.

She, Aspasia,[3] advocated partnership marriage for the wealthy Athenians, wherein the man and the woman would share in intellectual and philosophical friendships, as well as sexual intimacy—love and friendship combined.

Of course, these wealthy Athenian couples had slaves to do all the household work and nurture the children. Still, this was a radical idea. Greek men had not sought women's friendships, and they had pursued sexual fulfillment with hetaera—high-class "prostitutes"who were more like geisha girls in Japan than prostitutes, and many of them were temple priestesses of Aphrodite. (The book *Trying Neaira*[4] describes the hetaera in Ancient Greece.)

But Aspasia, who had a partnership relationship with Pericles, actually taught young couples to share intellectual and sexual intimacies with each other.

Partnership marriage did not catch on in Ancient Greece, and it did not become a major social trend until the 1980s in the USA, and then it caught on around the world, wherever women's liberation impacted a society.

So what is the problem? What is the unintended effect?

Partnership marriage is the most wonderful form of marriage—if it works! It thrives if the couple become close friends, fulfill their sexual needs, share the chores of marital and child care, and is financially and equally successful.

The problem is that in the old-fashioned role—enmeshment is missing—there are no interlocking roles: Who cooks? Who cleans? Who shops? Who changes the diapers? Who feeds the children? Who cares for the children? Whose career is more important? Whose job comes first?

None of this is worked out in advance. All of that has to be worked out between the individual couples—they have to struggle to determine who does what and whose priorities come first.

---

[3] Aspasia.

[4] Debra Hamel, *Trying Neaira*, New Haven, Yale University Press, 2003.

All of this is very stressful. Yet many couples work it all out. Unfortunately, some couples cannot work things out. Therefore, the divorce rate has skyrocketed since the women's movement expanded in the 1970s. The divorce rate in the USA in the 1950s was 7 percent; in the 1990s, it became 50 percent! Now, in 2023, it is above 40 percent—still higher than at any time in human history. And this rising divorce rate has occurred in all nations, where women have been liberated from their traditional wife/mother roles and into the economic, political, military, and athletic worlds.

The liberation of women is a good thing for society at large, but the unintended negative effect has been the divorce rate.

Expectations in partnership marriages are so high—the demand for fully equal roles are so strong and so difficult to achieve—that if the partnership does not work out, the couple split up.

And the couple can split up because neither is dependent on the other financially. Women used to be trapped in bad marriages because, financially, they could not do it alone—they were dependent on their husband's economic support. Now, women have their own careers, so they can leave a bad marriage, and they do.

Men used to be trapped in bad marriages as well and could not leave, too, because their wife cared for the children, she cooked his meals, and she washed his clothes. Now, men cook for themselves, have their clothes cleaned and delivered, and oversee the care of their children. So men do leave partnership marriages, even though they do not like it.

Further, some men are raised and "spoiled" by their mothers. When their partner-wife does not nurture them as their mother did, they feel that their wife is not fulfilling their needs. They divorce them because all they wanted was, not a liberated wife.

This syndrome is common in the USA, but it has become a national tragedy in Italy, where the newly liberated women call the men "mammone" because they are so linked to their mothers for nurturance.

In Italy, the women choose not to marry the men; they give them sex and accompany them to cafés, to shows, and on travels, but they prefer no marriage and no children as these Italian women do not want to become their mothers nor take care of their husbands as if they were children. So they choose not to marry at all, causing the birth rate in Italy to plummet.

In the USA, the women do marry, and they seek partnership marriage. If they get it, they are happy; if they do not, they leave—hence the high divorce rate.

Traditional men do not seek partnership marriage; they are like Italian men—and Japanese men as well—they want a wife, not a partner. So if they do not get a wife, they divorce—hence a high divorce rate.

To sum up, if partnership marriage works, it is the most fulfilling form of marriage in human history. Unfortunately, because of the lack of role integration, partnership marriages are difficult to maintain, and since both partners are equally financially independent, leaving the marriage becomes possible.

Is leaving emotionally easy? No, it is emotionally wrenching, disturbing, and problematical. And if there are children, then it is all the more difficult.

Yet with a divorce rate of over 40 percent, one can see that leaving a "bad "partnership marriage may be easier than staying in it.

8.2.2 Partnership Marriage and the High Rate of Remarriage

Though the divorce rate is very high, strangely, the remarriage rate is also high.

It seems that the search for a better partner continues to be strong, even after a partnership marriage fails.

People stay young and attractive-looking into their sixties these days. The new generation go to gyms, jog, ski, bike, do aerobics, and more. They stay good-looking, and therefore, they are "marketable" as possible partners for a partnership marriage.

Having children does not seem to be a deterrent. Children these days seem far more likely to bond with a stepparent than in traditional times. This is because the clan, as an extended family, is nonexistent in the modern urban setting. There are grandparents who have an important babysitting role, but the partnership couple usually exist in a nuclear family setting.

Therefore, the children sense the loneliness of the remaining parent—sometimes they themselves have a longing for the lost parent—even if that parent is still in the picture on weekend occasions.

Thus, not only is the remarriage rate high, but "merged" families are also common. In these merged families, the children of one partner are merged with the children of the other partner, such that there is a stepfamily unit. These merged stepfamily units have been successful in that the children seem to bond rather than conflict.

Thus, the remarriage rate has compensated for the high divorce rate, creating a situation wherein partnership marriages—though difficult to maintain—have continued to be highly sought after and have become the new norm.

So the high divorce rate, which has occurred as an unintended effect of women's liberation, has been partially offset by the high remarriage and merged family trend.

8.3 The Low Fertility Rate as an Effect of Women's Liberation

The declining birth rate—fertility rate—in modern societies is both a bad and a good thing.

It is good because the world is overpopulated with humans—countries like China, India, and Japan are dangerously overpopulated. Let us discuss overpopulation before we discuss the negative effects.

8.3.1 The Population Explosion of the Twentieth Century: The Declining Death Rate and the High Birth Rate

The introduction of modern medicine into traditional, premodern societies in the nineteenth and twentieth centuries produced a universal effect that do-gooders, scientists, and healthcare workers did not anticipate. They thought they were doing very good deeds by vaccinating against plagues, curing diseases with antibiotics, and introducing sanitary conditions in Third World countries.

They, of course, were doing good. However, they had inadvertently lowered the death rate drastically, especially the infant mortality rate.

But with the death rate falling and babies surviving in greater numbers, the population exploded because the birth rate was still in the traditional extended family system—in other words, the birth rate was very high.

Women average six to ten children, but half of them used to die before the age of 3. With modern medicine and sanitation, six to eight children were surviving and people were living longer.

The population of China and India went over 1 billion, and the Japanese islands were wall to wall with people. The population of Mexico, Nigeria, and Brazil exploded, and so did that of the Philippines, Indonesia, and more Third World nations.

8.3.2 The Demographic Transition[5]

A countertrend, linked with urbanization, and the decline of the extended family, along with the invention of contraception, engendered a decline in the birth rate, which eventually reduced the population explosion to at least manageable levels of fertility.

This urbanization trend, along with the introduction of contraception, combined with explicit government programs, aimed at reducing the birth rate. Countries like China infamously introduced and enforced the "one child" policy. Other nations, such as Indonesia and the Philippines, attempted similar programs but without the totalitarian control of China. India did nothing.

World population, as we entered the twenty-first century, was still a global problem. Would humans outrun their food supply, as Malthus[6] had predicted?

No it would not because modern science—as applied to agricultural production—has produced a super abundance of food.

However, globally, the human population is still a major social and economic problem.

---

[5] Dennis Wrong, *The Theory of the Demographic Transition.*

[6] *Malthus.*

Enter the women's movement. How has women's liberation unintendedly affected the world birth rate?

8.3.3 Liberated Women Opt to Control the Number of Children They Give Birth To

In order to have a career, modern women have chosen to limit the number of children they have. Liberated women want one or two children or no children at all. This allows them to become mothers, if they want to, and also keep their full-time career jobs.

Of course, "parental leave "becomes a major economic goal as a policy issue in most modern societies. Some nations, such as the EU nations, have very generous parental leave policies, allowing men, as well as women, to stay home and care for their children for months while still being paid.

The USA has a less generous parental leave system, allowing only a few months of paid leave, depending on the corporation involved.

Once the children reach the age of 3, daycare and nursery schools take over, and the parents can go back to work full time.

Again, the EU and the former Soviet Union nations have very inexpensive daycare and nursery schools, while in the USA, nursery schools are expensive for the middle and working classes but free for the poor. The quality of free daycare centers for the poor is not good, while expensive nursery schools for the middle classes are excellent but too costly.

In any case, liberated women do not want to have more than two children because they wish to pursue their careers as seriously as men.

Because of this, the birth rate has declined dramatically in all modern societies.

The good thing about this is that the world is overpopulated, so reducing the fertility rate is a good thing for the global condition of *Homo sapiens*.

There are problems with a low birth rate, however.

One problem is that the population of a given nation becomes tilted to the aging end. Too many old people remain alive, while not enough young people are around to fill all the jobs and provide the tax base for caring for old people.

This problem is becoming extreme in Japan and China. The birth rate is one or two children per couple, and the old people are multiplying, while the young people are not.

Italy is also experiencing this problem. So, too, are the Germanic societies—that is why the EU adopted a liberal parental leave policy and established excellent daycare centers and nursery schools.

To conclude, the demographic transition has already occurred worldwide. That is, urbanization and the modern economy had eliminated the extended family and had created crowded, living spaces. So the population explosion was already easing off. But the liberation of women has helped immensely in reducing the birth rate.

Since the death rate has also been reduced by modern medicine, the problem of too many old people will get worse.

However, with the low birth rate, at least *Homo sapiens* will not outrun its food supply. We have taken Malthus's warning and reduced our birth rate. The modern family consists of a partnership marriage and one or two children. If the grandparents are available and nearby, they will be involved in the child-care process. And the latter is very helpful to the partnership couple.

Unfortunately, many modern nations are very large, geographically, such that in the USA, grandparents are often retired in the Sun Belt—Florida, the Carolinas, Arizona, Nevada, or California—far away from the partnership couple.

In China, the grandparents are often in the countryside and the couple and the kids in the cities—far away.

Even in Germany, grandparents may be in Hamburg, while the couple and kids are in Munich—far away.

Where grandparents are available, they can be an important source of nurturance and support for the new nuclear family.

In today's world in modern nations, the birth rate is too low—families are not reproducing themselves, and there are too many old people. Modern liberated women should be encouraged to have children along with their careers, such that human beings will maintain their population at a moderate rate and educated women will produce their share of children in this new global high-tech world.

8.4 Some Wonderful Unintended Effects of Women's Liberation

8.4.1 Marathon Running and Pole Vaulting

When women were liberated in the 1970s, women's sports became an important area for women to explore.

Everyone knew that women could run, jump, and play ball in sports. But it was believed that there were limits to women's abilities. The World Olympic Committee—made up of men—insisted that women could not possibly run a marathon—they simply did not have the endurance to do so—and they believed that women did not have the upper body strength to compete in the pole vaulting event.

Well, modern liberated women have proven the World Olympic Committee wrong.

Women can run a marathon and can do so quite well. And it is not only the elite athletic women who can run marathons. This year, 2023, in the New York Marathon, out of the 50,000 individuals who ran the marathon, 25,000 thousand were women! It was a remarkable phenomenon for women, given that a few decades ago, it was believed they could not run a marathon at all.

Similarly, with the Olympic pole vault event, women not only can do pole vaulting, but they are also great at it. Women pole vaulters are breaking records year after year as they raise the height of the bar.

8.4.2 *Liberated Women Saving Democracy Globally*

In the year 2020, American women soundly defeated election deniers and political dictator supporters in the USA. The issue the American women came out to vote for was abortion rights, but the women saw this as not a specific issue but rather a leading one in an attempt to control women's bodies—was contraception to be banned next? Was women's health—and their very lives—to be controlled by the government of this state or that?

So the women voted for their own freedom and control over their own bodies, and in so doing, they protected American democracy from the right-wing anti-democratic movement in America.

At the same time, the women of Iran risked their lives and came out in full force on the streets of all Persian cities demanding the right to dress as they pleased and not to have to be covered up from head to toe.

The Persian women performed demonstrations en masse day after day and week after week. They have not been able to overthrow the theocratic dictatorship of the ayatollahs, but they did force the theocrats to ease up on the people—to allow at least a modicum of freedom.

Similarly, in Afghanistan, women are trying to oppose the rigid authoritarian government of the Islamicist Taliban dictators.

All across the globe, women are speaking up for their rights. And in doing so, they are risking their lives in the vanguard of a democratizing movement in nations where democracy is not yet established or is opposed by dictatorial regimes.

In Myanmar (Burma), Aung San Suu Kyi has led the movement for democracy. And even in a modern nation as in Germany, Angela Merkel helped establish long-term political stability.

Of course, Georgia Meloni in Italy, leading a fascist revival, presents us with a warning that women can be dictatorial as well as democratic. But the point here is that the women's liberation movement, by demanding the "rights of women," is inadvertently supporting "the rights of men."

The protection of women's rights expands the protections in the Bill of Rights and, therefore, pushes modern societies in a democratic direction.

Chapter 9
Gay Liberation in Sociohistorical Perspective

9.1 The Jewish Bible: Sodom and Gomorrah[1]

The earliest written record of homosexual activity occurs in the Jewish Bible in the story of Sodom and Gomorrah. In this story, a group of sodomite men accost the Hebrew tribes encamped near the city of Sodom. They grab a group of Hebrew boys and attempt to rape them. Lot, Abraham's cousin, is alerted by the tumult and, in shock over what he is seeing, blurts out, "we have girls, why are you trying to rape boys?"

He does not mean that the sodomite men should rape the Hebrew girls. He is just "culture shocked" that men would want to have sex with boys.

Significantly, for the modern world, the Jewish Bible then condemns homosexual activity. In Leviticus,[2] the prohibition states: "A man should not do with a man what he should do with a woman, for, this is an abomination against God."

Millennia later, Christian monks, during the Middle Ages, called homosexual behavior "sodomy," and anal intercourse in general came to be called "sodomy." And in the Jewish Bible, God destroys the city of Sodom and kills its residents with "fire and brimstone" because of their wickedness, especially their fertility festivals and their homosexual activities.

---

[1] The Bible, *The Story of Sodom and Gomorrah*.

[2] The Bible, *Leviticus*: "A man should not do with a man what he should do with a woman, for this is an abomination against God."

R. M. Glassman, *The Great Global Transformation*, Contributions to Political Science, https://doi.org/10.1007/978-3-031-90566-7_9

9.2 St. Paul and Christianity

Long before the term "sodomy" had been coined, Saint Paul, a Pharisee-trained Jew who grew up in Tarsus, a Greek trading city, studied with the Pharisees in Jerusalem. He later converted to Christianity and repeated the Biblical condemnation of homosexuality as sinful—an abomination … against God.[3]

Saint Paul took on the task of converting the Greeks to Christianity. He knew Greek culture, having grown up in Tarsus. And he knew the Greek language well. He also knew the Greek "mystery cults," focusing on the death and resurrection of the god Dionysus, a son of Zeus and a human mother.

It was Saint Paul who "invented" Christianity. He took the Jewish zealot notion of the "Messiah,"[4] a young man born of the House of David whom God anointed as the chosen one to signal to the Jews that the world would end and the good people would be raised up—body and soul—to heaven, while the bad people would be cast down into a fiery hell.[5]

Saint Paul added that the anointed one—the Messiah—was Jesus of Nazareth and that he was the son of God born of a human woman through "immaculate conception." Yes, he died, but he was resurrected—body and soul—and sits at the right hand of God, the Father.

Along with this new Christian theology, which Saint Paul knew would appeal to the Greeks, he withdrew the food taboos—on pork and seafood—which he knew would turn away the Greeks. However, when it came to homosexuality—which Saint Paul knew the Greeks had culturally fostered in the male warrior organization, with men being encouraged to have sex with the boys they were training to fight in the *hoplite phalanx* (which I will discuss later)—Saint Paul did not accommodate the Greeks on this phenomenon.

Instead, Saint Paul repeated the prohibition in Leviticus that homosexual activity was sinful—an abomination against God.

The Greeks could have rejected Christianity because of this conflicting cultural norm. However, they did not reject Christianity, for it seems that after centuries of Roman domination, the Greek warrior organization had declined, and even though the Olympic Games were still done fully naked,[6] the Greeks had begun to let go of their homosexual warrior attachments, for all Greek men were required to marry women at the age of 30. After all, without heterosexual activity, there would be no new warriors born, and the Greeks would have died out.

So the Greek culture was always bisexual—to use a modern term. As such, when the Greek warrior association was overridden by the Roman legions dominating the Greek lands, the Greek heterosexual bonds were made more central.

---

[3] The Gospels, St. Paul Letters; also, the Acts of St. Paul.

[4] The Bible, Isaiah, The Messiah.

[5] The Dead Sea Scrolls, Heaven and Hell (borrowed from *Zoroastrianism).*

[6] Stephen G. Miller, *The Olympic Games, Ancient Greek Athletics,* Amazon, 2004.

Hence, when Saint Paul banned homosexuality, the Greeks converted anyway—in great numbers. The Greeks loved the new Christian theology of death and resurrection and the young God—Jesus—as the Savior, the anointed one, the "Christos."

However, when the Greeks converted, a cultural paradox emerged. Greek homosexual behavior did not disappear; it became hidden in priesthood under the cloak of "celibacy."

So whereas the Jewish ban on homosexuality was direct and unequivocal, the Christian prohibition was problematical from its inception. Greeks (and Romans) converted to Christianity and banned homosexual behavior, but the institutionalization of the celibate priesthood, monkhood, and nunhood and the church hierarchy allowed homosexual behavior to continue on, hidden within the church—condemned outside the church but secretly encouraged inside the church.

How did such a strange hypocritical phenomenon occur?

It emerged, as I have already established, from the Greek warrior society and its naked athletic games.

9.3 Greek Bisexual Culture

Aristotle[7] tells us that warrior societies often exhibit homosexual activity. Greek and Roman historians tell us that the Celtic-Gaul exhibited homosexual activity.[8] Strabo,[9] a Greek, describes this with no moral rejection, while Tacitus, a Roman, condemns this Celtic Gaelic behavior.

In the earliest law code of the Greeks—the Gortyn Law Code of the Spartan Greeks,[10] who took control of Crete—it is stated that "If a man rapes a man or boy, such and such a fine is demanded." And "If a man rapes a woman (or girl), a fine is also demanded."

The Gortyn Law Code clearly shows us that the Greek men were as likely to rape a man as a woman.

The Greek Olympic Games were undertaken naked. The athletes were naked, their bodies oiled and perfumed, and their penises decorated with beautiful bows and other adornments. Graffiti at and around the games—and at other athletic games in other stadia—tell us that men fell in love with the athletes and wanted to "sexually intimate with" them—the Graffiti is colloquial, of course.

How did this homosexual culture emerge, and why does Aristotle link it to the warrior culture?

In order to remove the fear of death among the warriors, attachments to women and children were prevented through the institutionalization of late marriage among

[7] Aristotle, *Politics*, Barker Translation, Oxford University Press, London, 1960.

[8] Tacitus, *Celtic Gaul Homosexuality in the Conquest of Gaul*, London, Penguin Classics, 1952.

[9] Strabo, Celtic homosexuality.

[10] The Gortyn Law Code, the Great Code of Crete.

men. Men were not to marry until the age of 30. And they were encouraged to have sex with the boys they were training. The boys kept their hair long and were used as if they were girls. In this way, a bisexual culture was established wherein the men were having sex with boys, but since they looked like girls, they were being trained to have sex with young women, whom they would later marry.

Women were to marry young—fertility was understood to be greater among young women, and new warriors had to be produced for the Greeks to survive.

Nonetheless, given the homosexual activity of men, women—especially upper-class women—had a license to have sex with girls while preparing to have sex with men after they married.

Sappho's poetry exhibits this latter phenomenon.[11] At her school for girls, she fell in love with some of the girls, yet at the same time, she taught them to love men and prepared them to marry. Sappho describes the girls sensually and spectacularly, but she also describes the men as Apollos with rippling muscles, glorious hair and eyes, and warrior skills.

So the bisexual culture existed for both men and women in ancient Greece.

How could the Greeks convert to Christianity given this culture that stood against the Leviticus ban?

The Greeks—and poorer Romans—needed a religion of hope and salvation. They were already deep into the mystery cults, which focused on death and the hope of resurrection and redemption.

Because of the Ten Commandments and the strong moral strength of Judaism, which carried over into Christianity, Christianity offered even more hope and better moral support than mystery cults.

The salvation and hope offered by Christianity were so strongly desired by the Greeks and poorer Romans that they converted in great numbers—even though the prohibition on homosexual behavior was problematical.

I have already suggested that this paradox was overcome by the establishment of celibacy in the priesthood and leadership hierarchy of the Christian Church.

However, the hiding of homosexual activity within the Christian Church created a cultural confusion in all of Christian society.

Homosexuality was explicitly condemned yet was rampant within the church hierarchy and religious orders—monks and nuns.

Eventually, the Protestant Reformation eliminated celibacy and established sex as part of the natural biology of humans. But with celibacy eliminated in Protestant countries, what about homosexuality?

[11] Sappho poetry.

9.4 The Protestant Reformation

Once the Protestant Reformation removed celibacy from Christianity in Germanic Europe, what happened in regard to homosexuality?

Martin Luther asserted that sex was normal and not sinful; therefore, celibacy was abnormal and unnecessary. However, Luther also demanded a more literal reading of the Bible—both the Old and the New Testaments. Luther went so far as to translate the Bible into simple, readable German in order to facilitate the reading of the Bible for all people, not just the priests.

If one reads the Bible literally, one reads in the Old Testament: "A man should not do with a man what he should do with a woman, for it is an abomination against God." And this is repeated by Saint Paul in the New Testament.

So homosexuality is banned as sinful in Protestant Christianity as well as in Catholicism and Greek Orthodoxy.

This condemnation of homosexuality was consistent with Germanic culture, for in the Icelandic sagas,[12] there are stories wherein men ridicule other men by saying that they were the "bottom" in regard to other men who used them homosexually—these were insults. Further, some women were accused of being "masculine women," and their reputations were ruined by this slur.

So homosexuality and lesbianism were known as far back as the Viking times, but they were negatively stigmatized in Germanic culture.

Therefore, when Luther eliminated celibacy, homosexuality and lesbianism remained negatively stigmatized in northern Europe.

9.5 The Celtic Culture of Great Britain

As far back as Tacitus, the Celtic Gauls were criticized for preferring sex with men even though their women were very pretty. Tacitus, unlike Herodotus, who wrote centuries earlier, was judgmental in his descriptions of tribal peoples—the Celtic Gauls and the Germanic Norse tribes. Herodotus is not only the "father of history" but also the father of anthropology because he describes all the peoples he observed without any negative stigma; even when he is describing something like the head-hunting of the Scythians of southern Russia, he describes the custom in detail but does not stigmatize it.[13]

Tacitus is often judgmental and was negative in terms of the Gauls' homosexuality.[14]

Needless to say, once France, England, and Ireland were converted to Christianity—Roman Catholicism—the institutionalization of celibacy hid

[12] *The Icelandic Sagas*, edited by Orlinorfur Thornsen, London, Penguin, Deluxe edition, 1997.

[13] Herodotus, *Histories* (on Xerxes), London, Penguin, 1951.

[14] Tacitus, *On Gaul*, SPG, Germany.

homosexuality within the Catholic Church. It remained hidden in Ireland into the twentieth century, after which church "scandals" about sexual child abuse became front and center and problematic for the Catholic Church.

What about England and Scotland, which went Protestant after Henry VIII divorced his Spanish wife?

England and Scotland not only went Protestant, but they also went Calvinist Protestant. That is where Luther called sex normal and not sinful, and the Calvinists went back to Saint Augustine's condemnation of sex as sinful.[15]

Calvinists came to be termed "Puritans" for their conception of sexuality. One did not speak of sexuality, one did not admit any pleasure in sexuality, and one did not write about sexuality. Sex was for the reproduction of children in marriage and for nothing else.

With celibacy removed and sex repressed, what happened to homosexuality in England and Scotland?

New social categories emerged: bachelors for men and old maids for women. Some people simply did not get married. Homosexuality and lesbianism continued, but it was never talked about or written about, and it became quite scandalous if it was somehow uncovered and became openly known. Homosexual scandals occurred, but in most instances, the whole topic was covered up.

The North of the United States, including New England and the Midwest, was settled by Puritan Calvinists. Therefore, the hidden nature of homosexuality and lesbianism continued, as in England and Scotland. There were occasional scandals—the Salem "Witch" Trials among them—in which homosexual or lesbian behavior was condemned. But by and large, homosexual and lesbian activity remained hidden; as with *all* sexual behavior, it was not discussed or written about.

So how did it finally emerge into social consciousness? And why did it emerge first in the 1960s in the USA?

9.6 The Hippie Counterculture and the Sexual Revolution of the 1960s

After World War II, the United States experienced a series of revolutionary changes driven by various revolutionary movements.

The Black civil rights movement came first, emerging from the American South, where "Reconstruction" had never occurred and Black Americans did not have any of their constitutionally guaranteed rights.

The Black civil rights movement spread to the North and West, absorbing many young White people into its midst. The young White people marched with the Black radicals, demanding that America change and guarantee the constitutional rights of all Black people.

[15] St. Augustine, original sin in the City of God.

The young people became radicalized and began to demand more changes in America. They began to attack the Calvinist puritanism of American Christianity.

They formed into a "counterculture," which insisted that the human body was beautiful, that nakedness was natural, and that sex was good—"Make Love, Not War" became the mantra of the "hippie" counterculture as the newly radicalized youth of America opposed the Vietnam War and flaunted their newly found pleasurable sexuality.

The Black civil rights movement and the anti-Vietnam War movement converged into a new movement asserting sexual liberation. The sexual revolution expanded—"If it feels good, do it!" became the new mantra, along with "Make Love, Not War."

What emerged from the sexual revolution was a whole new set of social trends: the rejection of Christianity altogether as puritanical, "uptight," and foolish, with a movement toward Zen Buddhism and other forms of Eastern-oriented meditation, with Hindu gurus imported to instruct the young people in these new religious rites.

The "discovery" of the female orgasm and the clitoris also emerged, leading to the expansion of the women's liberation movement, which had become recessive during World War II, and the 1950s return to family normalcy. The "Big O" became a demand of the young women released from puritanical bondage and freed from the fear of pregnancy by the invention of "the pill," which put contraception into the hands of women and unleashed their sexual desires without the fear of unwanted pregnancy.

Lastly, along with the turn to Asian religions and other stranger religious cults and women's newfound sexual revolution, homosexual and lesbian sexuality "came out of the closet" and into the light of social discourse.

All the open talk of sexuality and female sexual satisfaction leads to talk of *all* sexuality as "natural." Humans were characterized as "polymorphously perverse"—whatever your sexual thing is, do it.

Thus, after centuries of hidden sexuality, the openness of sexuality that emerged during the 1960s counterculture brought the discussion—and the practice—of homosexual and lesbian sex into the open. Once openly displayed, it had to be evaluated. Was it socially acceptable or not?

Whether Americans accepted or rejected homosexuality and lesbianism, it was out there as a fact of social life in the new American society that emerged after the 1960s.

The counterculture is no longer a major force in American society, although "hipsters" still abound in Portland, Oregon; San Francisco/Berkeley, California; Seattle, Washington; and Williamsburg, Brooklyn, New York.

But the majority of the new generation is *not* Puritan. Yes, Puritan Christians still make up about 30 percent of the population, and they asserted themselves in the Trump phenomenon, gaining control of the Supreme Court (with the help of religious Catholics).

However, the new generation accepts the sexual revolution, including women's liberation and gay liberation.

9.7 The Gay Liberation Movement and the LGBTQ Revolution

Once homosexuals and lesbians were "out of the closet" and the phenomenon was being openly discussed, it became apparent that in the English language, there was no positive word for male homosexuality. Lesbian was a "polite" word for female same-sex activity, and I will describe its origin shortly. But all the terms for male same-sex activities were hostile terms: fag, queer, fruit, and worse.

Somewhere along the way, in the 1970s, male homosexuals began calling themselves "gay." The term stuck as it has a charm to it and a positive connotation.

As for the term "lesbian," it comes from the school of Sappho in the fifth century BC in ancient Greece. Sappho had her school for girls on the island of Lesbos. Lesbos was simply Sappho's home island. Her school for girls copied the schools for boys: she was a "sophist"—a teacher of wisdom—like her male counterparts. She taught the girls poetry, dancing, Olympic running, jumping, and wrestling; she also taught mathematics, logic, philosophy, and history.

Sappho, like her male counterparts, had love affairs with her students—she described the beauty and fragrance of her girls and her jealousies in love with them. Again, like her male counterparts, she also taught the girls to marry and enjoy heterosexual sex—Sappho's poems describe her love for men and her desire for their muscular Apollo-like bodies and their bravery in war.

The ancient Greeks did not call female-on-female sex "lesbian" sex. They simply accepted bisexuality as culturally normative.

It was Roman Catholic Christian priests and monks in the Middle Ages who, rediscovering the works of ancient Greek writers, found some of Sappho's poetry. It was these Christian monks who stigmatized Sappho as "that lesbian woman" who sinned against God by her sexual conduct.

Thereafter, the term "lesbian" came to mean any woman who engaged in same-sex activity.

Since modern "gay" women accept the term "lesbian" as descriptive rather than negative, it has remained their term for themselves, along with the term "gay."

Lesbians today go so far as to gather on the Greek island of Lesbos and hold celebrations in honor of Sappho.

The modern terminology expanded as gay and lesbian activity became more open and talked about in modern societies. Now, the terminology includes gays, lesbians, bisexuals, transgender individuals, and those who are questioning their sexuality or those who want to use the term "queer"—LGBTQ is now shorthand for all of these.

Once gay liberation expanded out of the closet and into the mainstream of American society, the movement spread to the UK, the EU, and the entire global world.

The AIDS epidemic—emanating from Central Africa but afflicting male homosexuals in a global pandemic—almost destroyed the movement. However, the scientific control of the disease contained it enough such that the gay liberation movement took off again.

One effect of the AIDS epidemic was the unexpected movement of gay men toward gay marriage. Gay men have been known for their promiscuity, but AIDS pushed them toward more permanent relationships. Lesbians have been noted to form more permanent unions before AIDS, but afterward, they joined the men and championed lesbian marriage.

So a new form of marriage bonding became normative—accepted by the American Supreme Court—and generated a new global trend toward gay marriage and lesbian marriage worldwide.

Most nations of the world now support gay and lesbian movements—marches, "rainbow" coalitions in politics, gay rights demands, and openly gay activities.

Each nation, of course, has responded differently to these trends—some very positively and some very negatively.

Thus, for instance, whereas the EU countries have allowed gays in the military and gay marriage, Russia and Hungary have banned openly gay activity and utilized the Russian Orthodox Church and the Hungarian Catholic Church to reinforce heterosexual marriage and to repress gay and lesbian activities.

Interestingly—and this shows how powerful a trend the gay and lesbian liberation movement is—in Budapest, Hungary, in 2018, in defiance of dictator Orbán's ban on gay and lesbian activity, young people held a huge LGBTQ rainbow rally. The rally featured two young men kissing and two young women kissing—in close-up television view—and the whole crowd cheered wildly. So the young Hungarians were defying Orbán and his anti-gay and lesbian policies.

I saw the rally on television in Athens, Greece. My Greek hosts accepted that gay and lesbian activity was up to the individuals engaged in it, and it should not be banned. But they did not like the public displays. They criticized the marches and the demonstrations as "going too far" and also opposed any ban on private gay and lesbian behavior.

The attitude of my Greek hosts is typical for many other national groups—gay and lesbian behavior is accepted as a social fact that cannot be put back into the closet. However, they do not want the movement to push so openly and expansively.

Just to show the ambivalence still in the world, two summers earlier, a nunnery in Kalamata, Greece, was shut down by a Greek Orthodox bishop because of lesbian activity. A year later, it reopened, and none of the nuns were punished.

Both the gay liberation movement and the backlash against the movement are spreading globally.

In the USA, where it all began, gays and lesbians are gaining greater acceptance—being elected to public office, gaining economic equality, and even military acceptance. But at the same time, religious Christians and Jews do not want to accept gay and lesbian marriage or publicly visible gay and lesbian couples.

The Christian backlash and Orthodox Jewish backlash exist, but moderately in the USA. And the scandals in the Roman Catholic Church in the USA, Ireland, Italy, and other Catholic nations have forced the Catholic Church to tacitly accept the existence of gay and lesbian individuals and to *not* oppose them openly. Pope Francis has not changed the Catholic—biblical—condemnation of homosexual activity, but he has said that they should not be "judged" but rather accepted into the congregational community. Orthodox Jewish leaders have said something similar.

Interestingly, there is no biblical condemnation of lesbianism. Leviticus does say, "A woman should not lie down with a goat"—a condemnation of the Canaanite fertility festival in which the War God was envisioned as a he-goat and the fertility goddess copulated with him. This is condemned as sinful, but there is no mention of lesbian behavior.

Since women, in biblical times, were married off at puberty, it is possible that lesbian behavior was more hidden. Only in the harems of the great kings do we hear of lesbian sexual behavior. But no prohibition exists in the Jewish or Christian Bibles.

The Roman Catholic Church, however, after Sappho's poems became known to them in the early Renaissance, pointedly prohibited such "lesbian" behavior. Nonetheless, it was rampant in the nunneries, as was male homosexual behavior among the monks and priests. Celibacy was a cover for this behavior that blocked it from the common view for centuries.

Whether LGBTQ rights are accepted or rejected, they are impacting the nations of the world as a global phenomenon that must be addressed.

9.8 The Backlash and Populist Dictatorships

I have mentioned this backlash and its use by modern dictators in our section on race, ethnic groups, and tribal identity. It is also the case that clear gender rules—highlighting macho masculinity—including power, force, violence and the seduction of women for men and motherhood, submissive sexuality and subordination for women—that is, a caricature of traditional gender roles—is extolled and embodied by the modern dictators.

Putin, Orbán, and Duda all exhibit this masculinity and derision of gay men. The anti-political correctness (PC) reaction generates support for these dictators from among non-college-educated working-class men and non-college-educated women as well.

However, as the demonstration in Budapest shows, this backlash cannot push gays and lesbians back into the closet. The phenomenon is now openly known—no longer hidden away—and, as such, will continue as a global movement.

9.9 Population Reduction as a Global Goal and LGBTQ Activity

A causal factor that could fuel the acceptance of LGBTQ behavior is the need for population reduction globally.

"Population explosion" is a global phenomenon that occurred for "unintended" reasons. The science and sanitation discoveries of the twentieth century, when first extended to traditional societies, generated a population explosion. Why? This is because traditional societies had a high death rate and a high birth rate. The introduction of modern medicine and sanitation dramatically reduced the death rate, especially the infant mortality rate. But with the high birth rate continuing and fewer people dying young, a population explosion occurred.

China and India discovered that they had 1 billion people! Indonesia and Mexico were overrun, as was the Philippines. What actions can be taken to avoid mass starvation—the Malthusian nightmare?.

Science came to the rescue of its own dilemma through the mass introduction of contraceptive devices such as "the pill," the diaphragm, the intrauterine device (IUD), and the condom—all of which were introduced globally.

Slowly, contraception and urban crowding are encouraging fertility reduction. So, too, is the women's movement—women delaying marriage, going to universities, gaining careers, and reducing the number of children they wish to have.

Why is the LGBTQ phenomenon mentioned? It is because gay men have fewer children than the norm. Gay male couples use surrogate women, and they have children, though far fewer than heterosexual men. Lesbian couples do have children but, again, tend to prefer no more than one or two—as college-educated women now do.

So LGBTQ activity inadvertently leads to fertility reduction. In this sense, it helps reduce the population explosion that threatens the globe with starvation and death.

Chapter 10
Gay Liberation and World Religions

10.1 Gay Liberation Globally

Though there were societies such as ancient Greece, Biblical Canaan, and the Plains Indians of America, wherein homosexuality was open, in most premodern societies, religion and family norms kept homosexuality and lesbianism hidden.

In terms of the premodern family, girls were married off at puberty or no later than 17 years old. Since there was no contraception and girls were married young, they would be producing children for their clan and were honored for doing so. Whether they were enjoying the sex needed for procreation or not, their role was to produce children.

Lesbianism was noted among the harems of divine kingships but otherwise submerged culturally.

And remember that even Sappho, the great Greek poet from the island of Lesbos whose name was slandered by the Christian monks of the Roman Catholic Church in the Middle Ages—"That lesbian woman," she was called, and the name stuck—like all the Greek women of her time, encouraged her students and disciples to marry men and love men. She herself was bisexual, loving both girls and men, as her poems tell us.

What of gay men? In most premodern societies, boys were married off right after puberty or before 18 years old, just like girls. The boys were often put through vigorous rites of passage by older men and then married off.

Again, whether the boys liked sex or not, they were supposed to produce children for their clan.

So, in most premodern societies, the extended family, or clan, submerged homosexuality and lesbianism.

R. M. Glassman, *The Great Global Transformation*, Contributions to Political Science, https://doi.org/10.1007/978-3-031-90566-7_10

10.2 The World Religions and Prohibitions on Gays and Lesbians

10.2.1 Judaism

Judaism, one of the oldest world religions—perhaps the oldest, even predating Brahman Hinduism—has the oldest written account of male homosexuality that we know of: the story of Sodom and Gomorrah.

In the story of Abraham, he leads his Hebrew tribes into the land of Canaan, and at one point, they camp outside the city of Sodom. Lot, Abraham's cousin, is watching over his tribe's flocks with the help of a group of boys. Suddenly, a group of Sodomite men attack the camp and grab the boys and begin to rape them. Lot is so astonished by this behavior that he screams out something along the lines of, "We have girls here. Why are you raping the boys!?"

Of course, he does not mean that the Sodomites should rape his girls; he just does not understand how they could want sex with boys.

Along with this homosexual activity, the Sodomites also held fertility festivals, wherein women had sex with men who were not their husbands and men engaged in homosexual as well as heterosexual acts.

The Bible then tells us that God condemned all of this and vowed to destroy Sodom and Gomorrah.

The cities are destroyed by "fire and brimstone," and from then on, homosexuality—"sodomy," as the Christian monks of the Middle Ages called it—is condemned as "an abomination against God."

So Judaism considers homosexuality a sin. Lesbianism is not mentioned but was later included by the rabbis as a sin.

Christianity followed Judaism in condemning homosexuality. But in Christianity, the situation is far more complicated. The Greeks were converted to Christianity by St. Paul, but the Greeks were openly bisexual, especially in the warrior organization.

10.2.2 Christianity and Homosexuality

Most scholars agree that St. Paul "invented" Christianity. Before him, the Jesus cult was just another Messianic "zealot" group (as Flavius Josephus calls them).[1]

Now, St. Paul—Saul of Tarsus—grew up in the Greek city of Tarsus. He was Jewish and came from a well-to-do merchant family. He could speak fluent Greek and knew Greek culture well. Because he understood the Greeks, St. Peter chose

[1] Flavius Josephs. The Roman-Jewish War.

him to convert them. At first anti-Christian, St. Paul became a fanatical Christian after an epiphany.

In converting the Greeks, he told them they could ignore the Kosher food laws and continue to eat pork and shellfish, a big part of the Greek diet. He also told them they did not need to circumcise the boys—as the Greeks considered circumcision to be penis mutilation.

However, when it came to homosexuality, which St. Paul knew the Greek men practiced with boys—"pederasty" being institutionalized in the warrior organization and in the Olympic Games, the Naked Games—St. Paul said no.

In order to convert to Christianity, which many Greeks wanted to do, they had to give up pederasty and all homosexual activity. St. Paul insisted that this was sinful.

Later on in history at the time of St. Augustine—400 AD—celibacy in the Christian priesthood became mandatory among the Roman Catholics. Greek Orthodox priests can marry, but the bishops, archbishops, nuns, and monks must be celibate.

In any case, St. Augustine, in his later writings, considered all sex sinful—hence celibacy made one pure.[2]

What occurred, of course, is that homosexuality became hidden within the celibate priesthood, nunneries, and monasteries. Pederasty was commonplace in Italy, and lesbianism was commonplace in nunneries across Europe.

Therefore, though Christianity calls homosexuality and lesbianism sinful, it flourished within the church hierarchy itself. But it was hidden and not discussed openly.

10.2.3 Islam and Homosexuality

Islam, like Christianity, has its roots in Judaism. Muhammad—mingling with a tribe of Orthodox Jews who had taken up residence in Mecca—extensively quotes from the Jewish Bible in the Quran.

In terms of gays and lesbians, Muhammad repeats the biblical story of Lot and his tribal group, who accompanied Abraham into the land of Canaan and rested temporarily outside the city of Sodom.

The Quran repeats the story of how the men of Sodom attacked Lot's boys, who were tending the sheep and goats, and began to rape them—or "sodomize" them, as it would be called by Christian monks of the Middle Ages.

God condemns these acts, and Mohammed repeats this condemnation of homosexuality as an act against God and, therefore, a sin.

Lesbianism is not mentioned for, as with the Hebrew tribes, girls were married off at puberty as their role was to produce children. So whether they liked sex with men or not, they were married off.

[2] St. Augustine, The City of God.

However, as the Muslim caliphate developed and Arabic-speaking kings emerged, harems of women were attracted to these kings in polygamist marriages. Among harem wives, reports of lesbian activity emerged from travelers who somehow gained access to the harems.

Even today, in Saudi Arabia, American social workers—women in full Burka covering—have told of lesbian activity in the twenty-first century, where the Saudi harems still exist as part of the Royal Family.

Of course, this lesbian sexuality is condemned, but it occurs nonetheless.

Still, as with Judaism, in Islam, there is no Koranic condemnation of lesbianism. In Christianity, there is condemnation—medieval monks created the term "lesbian" after reading the poetry of Sappho, referred to as "that lesbian woman!"

Of course, ironically, the Christian nunneries are a hotbed of lesbian sexual activity, with scandals emerging and then being suppressed from time to time into the modern era. In 2015, for instance, such a lesbian nunnery scandal emerged in Kalamata in the south of Greece. In the Irish Church—in Ireland and in America—such scandals have been numerous.

So all three "Abrahamic" religions follow the Old Testament in condemning homosexuality. Thus, in the twenty-first century, all three religions have had to come to grips with gay liberation.

Now, let us look at the great Asian religions.

10.3 Asian World Religions: Extended Family and Ancestor Worship

10.3.1 Hinduism

The *Kama Sutra*[3]—that great sex manual, the world's first sex manual—describes all manner of human sexual activity. If it can be done, the *Kama Sutra* describes it.

And, yes, male-male and female-female sexual activity is described. Male-male fellatio and anal intercourse as well as female-female vaginal touching and kissing are all described.

The *Kama Sutra* is not judgmental, just descriptive. However, homosexual men and lesbian women are called the "third sex." They are recognized as different. And homosexual and lesbian sex acts are condemned in other Hindu sacred books. "Non-vaginal" sex is condemned for men and punished with hefty fines. While lesbian sex acts are also condemned, women are being urged to marry men and produce children for their families.

Thus, "third sex" activities are recognized as occurring but rejected as normative and condemned as deviant. Yet there are Hindu temples with sculptures and

[3] *Kama Sutra*, Hindu Sex Manual.

paintings depicting fellatio between men and vaginal kissing among women. And maybe at these temples, gays and lesbians could gather and gain some acceptance.

However, into the British period, homosexual and lesbian activities were considered criminal behavior and fined heavily. Such behavior brought shame to one's family.

Interestingly, the Victorian British translation of the *Kama Sutra* translated the "third sex" as "eunuch." This is not correct as in the *Kama Sutra*, the so-called third-sex men engage in fellatio and anal sex—they were not eunuchs. And, of course, neither were "third sex" lesbians.

The Victorian British, whose upper-class boarding schools were full of homosexual and lesbian activities, would not own up to these practices even into the twenty-first century. Even now, gay liberation in the UK is problematical in boarding schools and in the church. As late as the 1950s, the man who helped save Britain from a Nazi invasion by breaking the German Code (and inventing the computer on the side) was later arrested and jailed for homosexual activity.

Modern India, with Modi's Hindu Party dominating the country, is having difficulty accepting gay liberation as well.

10.3.2 Buddhism

Buddha—the man himself—mentions nothing about homosexuality or lesbianism, for Buddhist monks gave up all sexuality and concentrated on spirituality—transcendental meditation—above all else. No matter what your sexual desires let them go, with all other earthly desires, and focus on "oneness with the universe"—"lose yourself and all self-centered desires—through transcendental meditation—become free of all cares, free of all anxieties, and one with the greatness of the universe.

However, outside of the monastery, in the everyday world for everyday people doing everyday chores, family and marriage were emphasized by Buddha.

Marriage and family were considered the core of society, along with the economic activities that produced the food and clothing for the Buddhist monks.

Thus, homosexuality and lesbianism were not mentioned. Rather, if you were not a monk, you should marry, produce children, and work well in your economic activity.

At any time, if life proved too difficult, an individual—male or female—could come to a Buddhist monastery to retreat from life's difficulties and find spiritual renewal. And since all sexual activity is given up at the Buddhist retreat, homosexuality and lesbianism are simply not mentioned. Such activity, however, would have been considered deviant from family and marital norms in Buddhist societies, and so individuals with such inclinations kept them hidden. Homosexuality and lesbianism were definitely "in the closet" in Buddhist societies and were nonexistent in Buddhist monasteries, along with all other sexual activities.

10.3.3 Confucius and Homosexuality

Confucianism, as scholars agree, is not really a religion, for Confucius said, "Do not ask me about the afterlife, I do not even understand this life." So neither God nor the soul is discussed in Confucianism.[4]

However, Confucius emphasized the extended family, or clan, as the basis of society. He encouraged ancestral worship. He said that marriage was the basic institution upon which all else is built. He encouraged the keeping of all rituals surrounding ancestor worship and family solidarity.

Confucius does not mention homosexuality or lesbianism. Rather, he defies heterosexual marriage and "pecking order" role relationships—where the father is dominant, the sons next, and then the mother.

The state and politics he envisions are a paternalistic extension of patrilineal family relationships. The Emperor rules the nation as the father rules in the Chinese extended family.

Women are subordinate—Confucius had no female disciples (Plato did)—although the mother of the family was held in high esteem over the daughters and concubines.

Nothing is explicitly said about homosexuality or lesbianism. These were deeply hidden in the closet.

Even today, in surveys in 2021, a great number of Chinese peasants and villagers answered "Don't know" about gay or lesbian issues.

South Korea, which absorbs Confucius's ethics and values, is similar to China, except that women have a higher status and are far more aggressive. And American influence has helped the gay and lesbian issue come into the open, such that it is considered legal—gay marriage, gay adoption, and gay rights are recognized in South Korea, under American pressure. But the majority of South Koreans, when asked about gays and lesbians, said it was not a good thing—not a good place to be socially. So Confucius' emphasis on family and marriage is still very strong in both South Korea and China.

Japan is similar, but male dominance and "Samurai" macho masculinity prevail in Japan.

---

[4] Confucius, *The Analects*, NY, Amazon, 2000. Neither God nor the Soul are discussed.

Chapter 11
Gay Liberation and New Definitions of Gender

11.1 From Homosexual to Gay, from Gay to LGBTQ

When homosexual men altered the terminology to "gay," they provided a nonstigmatized way to refer to themselves. "Gay" caught on; lesbians adopted the term as well, such that "gay" refers to both gay men and women—the "gay community."

This was good and created an image of gays as normative citizens rather than deviants.

Further, when the AIDS epidemic scared gay men into more permanent relationships than previously had been the case, gay marriage emerged as an institutional trend.

This was also accepted by the "straight" community because it reinforced the normative mainstream marriage pattern. Both straight couples and gay couples formed monogamous, dual-career couple bonds. The pattern was identical among straight couples and gay couples, even in terms of child rearing. And among lesbian married couples, the fertility rate is the same as for straight couples. With gay married men, the fertility rate is lower because the men cannot get pregnant and must either find a surrogate woman or adopt.

Gay marriage and the designation "gay" did much to create an acceptance of gays in all of the industrialized countries. It was a very positive trend, which removed the stigma of deviance from the gay community.

However, the new trend—generated by the gay community itself—of renaming themselves "LGBTQ" has had the opposite effect of the "gay" terminology.

"LGBTQ" extends the social definition beyond gays and lesbians. Bisexuals are now given their own designation. This is not a problem, though it is a new designation. Bisexuals are attracted to both sexes and could go gay or straight.

This category has also been accepted as part of the gay category and, therefore, has become acceptable to the straight community in advanced industrial countries.

R. M. Glassman, *The Great Global Transformation*, Contributions to Political Science, https://doi.org/10.1007/978-3-031-90566-7_11

When we come to transgender and "queer," however, they are seen as problematic to the community at large, for being transgender requires medical alterations of a major nature—hormone and surgical medical procedures, which are complicated and expensive. And such procedures raise medical and social questions such as "At what age should such procedures begin?" "Should they begin at all?" "What are the psychological implications involved in transgender self-identification?" "Are the old psychoanalytic theories of Margaret Mahler (i.e., "separation individuation and gender identification") and Sigmund Freud (theory of the resolution of the Oedipus complex and Electra complex) relevant?"

Further still, the designation "queer"—insisted upon by the gays themselves—attempts to normalize "drag queens" and "dykes" and to normalize cross-dressing.

The "straight" community is confused by the queer category—How can we normalize queers? Queers, by definition, cannot be normative; they must be deviant.

But this ruins the acceptance created by the category "gay." Gays worked to normalize homosexual men and lesbian women. And gay marriage doubled down on this normalization.

Queer does the opposite—it insists on deviance and creates confusion in the perception of gays. The category queer leads to such confusing activities as drag queens reading children's stories to children at libraries nationwide in the USA.

Actions such as that lead to definitions of gays as social deviants and reduce their acceptance in modern societies.

In fact, the new categories of transgender and queers have so confused modern society that the whole concept of gender has become blurry—not clarified and totally confusing.

What, for instance, does "nonbinary" mean? Are men's and women's genitals and hormones the same?

Just because, in modern society, we insist on equality between the sexes in the career world, the political world, and the family does not mean that women do not have vaginas and men penises or that estrogen and testosterone have the same effect.

Ninety-nine percent of all murders worldwide are committed by men, and the last time I looked, it was women who were pregnant carrying babies to term and giving birth.

As the French say, *vive la difference*.

Men and women are different, but this need not affect the dual-career couple, the workplace, the parliament, the Olympics, and other institutional spheres in society.

Women do, however, buy cosmetics in enormous amounts, and women's fashions, including clothing and shoes, are—cross-culturally— elaborate and ever-changing.

Gender differences are real—nonbinary is a false category that is creating confusion and backlash rather than the acceptance of gender potential and the acceptance of gays.

So the alteration of the designation from "gay" to "LGBTQ" has lessened the acceptance of gays and lesbians and totally muddled the conception of gender.

Gender differences are both biological and social—there is a complex interaction in the two spheres. These influences are difficult to sort out, but saying they do not exist is not helpful, and it certainly is not scientifically acceptable.

To conclude, the social definition of "gay" as applied to gay men and lesbian women was very successful in producing acceptance for the gay community in modern society. And gay marriage also strongly reinforced the social acceptance of gays.

However, the new designation of "LGBTQ" has had the opposite effect. It creates a vision of deviant behavior and completely confuses gender identity. Both of these trends lead to less social acceptance in modern societies and to higher rates of behavior designated as deviant—the designation of deviance comes from the transgender and queer designations created by the gay community itself and not from the straight community. In fact, the straight community is left confused and uneasy about the gay community and about the concept of gender itself.

Finally, gay liberation has emerged in the modern world. Our consciousness has been raised, and our scientific rationality has been applied to the further understanding of this phenomenon.

World religions have had to cope with this out-in-the-open phenomenon, and they are struggling to cope with it, based, as they are, on the traditional family. Lastly, all cultural complexes globally have to deal now with the issue of gay liberation because the gays are out of the closet and cannot be put back in.

Chapter 12
The Remarkable Case of Greece: Ancient, Byzantine Christian, and Modern

Ancient Greece is one of the few societies that openly displayed homosexuality. The male body was held up as astonishingly beautiful, while women were covered up. The male penis was displayed in statues and paintings, as well as on "Hermes" burial stones with the head of the dead man and an erect penis protruding below it.

The Olympic Games were held naked, with the athletes' bodies glistening with perfumed olive oil and some wearing ribbons on their penises.[1]

If most of the ancient societies actively banned homosexuality, how did the Greeks survive while enshrining it?

Greek homosexuality was institutionalized within the warrior organization. The older men took boys under their wings and trained them for fights within the phalanx.[2]

Men were not allowed to marry until the age of 30 for it was believed they would fight more heroically if they had no family ties and were less afraid to die.

In the meantime, these unmarried men were encouraged to have sex with the boys they were training. "Pederasty"—sex with boys—was institutionalized. As long as the boys had no beard, they were in play as sex objects.

In his *Histories*, Herodotus marvels that "these Persians do not practice pederasty."[3]

So how did Greek society survive? At age 30, these men who lived through the wars had to marry and did marry. And the Greek men were trained to be bisexual. That is, they loved boys—who kept their hair long and had no beards—but they also loved women, who kept their hair long and shaved their pubic hair, making them seem more childlike. Sex from behind was also popular among Greek men.

---

[1] *Stephen G. Miller, The Olympic Games, Ancient Greek Athletics, Amazon, 2004.*

[2] Xenophon, The Spartan Constitution.

[3] Herodotus, *Histories*, (on Xerxes) London, Penguin, 1951.

R. M. Glassman, *The Great Global Transformation*, Contributions to Political Science, https://doi.org/10.1007/978-3-031-90566-7_12

So the men did marry, and they did produce children so that society could reproduce itself. The duty of women was to produce a new generation of warriors, and the women were married off much younger than the men to ensure fertility.

What of lesbianism? This was never institutionalized, but with the men prohibited from marrying until age 30 and having sex with boys, women followed suit and began having sex with girls.

Sappho, of course, is most famous for having a school for wealthy girls. In that school, she encouraged Olympic-style athletics for her girls, including running, jumping, and wrestling—but not boxing for she did not want the girls' faces disfigured.

And she taught philosophy, poetry, dancing, and rhetoric.

She, as with the men, was bisexual. She loved her girls jealously but also loved men. And she encouraged her girls to marry and to envision their husbands like Hercules and Apollo—muscular and beautiful—all this while pursuing them sexually.

So Greece flourished as a bisexual culture in which male bodies were openly displayed naked, and male warriors were the heroic social cynosures of all the Greek society.

12.1 Christianity and Greek Culture

As we have described, when St. Paul sought to convert the Greeks, he dropped circumcision—because he knew the Greeks worshipped the penis and considered circumcision "penis mutilation"—and the food taboos—because he knew that shellfish and pork were essential to the Greek cuisine. But he kept the ban on homosexuality. It was considered a sinful behavior.

Why did he keep the ban on homosexuality? My theory is that during this Roman era, the Greek warrior organization no longer existed. The Greeks were recruited by the Romans but not in large numbers. The Romans demilitarized Greece because they did not want a Greek rebellion. Knowing that the Greek warrior organization was no longer functioning and that the Greek marriage and family institution no longer demanded late marriage or included pederasty, St. Paul seemed to know that he could ban homosexuality and still convert the Greeks.

He was correct. And he went further to entice the Greeks by creating a Christian narrative of the death and resurrection of Jesus that paralleled the "mystery cult" narrative of the death and resurrection of Dionysius and his return to the side of his father, Zeus. Dionysius had a human mother, who, like many, was impregnated by a father god.

However, though the conversion of the Greeks was quite successful, it had an "unintended consequence" (as Max Weber would call it) in that because homosexuality was banned but still existed against the Greeks, celibacy for "pure" Christians became a feud against the newly converted Greeks.

12.2 Byzantine Christianity

When Constantine made Christianity the official religion of the Roman Empire and moved the capital from Rome to Byzantium, Constantinople, the new capital, became the center of all Christianity. And Constantinople became a Greek city, even though it was the Roman capital.

The church structure and ideology were developed in Constantinople. Priests, bishops, and archbishops were created. And most interestingly for us in this treatise, male and female celibacy orders were institutionalized.

At first, it was only male celibacy that was enshrined as spiritually pure. Since sex was a bodily function—which even animals engaged in—the functions of the mind were elevated above these. So no sex meant purifying the soul.

Honored men flocked into the celibate orders. Priests were allowed to marry, but bishops were not, and, of course, monks—such as those of Mount Athos—claimed pure celibacy.

With the establishment of celibacy for bishops and orders of celibate monks, women began to organize celibate orders of their own.

Over the centuries, then, in both Greece and Rome, homosexual men and lesbian women could feel pure and saintly by joining a celibate order. Within the secrecy of their order, if they engaged in same-sex sexuality, nobody knew about it.

Thus, St. Paul's ban engendered an unintentional institutional effect of homosexuality and lesbianism being acted out within the context of holy, celibate orders of monks and nuns.

12.3 Twenty-First-Century Greece

Today, in Greece, the attitude toward gays and lesbians is similar to that in Italy. Gay marriage is accepted, gay adoption is legal, but gay pride demonstrations are not encouraged. Because Greek Orthodox priests can marry, there is much less of a scandal surrounding celibacy. No one goes up to Mount Athos to create a scandal. However, in 2020, a nunnery in Kalamata was closed down by the church because lesbian sexuality was discovered. Then 2 years later, the nunnery reopened. Is it still a lesbian haven? No one wants to talk about it, and no one cares.

Also, it should be asserted that the homosexual aspect of ancient Greek culture is played down or denied in Greek schools. There is real denial about homosexuality and lesbianism in ancient Greece among modern Greeks. They want their warrior heroes, but they view them through a Christian lens.

So there is a great deal of ambiguity toward gays and lesbians in modern Greece.

Part IV
Science and Secular Humanism as the New Global Zeitgeist

Chapter 13
The History of the Rational-Scientific Worldview

13.1 Hegel and the Zeitgeist: The Stages of Human Development

Hegel gave us a theory of "all of history."[1] The stages of human development were based on humans increasing consciousness of self in relation to the natural world.

Primeval humans were frightened of nature. They experienced storms, earthquakes, volcanic eruptions, and diseases, for which they had no explanation. People died in hurricanes, rivers flooded and killed people, and earthquakes and volcanoes terrified tribal people—they terrify us now, so imagine how much more terrifying they were when no causal explanation for them existed. And diseases seemed to attack people from nowhere, causing illness in some and deaths in others, while some people were spared.

Hegel correctly observes that early humans were afraid of nature—they conceived of themselves as weak and vulnerable, while the "spirits" of nature were all powerful.

In the era of civilization, Hagel tells us that humans gained some control over nature. River flood agriculture was developed, wherein the control and utilization of water supply were achieved through human engineering. Further, huge amounts of food were grown, and animals were domesticated. The forces of nature came partially under the control of humans.

Humans conceived of themselves as partially dominant over the forces of nature. However, with the vast population growth that occurred, human life was not fully valued. War captives were enslaved, and miners worked to death in the mines and on construction sites.

Furthermore, nature gods and goddesses were worshiped, and though these were anthropomorphized—made into human form and pictured in statues and

[1] George Hegel, *The Philosophy of History*, NY Amazon, 2011.

R. M. Glassman, *The Great Global Transformation*, Contributions to Political Science, https://doi.org/10.1007/978-3-031-90566-7_13

poems—these nature gods and goddesses were all powerful over humans. Humans had to build houses for them, feed them, pray to them, and make sacrifices to them, or they—the gods and goddesses—would harm humans by sending storms, earthquakes, droughts, floods, and diseases to destroy them.

Not only did humans sacrifice animals for the gods and goddesses, but they also sacrificed other humans—sometimes war captives, sometimes slaves, but often enough a first-born son, a daughter, or a chosen one from among their own people.

Human sacrifice, slavery, and warfare took their toll on humans, such that human life itself was not valued in the ancient empires, even though humans had gained some control over nature.

Hegel then makes central two different ideological movements that improved the human conception of self.

First is the Judaic idea that "humans are made in gods image,"[2] and therefore, since every human life is "godly," every human life is important. This, according to Hegel, raises up the human conception of self—human self-consciousness is raised to center stage because every life is considered valuable, worth saving, and worth preserving.

Second—and suddenly Hegel moves away from the realm of the religious conceptions of humans—the Greek idea of attempting to understand the natural world logically, mathematically, and rationally leads to the human understanding of nature in nontheistic terms.[3]

The human mind is elevated to its most rational level, and the universe becomes less frightening as our rational knowledge of how it works increases.

So Judaism raises up every life as a valuable entity worth preserving, while Greek science gives the human species the beginnings of an understanding of the natural world we live in and are part of.

Hegel then goes on to establish that Protestant Christianity and "modern" science—the science of the Enlightenment period at the tail end of which Hegel lived—raised human self-consciousness to its highest pinnacle. Why? This is because in Christianity, a human being—Jesus—is raised to godly status, thus enhancing the valuation of human life even more than under Judaism, and modern science has produced a far better understanding of the natural world than its Greek predecessors.

Furthermore, German Protestant Christianity emphasizes "individualism"—every individual has the ability to understand and interpret scripture on their own—they do not need priests, popes, or rabbis to interpret scripture for them. Hence, every individual is not only godly but also intelligent and competent in themselves.[4] Hence, German Protestant Christianity raises the human consciousness of self to its highest level.

---

[2] Oxford Study Bible, "Humans are made in God's image" (Genesis).

[3] John Burnet, in Early Greek Philosophy, Google Books, 2000.

[4] Martin Luther, The Protestant Reformation.

At the same time, the growing body of scientific knowledge gives human beings an ever-increasing understanding of the natural world.

13.2 Beyond Hegel to Marx and Maslow

Hegel has emphasized the human progressive stages of history based on ideas that gave us a heightened sense of individual self-consciousness and a greater understanding of the natural world of which we are a part.

Marx, of course, famously "stood Hegel on his head"—figuratively—by emphasizing the material causes of the progressive stages of history.[5]

Marx's stages of history have proven more useful than Hagel's social science categories of progressive human change. However, again, as is so well known, Marx's utopianized last stage of history consisting of communistic sharing in economics and classless democracy in politics was ruined by Marx's intermediate stage, wherein a "dictatorship of the proletariat" temporarily ruled until the final stage of history was reached.[6]

Even though pure communism and classless democracy have not emerged and even though communist dictatorships still trouble the world and brutalize members of their own population, Marx's utopian idea of "species being"[7] has gained ground in a more rational-scientific formulation.

That is, by "species being," Marx meant that every individual could achieve their full potential in their lifetime. One could be a "farmer in the morning, a poet in the afternoon, and a musician at night,"—or whatever it is that allows an individual to reach their full potential. So one could be a corporate manager in the morning, a marathon runner in the afternoon, and a novelist at night.

Human self-consciousness has now—in this Marxian formulation—reached an even higher peak, for every individual is not only godly and important but can also achieve their full human potential. Both work, as one's vocation, and cultural and athletic proficiency, as one's avocation, can allow every human to feel fulfilled in their life potential. All their talents are allowed to flourish.

Now, this, of course, is utopian. The demands of work, family, and friendship often inhibit this kind of self-oriented fulfillment. A few of us can achieve the fulfillment of "species being."

Still, in the modern world of scientific psychology, the idea of "self-actualization," as presented by Maslow, has gained currency.[8]

---

[5] Karl Marx, Letters to his Father in on "Study Hegel on his ______(??), in *Works*. Karl Marx and Friedrich Engels, in *Works*(??).

[6] *Ibid*., The Stages of History, *Works*.

[7] Karl Mars, *Species Being*, *Works*.

[8] Abraham Maslow, *Self-Actualization*, An American J. of Psych, 1943 Hierarchy of Needs.

Why do I highlight this idea of "self-actualization"? This is because it operationalizes Marx's idea of species being and places it into a scientific framework in which it can be analyzed.

I am aware that Maslow and the psychologists who follow his views are focusing on psychological well-being and the reduction of anxiety, depression, and neuroses. However, if we place the idea of self-actualization in a social logical context, it comes close to Marx's idea of species being.

It is my view that part of the great global transformation we are living through will include individual self-fulfillment in work, play, and the cultural expression of talent.

Even though the world of work has become more and more specialized and even though workaholic demands are being made upon modern managers, technocrats, and white-collar workers, still, 50,000 runners—men and women alike—compete in the New York Marathon each year. And individuals do paint and sculpt and write poetry and novels and climb mountains and cliffs and surf and ski and pedal and paddle.

Human self-consciousness and human self-fulfillment are heightened in the modern world as the global high-technology industrial capitalist economy expands.

Part of this progressive process is driven by the increasing scope and effect of science. So let us look at the history of science and then analyze its effect on the modern world.

13.3 The Rational-Scientific Worldview Emerges in Ancient Greece

13.3.1 From Thales to Pythagoras to Leucippus[9]

Thales is credited with initiating the rational-scientific worldview. His home city was *Miletus.*

The Greeks on the Asia Minor coast of the Aegean Sea began trading with the great empires of the Middle East and North Africa. They followed the Phoenicians in this trade—learning how to trade from the Phoenicians and then competing with them. The Greeks, according to Hecataeus, even learned how to pack a ship properly so that the cargo was secure and the ship would not be destabilized.

Not only did the Greeks learn to pack ships from the Phoenicians, but they also learned to write down the geography of the seacoast and port cities, record the cultural norms of the people they would be trading with, and even compile accounts of the history and myths of the regions they made contact with.

The Phoenicians did all of this but kept their work secret so as not to encourage competitors. The Greeks, on the other hand, wrote openly and enjoyed the

[9] John Burnet, in Early Greek Philosophy (see Thales Chapter), Google Books, 2000.

competition. Hence, books of geography, anthropology, and history were made public by the Greeks such that their work could be built upon. Thus, from Hecataeus to Herodotus and from Plato to Aristotle, a foundation for social sciences emerged.

In this context of growing and lucrative trading, Greek intellectuals traveled along with trade merchants visiting the Aegean and Mediterranean regions—and even the Black Sea coast—and wrote down the geography, history, culture, and religious beliefs of the people they encountered.

Thales of Miletus traveled to Egypt for trade. He brought back more than the magnificent craft goods of Egypt. While there, he learned from the Egyptian priesthood the principles of geometry and the mathematics of measurement involved with geometry. The Egyptians used such mathematics and geometry to build perfect pyramids and huge temples.

Thales, however, became interested in geometry as both an abstract exercise in logic and as a practical predictor of distances. Thales became famous for being able to predict exactly at what distance and position a ship approaching Miletus would come into view. He also utilized his Egyptian geometry to help in bridge building for military purposes.

While in Egypt, Thales learned more—he learned the principles that would establish the beginning of the scientific worldview. That is, the Egyptians believed that all the world was created from the mud of the Nile River.

Now, all the peoples of the Middle East had creation myths: the sky god had sex with the earth goddess, and the universe was created, or the great Cackler—a bird goddess—laid an egg, and the universe was hatched from it. But the idea that a substance—such as the Nile mud—was the primary substance from which all other substances were made fascinated Thales.

He knew from his travels to Babylon that fire, air, earth, and water were all candidates for the "primary substance" out of which all other substances are made.

Returning to Miletus after extensive travels to all civilizational areas near Asia Minor, Thales gave lectures and attracted a group of young disciples.

He put forth "water" as the primary substance because water existed in many forms—liquid, solid (ice), and gas (water vapor)—and he encouraged his students (1) to experiment with water—watch it vaporize, watch it freeze, and liquefy it again—and (2) to *disagree* with him—prove him wrong by choosing air, fire, or earth and demonstrating that it is a better choice.[10]

Rationality, logic, experimentation, and disputation were encouraged by Thales. This is the beginning of the scientific method.

His students, such as Anaxagoras and *Anaximander*, took him up on his challenge. Perhaps it was air, not water, that is the basic substance—we breathe air in order to live, do we not? Or perhaps it is an unknown substance—not fire, air, water, or earth but an infinite substance ubiquitous in the universe from which all known substances emerge.

---

[10] John Burnet, in Early Greek Philosophy (see Thales Chapter), Google Books, 2000.

Pythagoras heard Thales' lecture, and he—fleeing the democratic revolution in Samos—then traveled from Miletus to Egypt. There, he, too, learned Egyptian geometry and mathematical measurements. He then fled further to the Italian coast facing the Greek mainland and the city of Croton, famous for its Olympic champions.

In Croton, Pythagoras developed his theory that the key to understanding the universe lay in numbers. Pythagoras believed that the application of mathematical measurements and calculations could help us understand the universe—the distance to the sun, the moon, and the planets; the shape of these objects; the movements of these spheres; and more.

When Pythagoras discovered that the secret of musical harmonies could be determined by measuring the length and width of stringed instruments, then he truly believed he had found the key to the universe in mathematical formulations: musical harmonies, godly beauty, the music of the spheres, and the movements of the planets.

So with Pythagoras, we add to Thales' method of observation and experimentation the mathematization of the world. The scientific method is emerging.

Pythagoras also believed that the soul lived on beyond the body—also an Egyptian belief—and his school was both scientific and religious in its orientation. I shall come back to this.

First, we must look at the ideas of *Heraclitus*, *Leucippus*, and *Democritus.*

Heraclitus came from a city north of Miletus, *near the Phrygian, Lydian, and Hittite civilizations. He may also have traveled east to Persia because he seems to have been influenced by the ancient Persian fire religion.*

Heraclitus believed that it was "fire" that was the basic substance.

The reason he chose fire is because Heraclitus believed that change was the most important fact about the universe. He said, famously, "The same man cannot walk into the same river twice. For it is neither the same man nor the same river."

Think of yourself as a baby, a child, an adolescent, an adult, and a senior citizen—we are all in flux, always changing. And, of course, the river flows by—it is not the same water or silt as it was a moment ago.

The fact of a universe constantly in motion, constantly changing, yet seemingly unchanged on the surface is another basic scientific conception.

In fact, this conception was then made more precise with the introduction of atoms as the basic substance from which all things are made. The term "atom" comes from the Greek word that means the smallest possible "uncuttable" particle.

It was Leucippus from Miletus *again who has been credited with inventing the atomic theory. He traveled to Athens, and there, Democritus took the theory and expanded upon it, such that it came as close as the ancient Greeks would get to the modern scientific theory of atoms—and now, even smaller particles, such as electrons, protons, neutrons, quarks, antiparticles, and more.*

With Democritus, the method and theory of science became established. It all began with Thales, then Pythagoras, and then many more Greek observers, experimenters, logicians, mathematicians, and theorists.[11]

Thales set the standard that differentiates science from religion: a theory can and should be challenged and disputed. If observations, experimentations, and mathematical calculations show that a theory is wrong, then change the theory. Theories are based on hypotheses, and hypotheses are only temporary assumptions.

What about religious beliefs? Does the rational-scientific worldview undermine religious beliefs?

It did in ancient Greece. Enter Xenophanes and Heraclius once again.

Xenophanes also came from a city north of Miletus.[12]

He looked at the portrayal of the gods and goddesses in Homer's Iliad and the Odyssey. The gods and goddesses behaved immorally—they exhibited every human foible, and they were jealous, angry, irrational, and certainly not a role model for human behavior.

Xenophanes railed against the Greek primitive tribal religion with its Olympic gods and goddesses acting badly.

Xenophanes completely rejected the belief in the gods and goddesses of the Olympic pantheon. However, he did not advocate atheism; rather, he advocated the belief in a moral god—one god—one moral god with a truly moral code of ethics.

Did he know of the Jews? The Phoenicians traded with the Israelites, but of course, the Phoenicians, who called themselves Canaanites, believed not only in a pantheon of gods and goddesses but also in human sacrifice—the sacrifice of babies to "the flames of Moloch." Still, *the Phoenicians traded with the Jews, so their views could have been known.*

The Egyptians, before and after Akhenaten, were developing a new theology—Amun, the creation god who brought himself to existence by the power of his mind, the self-created creator, and the god who is pure spirit and of whom no image can be made.

However, after Akhenaten, who believed that the sun god—the Aten—was the only true god, the Egyptians went back to their full pantheon, naming the high god, Amun-Ra, combining Amun with the sun god, Ra.

Did Xenophon encounter Zoroastrian beliefs—such as Ahura Mazda, the god of good, versus the devil, the god of evil? We do not know, but this is possible.[13]

Whenever *Xenophanes got the concept, the idea of a high god who is a moral god would eventually gain some adherents in Greece.*

Heraclitus also became an advocate of the one true moral god.

Along with Xenophanes' rejection of the Greek pantheon of gods and goddesses, the rational-scientific worldview was also undermining Greek religion.

---

[11] *Ibid.*

[12] *Ibid.*

[13] Zoroastrianism: God and the Devil, Heaven and Hell. See Wikipedia.

Thus, Democritus, in his atomic theory, also believed that the gods and goddesses do not care about humans. Whether they exist or do not exist cannot be proven, but either way, they do not affect our lives in any way.

This "atheistic" ideology would be expanded upon by Epicurus. He believed that since we could not prove the existence or nonexistence of gods and goddesses, we should ignore the topic completely. What is then left for humans? Humans are left to gain pleasure and avoid pain.[14]

Epicurus' pleasure garden became a favorite haunt for Athenian intellectuals. However, the ordinary people in all Greek city-states continued to believe in the Olympic gods and goddesses and to build their temples and celebrate their festivals.

13.3.2 Pythagoras, the Soul, and the Mystery Cults

As the *rational-scientific worldview was spreading, it did undermine the Olympian religion. Even though the majority of Greeks still believed in the Olympic pantheon, other religious trends were emerging.*

Pythagoras emphasized not only the mathematization of the universe but also the idea of the soul living on beyond the body. He probably got both ideas from his stay in Egypt.

The notion of the soul living on after death is a powerful idea that has arisen in many cultures. The ancient Celts believed it, if we can believe Tacitus.

Pythagorean-teaching groups spread out across Greece. And since Pythagoras' wife outlived him, she taught both his mathematics and religious ideas. Her presence encouraged many other Greek women to join the Pythagorean schools in many cities, including Athens. In Athens, we believe Plato's mother became a Pythagorean after her husband's early death.

In any case, Plato became a strong advocate of both the study of mathematics and the idea that the soul lives on after death.

Pythagoras' and then Plato's ideas on the ever-living soul influenced Christian thinking centuries later and also the thinking of the Stoics.

Led by Zeno—a name for a man that is not a Greek name but probably Phoenician—the group met on the porch of the Stoa, a magnificent building still intact below the Acropolis in today's Athens.

Zeno and the Stoics believed that the soul lived on after death and amalgamated with a "world soul" that pervaded the universe.

The Stoics also believed in a moral god who judges us. Further, they believed not in pleasure but in acting modestly, avoiding luxury and debauchery, and living simply in a healthy way.

They are usually contrasted with the Epicureans, who advocated pleasure and believed life ended with death and that there was no soul that lived on.

[14] Epicurus. The Philosophy of Epicurus, Stanford Encyclopedia of Philosophy, 2005.

However, Epicureans did not advocate debauchery—overeating or promiscuity or living luxuriously. One had to avoid pain; even those things could generate pain, for "any good done in excess becomes an evil"—as the motto from Delphi warned.

Still, the contrast between the Stoics' and the Epicureans' style of life was made in the ancient Greek world, and Stoicism was more popular. Epicurus was condemned as an atheist who criticized the gods and goddesses and lived immorally, while Zeno and his Stoics were seen as eschewing luxury and debauchery—something the Greek warrior culture railed against—and offering the hope of an afterlife.

Yet neither of these ideas created a movement that would replace the Olympic tribal religion. Nor did the rational-scientific worldview gain popular support. No, it was the mystery cults that swept up the Greeks in a new form of religious fervor.

The mystery cults were imported from Asia Minor. They featured the death and resurrection of the young god Dionysus. They originated in the fertility festivals of the earth goddess featuring the death of all life in the winter and the rebirth of life in the spring. These festivals included human sacrifice—either of a young man or a virgin girl.

In the Dionysus mystery cult, as it emerged in Greece, there was no actual human sacrifice. Instead, there was a symbolic sacrifice—the acting out of the death of Dionysus at the hands of the female goddesses—"the Furies." Then there was a symbolically acted out sexual orgy—in Asia Minor in the Middle East—the war king and the high priestess dressed up as the god and goddess who would act out the sexual union that produced the creation of the world.[15] *In Greece, the sexuality was acted out with leather phalluses and vaginas and was led by women priestesses from certain aristocratic families.*

But the key element was the rebirth—the resurrection—of Dionysus and his assent to the side of his father, Zeus, for Dionysus had been the son of Zeus and a mortal human mother. He had been killed by Hera, jealous of his birth mother and his handsome success as a demigod. His mother pleaded for Zeus to raise him from the dead, and Zeus did so. Upon his resurrection—body and soul—he became a god ruling alongside his father, Zeus.

The parallels with Christian theology—developed by St. Paul—are obvious. And it is probable that Saint Paul, raised in the Greek city of Tarsus, was quite familiar with the Greek mystery cult of Dionysus.

What is important for us here in focusing on the effect of the rational-scientific worldview is that the growing rationality did create a crisis in Greek religious belief. And this crisis led to (1) a rational-scientific view of the world, (2) atheism and agnosticism, (3) a monotheistic moral god, (4) the Stoic belief in a moral universe and an ever-living soul, and (5) a new religion (not rational at all)—the Dionysus mystery cult.

In the play The Bacchae, *Euripides*[16] *tells his audience that the rational view of the world is not enough and that as strange as the mystery cults are—involving*

[15] James George Frazer, *The Golden Bough*, New York, Amazon, 2011 (1890).

[16] Euripides, *The Bacchae*.

violent death as well as resurrection—they are all we have to alleviate our existential pain.

It needs to be pointed out, however, that The Bacchae *was not a popular play—Euripides was exiled for a while for writing it. And Aristophanes, in his play* Worshipping Women, *has the women of Athens put Euripides on trial for defaming them. In this comic play, women make it clear that an actual sex orgy or actual human sacrifice does not occur during the mystery cult festivals.*

All throughout the history of science—from the ancient Greeks to the Renaissance Italians and into the modern world—science and religion would collide, competing for the role of the dominant worldview. We shall describe the historical and modern collisions shortly.

First, let us emphasize the rise of the social sciences, along with the natural sciences.

13.3.3 The Rise of the Social Sciences in Ancient Greece: From Hecataeus to Herodotus to Plato and Aristotle

Why is there a need to present the origins of social science? It is because the human consciousness of self has been dramatically increased by our scientific understanding of individual psychology, social interaction, economic motivation, and political behavior.

Of course, after the work of Darwin, Marx, and Freud, it seemed as if human beings were diminished—by Darwin as animals, by Marx as part of a group dynamic, and by Freud as controlled by unconscious, irrational desires.

However, whenever human understanding is expanded, human control over ourselves and nature improves. So Darwin, Marx, and Freud, notwithstanding the development of the social sciences, have increased our consciousness of self—as individuals, as members of a group, and as part of the natural world.

So where did social science originate? With the natural sciences and act the same time period—they arose in ancient Greece.

It is not that the Egyptians, Babylonians, Phoenicians, Jews, Chinese, Indians, and other civilized peoples with a writing system did not understand human beings and did not make major contributions upon which the Greek intellectuals built. Rather, it is that the Greek intellectuals systematized the knowledge and presented that knowledge within a rational framework of discourse. They also attempted to analyze the material they accumulated in a value-free, nonjudgmental framework.

Now, of course, the latter is probably impossible to do, but the Greek intellectuals did attempt to do it. For instance, when Herodotus described the culture of the Scythians, he noted that they were headhunters. But he did not negatively stigmatize them because of it. And when he analyzed the Persian-Greek War, he presented both sides fairly—if Greeks acted treacherously, he described it; if Persians acted nobly, he described that.[17]

When we come to the Roman intellectuals, such as Tacitus, we will find something quite different. The Romans were totally judgmental in their analysis, though their descriptions seem accurate.

So where should we begin? The Greeks credit Hecataeus with establishing geography and anthropology. Hecataeus, like old early Greek scientific founders, came from the Asia Minor city-states north and south of Miletus, which was the center of scientific learning.[18]

Hecataeus, like Thales, learned seafaring trading from the Phoenicians (of Sidon, Tyre, Byblos, and other city-states—in what is now Lebanon). He learned to pack ships so that they would not list in rough seas, and he learned to make maps of the coastline and its port cities—contributing to geography. As mentioned, the Phoenicians brought this science to its early high point but kept all their knowledge secret, while the Greeks—competitive and expansionary militarily—made the knowledge public. So while Hecataeus became famous, the Phoenician geographers and ethnographers have remained unknown.

The Phoenicians taught the Greeks that geography was not enough and that knowledge of a people's culture was necessary. Why? The reason is that in order to trade successfully, you had to know what a given people wanted, what they needed, what they had, and whether they were belligerent and dangerous or open to peaceful trading.

Therefore, a careful ethnographic, economic, and political description of a given trading partner had to be developed. The Greeks, such as Hecataeus and, later, Herodotus, did this and then published their findings. They were so open about their observations that they lectured on them in the public squares of the Asia Minor Greek cities. Of course, this could be lucrative—they would be chosen to captain trading ships and gain profit, and they could receive payment for their lectures as "sophists"—purveyors of wisdom.

Hecataeus traveled to Egypt, Syria, and the Aegean region and wrote the geographies, histories, and ethnographies of the peoples he encountered during his trading ventures.

Many other Greeks followed in his footsteps, culminating in Herodotus of Halicarnassus—an ethnically mixed city of Greeks and Carians, who lived together peacefully since Mycenaean days.

Herodotus is called "the Father of History" because he did not just catalog the geography and ethnography of the peoples he observed. Rather, he framed his entire project around the Persian invasion of the Middle East, Egypt, and Greece, trying to understand why these wars happened and why the Greeks ended up winning.[19]

---

[17] Herodotus, *Histories* (on Xerxes), London, Penguin, 1951.

[18] John Burnet, in Early Greek Philosophy, Google Books, 2000.

[19] Herodotus, *Histories* (on Xerxes), London, Penguin, 1951.

When Herodotus was a boy, he remembered hearing over and over again, "Do you remember where you were when the Persians came?" The Persian invasion was traumatic for the city-states on the Asia Minor coast of the Aegean, for the Greeks lost in Asia Minor, and the city-states were dominated by the Persians. Democracies were overthrown, and Persian governors and local "kings" were installed to rule.

Thus, the defeat of the Persians, first at Marathon by the Athenians and later at Salamis and Platea, was a monumental phenomenon, freeing all the Greek city-states from Persian domination, allowing democracy to flourish again and projecting Greek culture into eventual dominance in the entire Middle East, Egypt, and Rome, after Alexander the Great invaded the Persian Empire victoriously (something Herodotus did not live to see).

So Herodotus did all the geography, ethnography, economics, and political analysis that his predecessors had done. But he carefully documented all the battles, all the dates, all the witnesses, and all the participants in this colossal set of wars between Persia and Greece.

In the nineteenth century, emerging modern historians called Herodotus "the Father of Lies" because he presented the myths the people spun, along with the actual events.

We know now, however, that most of what Herodotus tells us is quite accurate and that the myths were presented because that is what many people believed. Along with the myths, Herodotus presents the facts as accurately as he could. And his descriptions of the cultures of the Egyptians, Persians, Babylonians, Scythians, and even the Greeks themselves have also proven to be quite accurate.

So Herodotus is considered the father of history and the father of anthropology, and he did give us the first "dialogue on the forms of government"—he puts this discussion of democracy, oligarchy, and monarchy into the mouths of the princes of Persia, who were yearning for succession to the kingship. He knew the Persians never had such a discussion and that it came from the Greeks—he tells us that his countrymen said the princes of Persia never discussed this, but he says, "I think they did." Herodotus wanted to present this dialogue on the forms of government because he knew it was important, and he knew the Persians had fostered *only* monarchy. He knew that if the Greeks had lost, democracy and oligarchy might have been lost to the world forever. Hence, he presented the dialogue on the forms of government to make sure these ideas would be heard by all those reading his work.

The Athenians made Herodotus a celebrity—and made him rich. They encouraged him to write on the Battle of Marathon so that they—the Athenians—could look heroic and compete with the Spartans who had died heroically at the Battle of *Thermopylae* and who had been mythologized for it: "The Spartan 300."

Herodotus' fame encouraged others to follow in his footsteps. And so when, after Herodotus' death, the Athenians and Spartans split Greece into a horrific Civil War, *Thucydides, a disgraced general (disgraced falsely by his own Athenians), stepped up and wrote—in exquisite historical detail—the history of the Civil War—the Peloponnesian War.*[20]

With Thucydides, we do not get any mythology, only historical facts. So his work became the template for future historians—anthropology would continue with the Roman historians, but history and ethnography were, at least, partially supported.

From *Thucydides, we jump to Polybius.*[21] *He was not the last Greek historian by any means. Greek historians continue to write and to do geography and ethnography. From Strabo to Plutarch,*[22] *with many in between, the Greeks continued the tradition of* Hecataeus.

With *Polybius, we bring social science to Rome—for the Romans had never written their own history up to that era.*

Before jumping to Rome—from Polybius to Livy to Tacitus and Sallust and Cicero—let us first see how the social sciences expanded in Greece with Plato and Aristotle following after Herodotus and Thucydides.

13.3.4 Plato, Aristotle, and the Rise of Political Science, Sociology, Economics, and Psychology

Plato and Aristotle are the two greatest philosophers of all time, and libraries have been written about them. Since I cannot do them justice in a short sketch, I simply outline their contributions to the social sciences as we know them today.

Just as Hecataeus *and Herodotus established the groundwork for geography, history, and anthropology, Plato and Aristotle established the groundwork for political science, sociology, economics, and even psychology.*

Both Plato[23] *and Aristotle*[24] *also contributed to the expansion of the natural sciences: Plato taught mathematics and encouraged the Greek sophists to include Pythagorean mathematics as part of their teachings. Aristotle compiled books on zoology and anatomy and encouraged his students to catalog the animals, plants, and human cultures they encountered in their travels.*

Most of all, both Plato and Aristotle took off from Herodotus' dialogue on the forms of government and wrote expansionary treatises evaluating and describing democracy, oligarchy, monarchy, aristocracy, and tyranny.

Plato famously rejected all the existing forms of government and advocated a government of intellectually (and physically) gifted individuals who would run the polity as "guardians"—philosopher rulers. He fully believed that such a

[20] Thucydides, *The Peloponnesian War*, London, Penguin Classics, 1951.

[21] Polybins, Book VI, *The History of Rome*, NY, Amazon, 2006.

[22] Plutarch, *Plutarch's Lives* (Parallel Lives), London, Penguin Classics, 1951.

[23] Plato, *The Republic*, The Laws, London, Penguin Classes, 1950.

[24] Aristotle, *Politics*, Ethics, Barker Translation, Oxford University Press, London, 1960.

meritocratically selected group could rule better than anyone else—and significantly, he included women in the meritocratically selected group of "guardians."

Aristotle favored what he conceived of as a more practical solution to the problem of the best polity. He advocated a democracy wherein the middle class would be in a majority, as the middle class, he observed, tends to follow the law and is willing to compromise on key issues of governance, whereas the rich act as if they are above the law and the poor as if the law does not apply to them. Neither are the rich or the poor willing to compromise on contentious issues. Aristotle also theorizes that, along with the lawful guidelines of governance, middle-class democracy should include a leadership role, such as that exists in a monarchy—but elective; a democratic popular assembly that includes the poor and the rich, though stabilized by a middle-class majority; and leadership roles for the wealthy and well-educated, who, though not forming into a dominant oligarchy, could still contribute to the polity by the strength of their education and their training in the art of rhetoric or debate.

Aristotle even emphasized the idea of "consent" of the people as functional for good government. He also emphasized that tyranny—the worst form of government—was based on pure power, even though tyrants attempt to gain the consent of the people through clever acts of generosity and manipulative acts of propaganda.

So political science, including debates over the forms of government, emphasizing the strengths and weaknesses of each form, was established. It would not be expanded until the Italian Renaissance and the French and Scottish Enlightenments, but it was firmly established in the Hellenic Golden Age.

Aristotle, expanding on Plato's work—Plato was literally his teacher—also founded sociology by focusing on the class basis of politics in his analysis of the rich, the poor, and the middle class. Plato began this analysis, and Aristotle expanded upon it.

Along with class analysis, Plato emphasized social change—the dramatic alteration of norms and values within the family, relating to gender, and with economic roles as well.

Plato noted that the norms of the family were changing as a "youth-centered" culture replaced veneration for the elders. He also advocated women's liberation into all areas of social life: equality in the family—with nursery schools for the care of children such that women could engage in politics and economic roles and even participate in the military. Plato set the groundwork for sociology as a science of society, although its expansion would wait until the nineteenth and twentieth centuries with Comte and Durkheim and Marx and Weber.

Plato even set the stage for Freud's twentieth-century seminal work on psychology. Freud's notion of the id, ego, and superego can be traced back to Plato's idea of the "tripartite psyche." Even dream analysis and the Oedipus complex can be traced back to Plato, who, in his condemnation of tyranny as the worst form of government, described the actions of a tyrant as that of an individual in a bad dream who imagines having sex with his mother and murdering his father and others who have challenged him. Plato made the Oedipus myth part of our unconscious mind in the dream world, and Freud, of course—shocking to the Victorian era he lived in—insisted that all of us share this unconscious dream world wherein we act out our sexual fantasies and destructive passions.

Finally, Aristotle gave "economics" its name—"Oekos," which is the Greek word for a household farm or workshop.

Aristotle discussed trade, interest rates on bank loans, pricing, and profits. Taking off from Hesiod's Works and Days, *wherein sea trade—trade capitalism—was encouraged, Aristotle described the trade-capitalist economy of ancient Greece. He does not give us the systemized brilliance of his political analysis, but he does provide us with the beginnings of an economic analysis beyond that of the agricultural production of the river flood empires.*

Of course, Aristotle's economic analysis was not expanded upon until the Scottish Enlightenment, wherein Adam Smith, Ricardo, Malthus, Bentham, and others generated what we now call "classical economics." The Scots and the English Jews then described industrial capitalism, something Aristotle never saw and could not imagine.

Along with the natural sciences and mathematics, the social sciences created a rational worldview in which the universe, nature, and human beings were analyzed and better understood than ever before.

Of course, the knowledge, craft goods, art, and architecture produced by the great civilizations of Egypt, Mesopotamia, India, China, and Meso-America were spectacular in their own right.

But humans, as humans, gained a greater understanding of themselves and the natural world with the establishment of the Greek rational-scientific worldview.

13.4 The Decline of the Rational-Scientific Worldview and the Rise of Christianity

The Roman conquest of Greece did not end the scientific revolution. In fact, in the city of Alexandria, founded by the Greeks after Alexander the Great's conquest of Egypt, the scientific revolution continued. Mathematics was expanded, astronomy was enlarged, and medicine and physiology were improved. The theories of *Aristarchus and Ptolemy competed for whether the earth or the sun was the center of our planetary system.* Archimedes created a geared bronze "machine" that could predict eclipses and show the movements of the moon and the planets. He did this in Syracuse, his home city, but a large replica of his machine was kept in the library and school at Alexandria. Hypatia, the daughter of the man who headed the school at Alexandria, was the last Alexandrian—and the last woman—to move the scientific worldview forward.

Galen, a Greek doctor, produced a book of physiology and medical cures that became the standard for these subjects into the Arabic Golden Age and beyond into the Italian Renaissance.

Archimedes also continued to experiment, creating his famous equation on the displacement of water volume and the weight of the object displacing the water—"Eureka!," he shouted as he gained the insight for that mathematical formula.

So during the Hellenistic and then the Roman era, science continued to expand.

However, the violence, greed, and immorality of the Romans eventually generated a backlash against Greco-Roman culture.

Where the Greeks had the Olympic Games, the Romans had gladiator games. Where the Greeks built modestly, the Romans built on a grand scale. Where the enslavement and forced labor of conquered peoples was minimal among the Greeks, it was monumental among the Romans.

The violence and forced labor perpetrated by the Romans led to military rebellions and the theological rejections of all things Roman. Eventually, even the Romans themselves became shocked and morally outraged at excessive violence and the lack of morality institutionalized by the emperors.

Intellectuals, such as Tacitus,[25] rejected this horrendous display of perverted, immoral behavior. Both the Romans and their subjects were ready for a new moral worldview.

Christianity emerged from the zealot Judaic sect, whose beliefs are written in the Dead Sea Scrolls and whose actions and ideas were documented by Josephus[26]—the Jewish general turned Roman informer and then turned Greek-influenced historian.

With the destruction of Jerusalem and the expulsion of the Jews after 70 AD, Christianity—one of the zealot offshoots—began to take hold among the Syrians and Phoenicians and then, with Saint Paul's activities, among the Greeks.

Eventually, the poor of Rome—and many aristocratic women—converted to the new religion, a religion with a rigid moral code made explicit in the Ten Commandments of the Jewish Bible, along with the theology of redemption in the death and resurrection of Jesus, the Messiah, the Son of God.

The Greek word for Messiah is "Christos"—the anointed one—and this name caught on in Antioch, a Christian stronghold in Syria, where the population was bilingual in Aramaic and Greek.

The point for us here is that all things Roman were rejected by the Christians. In their effort to create a moral society, they closed down not only the gladiator games but also the Olympic games, which were played naked and did emphasize homosexual activities. The Christians also closed down all the schools of philosophy and science—Christians burned the library at Alexandria and murdered Hypatia.

From Constantine the Emperor who made Christianity the official religion of the Roman Empire and moved the capital from Rome to Byzantium into the Byzantine era—approximately 400 to 1453—Greco-Roman culture including scientific and philosophical activities was submerged while Christianity was elevated.

The rational-scientific worldview declined and almost disappeared forever.

It was not the Christians who revived it; it was the Muslims who did so.

---

[25] Tacitus, *The Annals of Imperial Rome*, London, Penguin, 1952.

[26] Josephus, *Roman-Jewish War*; *Jewish Antiquities*; London, Penguin Paperback 1953.

13.5 The Arabic-Muslim Golden Age and the Revival of "Greek Science"

While the Christians closed down all the Greek schools of science and philosophy, the Byzantine monks and the Greek Orthodox Christian hierarchy kept all the books of Greek science and philosophy in their libraries in Constantinople. They cherished these books of the Greek heritage, even though as Christians they would not disseminate them to their Christian parishioners.

When Islam swept from Arabia into the Middle East and North Africa, conquering these regions with lightning speed (after 650 AD), the one city the Muslims could not take was Constantinople.

By land, the walls were too thick, high, and well fortified. By sea, the Byzantine Greeks greeted the Muslim fleets with "Greek fire," a kind of napalm that was thrown from huge catapults onto the ships. The ships burned, and the fire could not be put out by water. Those ships that got through were stopped by giant golden chains, which sprung into effect when the enemy ships neared the harbor at Constantinople.

For years, the Muslims tried to take Constantinople, but they could not. Having conquered the whole Middle East, including Persia, the failure at Constantinople frustrated the Arabs. How had these Greeks created such a walled fortress, and how had they invented "Greek fire"?

Emissaries were sent to Constantinople to make peace and to inquire about Greek culture. The Byzantine Greek leaders were flattered by the Muslim Arabs' praise and curiosity. No longer fearing invasion, the Greek authorities—secular and Christian—decided that the spread of Greek scientific and philosophical learning could help the world.

Remarkably, they assisted the Muslims in translating the major works of the Greek scientists, mathematicians, medical doctors, and philosophers.

Arabic translations of Galen's book of medicine and human physiology, mathematical books from Pythagoras to Euclid, the entire set of books from Aristotle on logic, metaphysics, physics, and politics, some of Plato's dialogues—especially those concerning the soul, and the books of astronomy.

Greek science, mathematics, philosophy, and social science were all translated into Arabic, and a huge library was built to house them in Baghdad—it was called "The House of Wisdom."

Arabic-speaking intellectuals and Persian intellectuals (who had a love-hate relationship with the Greeks since the days of the Persian-Greek Wars) rallied around these scientific and philosophical books explaining them to the Arabic- and Persian-speaking world and adding important insights and improvements to the scientific and mathematical treatises.

The books of "Greek science" spread both east and west, influencing the Muslim world from Persia in the east to Spain in the west.

Avicenna (Ibn Sina),[27] a Persian intellectual and traveler, added two major breakthroughs: he added newly learned cures and treatments to the medical book of Galen, and most importantly, for the future of science, he added Indian numerals, including zero, to mathematics.

Having traveled in eastern Persia near India, he learned to utilize Indian numerals. These were much easier to use than Greco-Roman numerals, which are quite cumbersome. The Indian numerals became known as Arabic numerals because after Avicenna, his mathematical discoveries were published in Arabic and, as such, were circulated throughout the Arabic-speaking world.

The exciting new mathematical and medical knowledge was then spread from Persia—by way of Baghdad—all the way to Spain. In Spain, many Arabic-speaking intellectuals, including many Jewish intellectuals who spoke Arabic, became enlightened by the work of Greek science and by the Persian improvements in this project.

Averroes (Ibn Rushd),[28] also a doctor and influenced by the new medical and mathematical breakthroughs, became excited by—almost obsessed with—the works of Aristotle.

Averroes wrote a series of commentaries explaining the works of Aristotle. He went line by line with Aristotle's work—logic, metaphysics, physics, and politics—all of Aristotle's works. Avicenna believed that Aristotle was the greatest philosopher of all time. And, after him, so too did the European Christian world of the Renaissance.

Unfortunately, the "Arabic Golden Age," generated by the revival and translation of "Greek science," would eventually be cut off by two events: (1) the Muslim reaction against this secular "foreign" subversive knowledge led by Al-Ghazeli's writings and his subsequent Muslim followers and (2) the invasion and destruction of Baghdad by Genghis Khan and his marauding Mongol army, who burned down the "House of Wisdom" along with the rest of Baghdad.

The loss of Baghdad, however, was only temporary. It was rebuilt after the Mongols' withdrawal. And copies of the Arabic translations of the Greek books still existed in Antioch, Aleppo, Alexandria, Fez, and many cities in Spain.

It was the followers of Al-Ghazali who blocked any further expansion of Arabic contributions to the development of science, mathematics, and philosophy.

Averroes was threatened with death, as were many other Arabic-speaking intellectuals. In the long run, Al-Ghazeli's rejection of Greek science forced the Arabic intellectuals to give up their quest for secular scientific knowledge and to focus instead on Muslim theology.

The Arabic Golden Age was ending. However, Jewish intellectuals in Spain were still able to engage with Greek science, especially in medicine and mathematics, and they were also able to read the works of Aristotle as explained by Averroes.

---

[27] Ibn Sina (Avicenna), *Philosophy in the Arabic Golden Age*, NY, Amazon, 2013.

[28] Ibn Rushd (Averroes), *Philosophy in the Arabic Golden Age*, NY, Amazon, 2013.

These Jewish intellectuals later formed a bridge between the Arabic intellectuals and the emerging Christian intellectuals in Spain. I shall come back to this momentarily. First, let us look at the most famous of the Jewish intellectuals: Moses Maimonides.[29]

Maimonides lived in Spain, along with millions of other Jews. The Jews had been in Spain before the Muslim conquest.

Maimonides was influenced greatly by the work of Averroes. He became a doctor—one of the professions open to Jews in the Arabic world. He also fell in love with the works of Aristotle and the commentaries of Averroes.

Forced to flee Spain because of a Muslim fundamentalist invasion, he and his family took up residence in Fez, Morocco. However, he was forced to flee Fez when the fundamentalist Muslims took over there, too.

He attempted to live in Jerusalem—the holy city of Jews—but discovered that it was run down and neglected. Unable to reside in Jerusalem, he moved to Cairo, Egypt, where Saladin was King. He was the great Muslim hero of the Crusader Wars, who defeated Richard the Lionheart and drove the Christian Crusaders back to Europe.

Becoming the doctor of Saladin's Court, Maimonides gained enough wealth to live well and enough time to write. He was also protected by Saladin as an honored resident in Cairo.

Maimonides incorporated Greek science into his medicine. He advised his students to read the updated version of Galen's medical books. He also taught Aristotle's logic and Greek mathematics using "Arabic numerals."

His book *Guide for the Perplexed* explained to the Jews that one could combine Bible (Torah) study with the study of Greek science and philosophy.

The Jewish rabbis were not so sure that Maimonides was correct. They did not like the inclusion of Greek secular-scientific works combined with biblical exegesis. The head rabbis might have condemned Maimonides the way Averroes was condemned by the fanatical Muslims.

However—and this is important for the history of the world, as well as for the history of the Jews—Maimonides gained the favor—the adulation—of the rabbis by reorganizing the Talmud, the great set of commentaries on the Bible (Torah).

The Talmud had been compiled for centuries since the days of Babylonian captivity. It contained all the wisdom of the Jews. However, it was not well organized.

Maimonides used his background in Aristotelian logic to organize the Talmud so that it could be much more easily read. Talmudic study received a tremendous jolt of enthusiasm. And Maimonides became a hero of the Jews—the great "Rambam" and the pillar of Jewish intellectual learning.

So instead of becoming a heretic, Maimonides became a folk hero among the Jews. And instead of banning the study of Greek science, the Jews were allowed to continue such study.

---

[29] Moses Maimonides, *The Guide for the Perplexed*, NY, Amazon, 2014.

When the Jews entered the world of the European Enlightenment centuries later, they actively contributed to the fields of medicine, mathematics, science, and social science.

Now, let us go back to Spain so that we can take the science of the Greeks and the Arabic-speaking world into the European Christian world.

13.6 Greek Science and Philosophy Is Debated in Christian Spain and Carried Over to Rome

When the Spanish-speaking Christians reconquered Spain from the Arabic-speaking Muslims, the question of Greek science emerged as problematical once again. The Muslims had banned Greek science—Al-Ghazeli's positions triumphed over that of Averroes (Ibn Rushd). But the Jews, in revering Maimonides, had allowed for such study. Not only were the Jews allowed (but not really encouraged) to study Greek science, but they were also often bilingual in Arabic and Spanish (as well as the Hebrew of the Bible).

So the Jews acted as translators for the Christian Spaniards. But should the Christians allow the study of secular Greek science? This became the subject of debate in Spain.

The Roman Catholic Church of Spain, unlike the Muslim and Jewish religions, was strongly hierarchical. The Pope and the College of Cardinals in Rome were the ultimate authorities on all theological matters.

Therefore, the Spanish bishops and priests had to look to Rome for decisions on Greek science and philosophy.

The Pope and the cardinals did not know how to evaluate the Greek books—they could not read much Greek, and they could read no Arabic. What should they do?.

The Pope and the cardinals created a commission to look into this issue. The commission was led by Albert (the Great—Albertus Magnus), a noted German Christian theologian who was good at languages. Albert would become "great" in his incredible linguistic work, but the Pope wanted a trusted Italian in the mix who could keep him posted and whose judgment could be fully trusted.

Enter Thomas Aquinas.[30]

[30] Thomas Aquinas, *Summa Theologica*.

13.7 St. Thomas Aquinas Embraces the Work of Aristotle and the Commentaries of Averroes

With the help of Jewish translators from Spain, Albert, Thomas, and other members of the commission translated the works of Aristotle from Arabic into a vulgarized Latin, which they could read easily. The translations were rough but quite adequate.

Though Albert lead in the translation endeavor—which occurred in the city of Cologne—it was Thomas who, having come under the spell of both Aristotle and Averroes, legitimated the works of Aristotle and by association, other Greek works, to the Pope and the cardinals back in Rome.

Aquinas adored Aristotle's *Logic and Metaphysics*, expanding upon them to write his famous *Proofs of the Existence of God.*[31]

He called Aristotle "The Philosopher" and Averroes "The Commentator."

And most importantly, he convinced the Pope that Christians could safely combine the study of Aristotle with the study of the Bible. His *Proofs of the Existence of God* using Aristotelian logic convinced the Pope that Thomas Aquinas was giving him good advice.

So just as the rabbis gave in to Maimonides and his *Guide for the Perplexed*, the Pope and the cardinals gave in to Aquinas and his *Theologica.*

Science had died under the assault of the early Christians, but now, it would be resurrected by the Christians of the Italian Renaissance.

13.8 From Thales to Galileo: Science Reaches a New Level

Once the Pope accepted Thomas Aquinas' judgment on Greek philosophy being compatible with Christian doctrine, a great surge of translations followed. And along with these translations from Arabic to Latin, it was discovered that in the church archives, many Greek and Roman works already existed in Latin translation. Eventually, with the help of Byzantine Greek priests, more of the works of ancient Greek science and philosophy were made available, and the quality of Latin translations was improved significantly.

In this era of the rebirth of Greek and Roman knowledge, many intellectual achievements began to occur. For instance, with the development of scientific theory and mathematics, the work of Copernicus became foundational.

Copernicus[32] was a Polish priest who studied in Rome. He became interested in astronomy because he discovered that there were two different conceptions of the planetary system of which the earth was a part. The favored system was that of Ptolemy. He was an astronomer living in Alexandria at the height of Alexandria's era of scientific centrality during the Hellenistic period.

[31] Ibid., Proofs of the Existence of God in Theologica.

[32] Nicholaus Copernicus, *On the Revolutions of the Celestial Spheres*, 1543, Wikipedia.

Ptolemy described a planetary system in which the earth was the center and the sun and the planets revolved around the earth, with the moon separately revolving around it. Ptolemy backed up his theory with complicated mathematical formulas for calculating the orbits of the sun, the planets, and the moon. He also supervised the construction of geared bronze machines, which, when turned by hand, showed the movements of all the planets around the earth—and predicted eclipses of the moon. This geared machine was originally invented by Archimedes in Syracuse but was replicated at the University in Alexandria. Further, the data for predicting eclipses of the moon was originally discovered and written down by the Babylonian priesthood. This data was gathered by the Greeks and then further mathematized.

In Alexandria, another planetary system, different from that of Ptolemy, was currently debated. Aristarchus, years earlier, had theorized that the sun was the center of the planetary system and that the earth and all the planets orbited the sun. The moon, of course, orbited the earth.

The theory of Aristarchus gained currency in Alexandria and was discussed by Hypatia, the last astronomer and mathematician of the Alexandrian library. However, once Christianity dominated the thought of the Roman Empire, Ptolemy's theory prevailed because it was consistent with the biblical conception of the universe—the earth-centered universe was the biblical universe.

However, when Copernicus utilized the mathematics of both Ptolemy and Aristarchus and compared the orbits of the planets, he became convinced that Aristarchus had it right—the sun was the center of the planetary system, and all the planets, including the earth, revolved around the sun.

Copernicus improved the mathematics of the solar system and provided a clear description of the planetary orbits circling the sun.

However, Copernicus knew that his new mathematical description of the planetary system would contradict the Bible. Therefore, fearing that he would be condemned by the Church of Rome as heretical, he went home to Poland. There, he published his theory of the solar system with all its mathematics but told his publisher to put it out after his death.

This was done, and it created an enormous sensation among those studying Greek and Roman science.

Enter Galileo.[33]

Galileo Galilei of Florence accepted Copernicus' breakthrough and decided to build upon it. Galileo constructed a large telescope—the telescope had been perfected in the Dutch cities, wherein glassmaking was a craft industry.

Galileo improved upon the Dutch models and created a telescope that allowed him to view the moon and the nearby planets more clearly than the ancients ever could. He described the moon and planets, verified Copernicus' mathematics and descriptions, and brought astronomy to a new level.

Luckily for Galileo, at this time, when Galileo was a young man, the Pope and a number of cardinals knew him and encouraged him and did not accuse him of heresy.

[33] Galileo, *Notebooks*, NY, Amazon, 2010.

Galileo's works on astronomy were published, and he became a celebrity in Italy, Paris, and the Netherlands, where his work became known.

Even if Galileo had stopped at that point, he would already be considered an important figure in the emergence of modern science. However, he continued on to create even greater scientific breakthroughs.

Galileo began experimenting to try to understand the laws of motion and the process of gravity. Whether he actually dropped weights of various heaviness from the leaning tower of Pisa or whether this is an apocryphal story, it does not matter. What matters is that Galileo discovered the counterintuitive fact that both heavy and light objects fall to earth at the same speed.

Fascinated by this experiment—which he repeated many times—he followed this up with further experiments on motion. He used rolling balls of metal to help him describe mathematically the comparative speeds and acceleration of objects differing in weight and volume.

Galileo wrote down in his notebooks the experiments and mathematics involved in engendering his theories on motion. These notebooks were published along with his work on astronomy. Still, the Roman Catholic Church allowed him to continue his groundbreaking foundational scientific work.

Galileo became quite famous as he continued to innovate the experiment and generate scientific breakthroughs.

Then the Pope died, and a more fundamentalist Pope acceded to the role of head of the church. This new Pope had Galileo arrested for heresy. He probably would have been torched and killed if it not had been for his friends among the College of Cardinals. His life was spared, but he was relegated to house arrest in Florence.

Realizing that he could not continue his scientific efforts, Galileo had his notebooks secretly smuggled out of Italy to Paris and various Dutch cities. Though Paris and the Dutch cities were Catholic, the French king prided himself on his independence from papal control and encouraged scientific and philosophical activity in Paris, while the Dutch cities prided themselves on their independence from all the surrounding kingdoms and also encouraged scientific thought and discourse.

Hence, the great Renaissance of Greek and Roman knowledge would move north from Italy to France, the Netherlands, and then across to Great Britain and north to Germany and Scandinavia.

The history of science then takes off, with astronomy and mathematics being rapidly developed in the Low Countries, Germany, and Scandinavia and then culminating with the work of Isaac Newton of Great Britain in a full systemization of the theories of motion and gravity and the advanced mathematics of trigonometry—claimed contentiously by both Newton[34] and Leibnitz.[35] Historians give the breakthroughs to Newton, but Leibnitz did his part in publishing the new mathematics and bringing it to the attention of the French and German scientists.

---

[34] Isaac Newton, *Principia Mathematica*, 1687, Wikipedia.

[35] Gottfried Wilhelm Leibnitz. He invented calculus, Wikipedia, 1700.

From this point on, the history of science is well known. I shall only mention the Dutchman Antonie van Leeuwenhoek, who turned the telescope around and invented the microscope and subsequently saw, for the first time in human history, the "microbes" that existed by the billions in a world too small for the naked eye to see. This, of course, eventually led to the discovery of the cause of many diseases, and this brought biology and medicine to a new level.

The other major breakthroughs can be found in any history of science from the Enlightenment period onward.

Here, in this treatise, I would like to emphasize the conflict between science and religion that was generated by the Roman Catholic Church after Galileo's time. Remember that Al-Ghazeli's anti-Greek science theology put an end to the Arabic Golden Age, and Maimonides was almost censured by Jewish rabbis. So let us look at the Roman Catholic's rejection of science and then the Protestant-Christians' encouragement of scientific thought while remembering, as we shall show, that some Protestant sects rejected science.

13.9 The Roman Catholic Church Against Science

The Byzantine Greeks were conquered by the Turks in 1453. But they had long since stopped producing any new scientific works. Instead, Greek priests debated scriptural theological differences, such as the conception of Jesus—was he a man, god, or both? Should paintings and statues be used to adorn churches (the icon controversy)?

The Greeks preserved the ancient books but did not provide any commentary on them.

Though Greek priests did help the Italians during the early years of the Renaissance, it was the Italians themselves who pulled science up to a new level—improving art, architecture, music, and so much more at the same time.

The Italians proved creative, innovative, and masterful during the explosion of intellectual achievements that we call the Renaissance.

The Roman Catholic Church supported the effort for centuries, until the works of Copernicus and Galileo frightened the hierarchy and seemed to threaten their authority.

The Catholic Church did not rule through military power; the kings and city-states had that. The church ruled by controlling the theology of Europe—unifying it, ending the Greek disputes, centralizing its control, and punishing any dissenters.

The Inquisition terrified the Europeans. All heresies were punished with torture and horrible death—burning at the stake, beheading, and punishment for whole families and communities that defied the churches' authority.

Science seemed to threaten the Catholic Church. It described a different picture of the universe; it was creating what seemed like miracles in its public experiments and breakthrough discoveries.

So the Roman Catholic Church cracked down on science, even creating an "index" of books that were not allowed to be read by good Catholics. That index existed until the 1960s.

Thus, like Al-Ghazeli's Islamic fundamentalism, the Roman Catholic's rigidity turned the church against science.

Scientific discoveries dwindled in Italy and Spain and moved north, where Roman Catholicism was being rejected.

13.10 The Protestant Reformation and the Legitimation of Science

The trading cities of the German Hanseatic League, the river cities, and the Dutch cities all welcomed the Protestant Reformation. Free from the control of the Roman Catholic Church—and partially free from kingly control—these trade and craft-oriented cities embraced the rational-scientific worldview.

Merchants, bankers, and craftsmen of the "market cities"[36] of Northwest Europe were already rational minded economically. That is, they calculated profits and losses, pricing and interest rates, supply and demand, and market dynamics and performed bookkeeping and accounting. All these were rational, mathematical, and logical.

With no kings in these city-states, rational law—legal authority[37]—governed their actions.

Given the economic and lawful rationality commonplace in these independent city-states, the adoption of the scientific worldview seemed fully consistent with their already rational world orientation.

Thus, though the residents of these market cities were deeply religious and would embrace Lutheranism and then Calvinism, the central symbol in these German, Dutch, and Swiss cities was the clock tower, not the church. Instead of church bells, which they did have, the town halls—wherein governance resided—were adorned with elaborate clock towers. The clocks not only told time accurately, but they also exhibited the best in scientific engineering progress: the clocks had iron and bronze gears and were pendular, and when they chimed the hours, "glockenspiel" sculptures would automatically appear and circle around, providing a show of engineering excellence. At the same time, cuckoo clocks and large "grandfather" clocks adorned individual homes.

In many of these cities, signs were put up stating: "We are all mathematicians in this town." And while Protestant churches were small and modest—so as to show no Roman Catholic luxury living—the town halls were big and beautifully adorned,

---

[36] Max Weber, *The City*, NY Free Press, 1951.

[37] *Ibid.* See also *Economy and Society* (Gunther Roth and Claus Wittich, translators). NY: Bedminster Press.

and the clock towers dominated the town centers, sending the message to all observers that these cities were proud of their rational-scientific progress.

Further, all the citizens of these "free cities" received an education—even the girls—because Luther had taught that all Christians should be educated so that they could read the Bible on their own without the aid of a priest, bishop, or pope.

Luther had believed so fervently in this that he translated the Bible—Jewish and Christian—into German. No more Latin and no more domination from Rome—Christians must learn to read and write in their own vernacular language.

And, remarkably, the Protestant Reformation and the scientific revolution merged in Germany to create the printing press—this Gutenberg invention facilitated the massive dissemination of Luther's German Bible. Not only were millions produced, but they were also very inexpensive to buy.

The success of Luther's German Bible and the adoption of the printing press throughout Germany, the Netherlands, Switzerland, Great Britain, and Scandinavia led to vernacular translations of the Bible into Dutch, Danish, Swedish, Swiss, German, and English.

The Protestant Reformation and the scientific revolution were proceeding hand in hand. If the Roman Catholic Church opposed science and repressed it, the Protestant Church would encourage science and expand it.

The scientific worldview and scientific activities became fully legitimized for the first time in history. Remember, not even the Athenians condemned and exiled scientific intellectuals, even though it was believed that they were thought to be rejecting the gods and goddesses and advocating atheism and immoral pleasure seeking. Eventually, in ancient Greece, scientific and philosophical learning was accepted. But it was never enthusiastically encouraged and legitimated as it was in Reformation-era Northwest Europe.

Now, of course, there were fanatical Protestant sects that rejected science and rational thinking. Thousands of Protestants joined spiritual sects, wherein the Bible was read most literally, and all knowledge, save that of "scripture," was rejected.

The Anabaptists, the Shakers, and the many Calvinist-influenced sectarians rejected science, machines, and all things modern. The Amish, the Mennonites, and other sects adopted Protestant Christian theology and strongly rejected the rational-scientific worldview and all the technological progress of the emerging Industrial Revolution.

These fanatical fundamentalist sects, however, were not in the majority, and many were driven out of Germany, the Netherlands, and Great Britain. Sent to the New World of America to survive or die, they were fully marginalized in northwestern Europe.

The main trend of the Protestant Reformation was fully in sync with the scientific worldview, encouraging its expansion and celebrating its engineering successes. It was not just the printing press that was heralded, but every machine and technological improvement was also greeted with enthusiasm. Scientists and engineers were encouraged to do more, such as improving the theories and applying them to significant technological breakthroughs.

Eventually, the steam engine, the machine production of goods in factories (as opposed to craft production and small workshops), railroad trains, and other engineering "miracles" engendered the Industrial Revolution in Northwest Europe.

The Protestant Reformation encouraged and legitimated all of this.

13.11 The Compatibility of Science and Religion

Whereas the Roman Catholic Church set religion against science, Protestant churches preached coexistence. The Protestants maintained that one could be a religious, spiritual, and moral Christian believing deeply in the theology of Jesus as the Savior, the Redeemer, and the one who held out hope of resurrection and redemption from sin. Strongly moral—using the Ten Commandments and the Gospels as their guide—the Protestants believed one could be a good Christian—a spiritual and an ethical Christian—and still pursue scientific knowledge.

The astronomical discoveries of Tycho Brahe and Johannes Kepler were hailed as wonderful. Copernicus' mathematics were not rejected as heretical; rather, they were accepted as foundational and were improved upon. The laws of motion of Galileo were not rejected as anti-Christian but were taken to a new level that ushered in the modern scientific revolution by Isaac Newton.

There were those, such as Thomas More[38] of England, who worried that this rationality could lead to atheism and that atheism would lead to sociopathic behavior because there was no fear of punishment in the afterlife—no moral God to frighten us into moral behavior.

There were those who turned on Erasmus of the Netherlands because he advocated modernizing the Catholic Church and opening the world of scientific inquiry. They believed, like Thomas More, that Erasmus' reforms of the Catholic Church would lead to a total rejection of Christianity.

And, oh yes, the rabbis of Amsterdam excommunicated Baruch Spinoza for advocating the rational analysis of the Jewish Bible as a historical document and rejecting the notion of an anthropomorphic father god rewarding and punishing us for our behavior.

Though the rabbis during the Arabic Golden Age had rejected Maimonides' adoption of Aristotle's logic, Greek mathematics, and Greek medicine, they made him a hero of the Jews for revising the Talmud commentaries and organizing them into a more readable and useful form.

Spinoza got no such reprieve, and instead of a hero designation, he was banished from the Jewish community.

Yet though Spinoza was banished, Maimonides had already set the principle in motion that the Jewish Bible and Talmud could be studied simultaneously with Greek science. After Spinoza, a few Jews were condemned for scientific activities,

---

[38] Thomas Moore, *Utopia*, London, Penguin, 1949.

and Jewish doctors continued to have a high status in Europe. So compatible did Judaism and science become that—after Spinoza—Moses Mendelssohn was called "The Socrates of the Jews" and was heralded by both Christian Germans and Jewish Germans.

Thus, into the eighteenth and nineteenth centuries, during the Enlightenment and the Industrial Revolution, religion and science were encouraged as copartners in the emerging new world of modern society.

By and large, Protestant Christianity and rational science were accepted as compatible.

Chapter 14
Science and Religion in the Modern World

14.1 Science as Spectacular: Space, Medical Cures, and Atomic Energy

It was not until after World War II that science became a global worldview. The invention of the atomic bomb and penicillin created a mystique of science: the atomic bomb showing that science had the ability to destroy humankind and penicillin showing that science could save us.

The world's peoples did not have to be familiar with Einstein's theory of relativity—the existence of the atomic bomb and a hydrogen bomb was enough to catapult science into a realm of knowledge production never before conceived of: humans, as scientists, were beginning to understand the secrets of the universe—Thales' quest to find the "basic substance" of the universe and Pythagoras' vision of the universe as governed by mathematical measurements had come to fruition with modern sciences' conception of the universe. Modern science is using atomic theory—particle theory—and theories of energy—all envisioned through mathematical formulations.

And, along with the discovery of nuclear energy, the medical breakthroughs on disease causality and cures showed the world's people how science could save humanity.

Thus, as the twentieth century came to an end, the rational-scientific worldview began to take hold globally as a new and better way to view the universe and our place in it.

In the era of the twenty-first century, when an individual looks at the sky, they do not think of heaven; they think of blazing suns, black holes, galaxies, and an expanding universe extending beyond our comprehension into infinity. When modern individuals think about the creation of the universe, they think of the "big bang," not a fatherly creator god. When modern individuals feel sick, they do not go to a shaman—a witch doctor; they go to a scientifically trained medical doctor and to a

R. M. Glassman, *The Great Global Transformation*, Contributions to Political Science, https://doi.org/10.1007/978-3-031-90566-7_14

hospital staffed by scientifically trained nurses and doctors and equipped with the latest technology available to keep humans alive.

Not everyone but a growing number of individuals throughout the world are absorbing the rational-scientific worldview. For instance, though in China traditional drugstores still abound, modern scientific drug stores exist side by side with them, and when the Covid-19 (or SARS) pandemic broke out, the majority of the Chinese looked to their scientists for a vaccine cure and followed their orders on quarantine and social lockdowns. The Chinese example typifies the global response to disease—all the peoples of the world follow the guidance of scientists who specialize in the particular problem at hand, anti-vaxxers notwithstanding.

Along with atomic energy and medical miracles, our ascent into space has furthered the mystique of science as the best way to view the universe and our place in it.

The International Space Station, orbiting the earth and housing astronauts from all advanced scientific nations, along with the landing of humans on the moon and our proposed Mars ventures, has created a world of "Star Wars" and "Star Trek" fantasies—captured on films and science fiction novels. These fantasies have become realities and have given science even more legitimacy as the preferred way to view the universe.

The invention of computers and their dissemination to the world's population have also institutionalized science and science-based technology as a world-organizing phenomenon. The Internet has created a new human reality—a reality mediated by the virtual world of email, social media outlets such as Facebook and Instagram, Zoom meetings, and so much more.

Radio, television, and movies had already created a worldwide mass media phenomenon, linking the world's cultures together into a global "pop" culture unifier. Now, computers, smartphones, and social media apps have linked the world's population into an interconnected communication culture in which individuals can actively participate—as compared to the passive participation in radio, television, and movies.

A world culture is emerging, and all humans have now become interconnected to the World Wide Web. And as a central part of this world culture, the scientific worldview has now become institutionalized. Globally, humans are now socialized into taking the rational-scientific worldview for granted as the proper way to view the universe and our place in it. The universe, life, and human beings are scrutinized through the lens of the rational-scientific worldview.

This is the new "Zeitgeist" of the twenty-first century.

And along with the rational-scientific worldview derived from the natural sciences—physics, astronomy, chemistry, biology, medicine, and mathematics—social sciences have emerged also. These social sciences—political science, sociology, psychology, anthropology, and economics—have provided a rational-scientific framework for understanding human beings as individuals and as acting in groups. Though not as precise as the "hard" sciences, social sciences have given us a great deal of new knowledge about ourselves and have contributed to the rational-scientific perception of the world.

That is, we no longer say, "That person is 'crazy.'" We now say, "That person is suffering from 'manic and depressive disorder'" or from "OCD" (obsessive-compulsive disorder) etc.

We do not just say, "That person is poor." We say, poverty is linked with educational deprivation and childhood trauma, and these could lead to serious social problems if not attended to.

Further, though economics has hardly been successful in understanding the capitalist business cycle of boom and bust, when the American stock market crashed in 2008, a joint task force of republican and democratic economic and financial experts were able to "bail out" Wall Street and prevent the "Great Recession" from becoming another "Great Depression," like that of 1929.

So individuals in society, politics, and economics are being analyzed using the rational-scientific worldview. And, as we shall describe, the idea of self-fulfillment generated by the Marxism idea of "species being," and the modern psychological theory put forth by Maslow as "self-actualization," will take Hegel's idea of the growing "consciousness of self" to a new scientific level.

We shall come back to this idea of self-actualization—in its sociological and psychological designations—soon. First, let us continue our discussion of the clash between science and religion as to which worldview will prevail.

14.2 Religion and Science in the Modern World of the Twenty-First Century

We have established that because of the remarkable scientific achievements in atomic energy, medicine, space travel, and global mass media connectivity, the rational-scientific worldview has become the dominant worldview globally.

But religions still exist, and the great world religions still have a powerful hold on the human mind. Judaism and Christianity still create strongly held views of the world. So, too, do Islam, Hinduism, Buddhism, and Confucianism (Confucianism is not a spiritual religion but puts forth an ethical and moral standard for social and political behavior similar in its hold to that of world religions.)

Why do the world religions still have a powerful hold on the worldview of modern individuals? It is because science cannot answer certain questions that religions answer by way of faith rather than rationality, that is: Why do we die? Why are we born? How should we live together in our daily lives? Who or what created the universe and ourselves in it?

Science can tell us the *cause* of a loved one's death but not why they must die. Science can tell us how life is produced from an egg and a sperm but not why life is born—or why life came into existence from "dead" organic matter.

Science has theorized that the universe came into existence through the "big bang." But in the theory of the big bang, a "singularity"—containing all the energy and matter in the universe—is postulated as already existing, so where did the "singularity" come from? How did it get created?

The theory of the big bang[1] is wonderful for explaining how all the energy and matter in the universe evolved—from the first "nanosecond" through billions of years of change to today's galaxies—as they expand outward in every direction. But the existential question of "creation" is not answered.

Yet if one adds the religious answer, god—whichever god—created the universe. Then one must ask: Who or what created that god? It is no use trying to get around the Aristotelian logic by insisting that the god created himself or herself through the power of "mind" or any other power. One is faced with an infinite regress if one follows Aristotelian logic—Who created the creator? No answer.

Why do we die? We do not die; our "soul" lives on forever. This is comforting, just as the idea of a creator god is comforting. But it makes no sense. Where are the myriad souls? Where is heaven? It would be awfully full, we might think.

Belief in the world religions' conceptions of god and the soul are difficult to maintain in the face of the growing acceptance of the rational-scientific worldview.

Of course, there are religious revivals occurring among Orthodox Jews, fundamentalist Protestants, Orthodox Catholics, fundamentalist Muslims, and traditionalist Hindus and Buddhists. However, the rational-scientific worldview is expanding in its global acceptance, while these world religious revivals are limited in their appeal—held onto by the less educated citizens of their nations. But even these deeply religious individuals will go to a hospital or see a doctor if they become ill, and they are definitely linked into the global Internet world of mass communication.

Still, the rational-scientific worldview gives us no ethical and moral standards to live by. Science—by its own definition—is value neutral. Scientists will create atomic bombs that could blow us off the face of the earth, and they will create vaccines that can save us from deadly pandemics.

Because of science's value neutrality and the decline in world religious beliefs, some ideological system-generating humanistic ethics becomes necessary.

The humanistic worldview—added to the rational-scientific worldview—can be secular, that is, avoiding the question of god and creation and postulating our "existential" aloneness in the "infinite universe," as Sartre put it, or humanism can be spiritual, projecting a belief in something beyond ourselves with a transcendent meaning that we cannot grasp.

Both kinds of humanism exist today, and with the decline of world religions, these humanistic worldviews may join the rational-scientific worldview, together forming the Zeitgeist of the twenty-first century.

Let me use the example of the current Covid-19 pandemic to illustrate both the rational-scientific response and the humanistic response to this disease.

[1] Stephen Hawking on the *Big Bang Theory*, *A Brief History of Time*, 1988.

Chapter 15
Science and Humanistic Ethics

15.1 The Covid-19 Pandemic Brings the World Together in a Quest for a Vaccine

The rational-scientific worldview creates the human ability to invent a vaccine to save the world's population from disease. However, since science is *amoral*—it can create atom bombs as well as vaccines—a *humanistic* worldview is also necessary in order to generate a global effort to create a vaccine and to ensure that all the peoples of the world gain access to that vaccine.

Thus, the global Covid-19 pandemic provides a perfect bridge between our discussion of the rational-scientific worldview and the secular and spiritual-humanistic worldview.

Further, it is significant that even in totalitarian dictatorships, such as China under Xi Jinping, there is enough caring for the economy that Xi and the Communist Party have acted humanistically in terms of curing Covid-19. The Chinese leadership shared the DNA of the virus with the world's scientists so that a vaccine could be developed as soon as possible.

The world scientific community, after receiving this information from the Chinese, embarked on the most rapid development of a vaccine ever accomplished. All the world's scientific biotech corporations cooperated—and competed—for the invention and production of a vaccine. China gave out the information not out of humanistic concern but rather to avoid economic breakdown. Nonetheless, the end result has been humanistic—a vaccine has been developed, and it has been shared with all the world's nations. There have been numerous vaccines developed by different companies, with multinational corporations sharing their data cross-nationally.

This represents a wonderful humanistic trend in the newly emergent global world. The fact that the Chinese totalitarian government shared its knowledge in a

R. M. Glassman, *The Great Global Transformation*, Contributions to Political Science, https://doi.org/10.1007/978-3-031-90566-7_15

humanistic way with the world is a positive sign for global cooperation on other important matters threatening humankind, such as climate change.

Even totalitarian and dictatorial regimes become concerned—and even cooperative—when their own interests are threatened.

China, even though it is competitive with other nations economically, politically, and militarily, is also enmeshed in economic coproduction and international marketing. Therefore, it had to act humanistically for its own economic interest.

The fact that totalitarian China—and dictatorial Russia—rushed to get the vaccine out to their populations shows us that a world "humanistic" ethos is emerging, even in nondemocratic nations. Dictators usually want their populations healthy and productive. The motives in this may *not* be humanistic, but the result is humanistic nonetheless.

15.2 Why Has Secular and Spiritual Humanism Become a World Trend?

The rational-scientific worldview makes rituals such as worshipping anthropomorphic gods seem illogical.

One religion mandates that you must take your hat off when entering a temple, while another insists you must cover your head—so put your hat on. One religion mandates that you get down on your knees to pray to God, another that you rock back and forth. One religion mandates that prelates must wear black, another white.

Rituals, as Durkheim has shown in the *Elementary Forms of Religious Life*,[1] are comforting, and they create group solidarity. Rituals reinforce group identity and create a feeling of close community.

However, rituals, in themselves, are meaningless and nonrational.

The modern global citizen is steeped in the rational-scientific worldview and therefore finds religious rituals to be irrational and meaningless. As Durkheim tells us, this will cause a loss in group solidarity, which is disconcerting for modern individuals. Nonetheless, religious rituals lose their hold when individuals become rational minded. Does God care if I keep my hat on or take it off?

And what about God—is the conception of God as a father who punishes and rewards really meaningful? Is it even logical? A hurricane hits, and someone says, "My house was spared. Thank God." But your neighbor's house was destroyed—did God do that too, and should your neighbor be angry with God?

All things are done for a reason—only God knows the reason. Yet so many terrible things happen in the world. Is God evil as well as good? Is there really a "reason" for all the terrible things that occur, along with all the good things?

[1] Emile Durkheim, *The Elementary Forms of Religious Life*, NY: Free Press, 1952.

"If God is God, He is not good, if God is good, He is not God; take the even, take the odd"—Archibald MacLeish in his play *J.B.*[2] states the dilemma well.

A dualistic system of gods escapes the paradox: all good comes from God, while all evil comes from the devil, the god of evil—simplistic and logical but childish and absurd.

To the modern scientific mind, there is no rational conception of god. As Sartre put it, "God is dead, we are alone in the universe."[3]

Even the idea of a creator god winds down in a logical regress: God created the universe, but who created God?

"God is the self-created creator, who willed himself into existence through the power of his mind." So where did his mind come from, as well as his power?

If we are rationally scientifically minded, no conception of god or gods is sustainable. We find ourselves in a seemingly infinite universe in which we are alone in our conscious awareness of that universe and our place in it.

We have no idea why we are here, why we know we are here, why we are born, or why we die.

Science can explain the events in the universe, can explain how we are born and why we die, but science cannot tell us why we and the universe exist or, since we do exist, how we should behave toward one another and toward other animals and plants and planets.

Sartre's *"existentialism," though logically correct—we are alone in the universe, and there is no imminent father god caring for us—gives us no moral compass.*

As we have established, the rational-scientific worldview gives us enormous knowledge but no moral-ethical code of behavior.

Therefore, rationally scientifically oriented individuals have had to create their own ethical and moral norms. Hence, humanism has emerged. It has emerged in two forms: one is purely secular. There is no god; we make our own caring norms and values—this is "secular humanism." The other is "spiritual humanism," wherein some conception of a moral god is accepted, but humanistic norms and values are also demanded.

Secular humanism—wherein no god is projected as imminent in any way—has become a world movement. And following Søren Aabye *Kierkegaard*[4] *and Martin Buber,*[5] *there is also a humanistic movement that includes some conception of a caring god and its equally humanistic moral mandate for human behavior.*

---

[2] Archibald MacLeish, *J.B.*, 1958.

[3] Jean Paul Sartre, *Being and Nothingness*, NY, Amazon 2012.

[4] Søren Aabye *Kierkegaard, Christian Existentialism*, Wikipedia.

[5] Martin Buber, *I and Thou*, Penguin Classics, NY, 1953.

15.3 Thomas More's Rejection of Atheism as Engendering Sociopathic Behavior

In Utopia,[6] *one could absorb any set of beliefs—all religions were tolerated, except atheism.*

Thomas More maintained that if one did not believe in a punishing and rewarding god—as well as heaven and hell in the afterlife—then a person would simply act sociopathically—Why not? There would be no punishment.

In today's rational-scientific world, wherein a father god who rewards and punishes, and an afterlife that continues that process, is not accepted, how do we keep people from becoming sociopathic?

Secular humanism is one answer, for it teaches people to be kind and caring toward others. "Do unto others as you would have them do unto you"—as "the Golden Rule" of Judeo-Christian tradition says. And it is also the Confucian tradition: "Do not do to others what you do not want them to do to you."

Humanistic caring, thus, is a rational conception. However, humanistic ethics has to be carefully taught—it must be instilled in children and exhibited within the family and community.

Modern families—globally—do instill humanistic ethics in their children. Yes, modern child rearing tends to be "permissive"—kids are rarely punished and overly rewarded. However, these modern children are raised by caring parents who do teach cooperative norms to these otherwise self-oriented children.

The children are encouraged to "self-actualize" their talents—"Be all that you can be," from Maslow and "species being" from Marx. And modern children are often selfish and "spoiled" and self-centered—but they are also caring and kind for the most part.

What of "spiritual humanism"? Sigmund Freud could not understand how anyone—given modern scientific rationality—could have a "religious experience." But others, such as his student Jung, insisted that one could be both rational and spiritual. So, too, could Buber and Tillich[7] *be rational, logical, and scientific and still believe in some form of a "god" outside of ourselves that is somehow imminent in the universe.*

In actuality, we have no idea how we got here or what the universe means. But no conception of a creator god or an imminent god does leave us quite alone and possibly in despair. Therefore, spiritual humanism with some sort of conception of "god"—Buddhist, Spinozian, Stoic, or whatever conception makes personal sense for an individual—is an alternative, as long as it is coupled with humanistic ethics, the ethics of caring for other humans, animals, nature, and the world.

Sociopathic atheism, as More warned in Utopia, is not a viable option. Some sort of humanistic ethics must accompany the rational-scientific worldview for humanity to move forward progressively in terms of ethics, along with the scientific progress

[6] Thomas More, *Utopia*, London, Penguin, 1949.

[7] Paul Tillich, *The Courage to Be*, 1952, Yale University Press.

of increasing knowledge about ourselves and the universe and the remarkable technological progress generated by that scientific knowledge.

What good are computers, cell phones, and rockets to the Moon or Mars if we keep killing each other and polluting our planet? War and competition are part of our DNA, so some form of humanism must accompany the rational-scientific worldview if humanity is to survive.

15.4 The Optimism: The United Nations Universal Bill of Human Rights

As I write, it is December 10, 2020—"Human Rights Day." On December 10, 1948, the United Nations added to its Charter the Universal Bill of Human Rights. This Bill of Rights includes economic and educational rights, along with the political rights found in the American Bill of Rights.

This Universal Bill of Human Rights is the hallmark of humanistic ethics. Every human, regardless of race, ethnicity, religion, or creed, is guaranteed equal treatment under the law and equal opportunity educationally and economically.

Living up to the Bill of Human Rights is, of course, an uneven phenomenon. Nonetheless, the principles involved are clearly stated, and many nations are attempting to achieve the difficult goals set forth in the United Nations Bill of Human Rights.

Furthermore, the United Nations has passed two other humanistic law codes: the code of humane warfare and the prohibition of genocide.

Again, these have been unevenly applied worldwide. Nonetheless, there is a World Court at the Hague in the Netherlands that tries individuals and government officials who are charged with inhumane acts of war or, worse, genocide.

The use of poison gas, for instance, is considered inhumane or attacking civilian populations. Of course, both have been done in Syria and Iraq recently, yet no one has been forced to the World Court. Saddam Hussein, however, was killed after the American invasion in the Gulf War II, but Assad of Syria is being protected by the Russians at the moment.

The Chinese, here in 2020, have been actively suppressing the Uyghurs of western China. It is not genocide in that the Uyghurs are not being killed. But it is cultural and religious "genocide" in that the Uyghurs are being forced to learn the language and culture of the Han Chinese, and their religion—Islam—has been banned. The Chinese' actions toward the Uyghurs have been condemned by the United Nations. But the United Nations does not have the military power to intervene on behalf of the Uyghurs.

The United States does pressure the Chinese in terms of human rights violations. But, so far, the USA has not been successful in its efforts to instill the reality of the Bill of Human Rights into Chinese society. Under President Trump, no pressure was put on the Chinese regime regarding human rights violations.

Dictatorships, such as those in China, North Korea, and Russia routinely violate the human rights provisions of the United Nations Charter. However, as China and Russia are drawn into the world economic nexus, pressure to recognize human rights may resonate more effectively.

A hopeful sign, for instance, was China's rapid attempt to prevent the coronavirus from spreading in China and, failing that, China's very quick cooperation with the world's vaccine at Western pharmaceutical corporations, such as Pfizer—to help the scientists make an RNA vaccine by giving them the genetic code of the virus.

Now, this was self-serving—not humanistic—in that China wanted its world trade economy to resume full production as soon as possible. The Chinese regime also bore blame for allowing live animal markets, traditional in China, to remain open when the regime knew that exotic viruses were emerging from animals, especially bats but also other exotic animals and birds. They were also careless in their laboratory while experimenting with these viruses.

The global response to the Covid-19 pandemic must be seen as a humanistic response. Whatever the motives of the various world regimes are, the development of a successful vaccine is intended to save lives. And this phenomenon inadvertently reinforces the Talmudic, humanistic dictum that "every human life is important and worth saving."

Where did the idea come from?

15.5 The Jewish Bible and the Humanistic Ethic

Judaism, Christianity, and Islam all share the Jewish Bible—the Old Testament—as their basis for ethics. The Jewish Bible asserts that "all humans are made in God's image," and therefore, every human life is holy. Suicide is forbidden, for one's life is so important that one cannot take it away—this would be sinful. And murder is forbidden for the same reason. Paradoxically, murder is considered so terrible a crime that the punishment for it is death!

The death penalty was considered necessary in order to inhibit men from murdering. In the modern world, this paradoxical Old Testament dictum has been removed in many countries since World War II. Life imprisonment has replaced the death penalty, while the humanistic ethic that all human life is sacred has been retained.

So the Jewish biblical ethic of the sanctity of human life was partially compromised; nonetheless, this biblical ethic did become the foundation stone upon which the valuation of human life eventually became a global ethic—at least in principle.

Now, one can argue that murder is universally condemned by most cultures, though penalties for murder vary in their extremity. But in most of the ancient civilizations, human life was not held as sacred. Humans were routinely enslaved, worked to death in mines, sent to their deaths in endless wars, and routinely buried after death—unless they were members of the elite.

The Jewish biblical ethic that every human life matters—whether rich, poor, male, female, resident, or stranger—is different and important.

Further, the Jewish Bible also enshrines the prophets, who railed for social justice, including caring for the poor, the infirm, the widowed, the orphan, etc.

Again, this humanistic caring about social justice for all people was not a universal phenomenon. It came out of Sumer and Babylon, but it was stated much more forcefully in the Jewish Bible.

Hinduism and Buddhism do not really have such a humanistic ethic. The theology of the transmigration of the soul, good karma and bad karma, and transcendental meditation are explanatory in terms of good and evil and the achievement of personal tranquility, but in terms of the valuation of human life, this theology does not emphasize that "saving one life" is a marvelous and holy achievement, as said in the Jewish Talmud.

Confucianism in China and Korea contains two humanistic ideals: one is the concept of "benevolence"; the other is the Golden Rule stated negatively.

In terms of "benevolence,"[8] Confucius taught that both the Emperor (and his Mandarin officials) and the father of a family should take care of the common people and, in the family, their children.

This is a paternalistic ethic wherein the common people and the children are taken care of but wherein the elites that care for them are far more highly valued. The father has all the power over his wife and children, while the Emperor and his officials have all the power over the "common people."

Further, the fact that the Golden Rule is stated negatively—"Do *not* do to others what you do *not* want them to do to you"—shows that this is meant as a prohibition against crime and violence. And, yes, this is very good. However, it does not encourage *altruistic* behavior: "Do unto others as you would have them do unto you."

Further still, Confucian culture is a *shame* culture: if you shame your family or shame the Emperor, you must commit suicide. Suicide is almost mandatory under certain circumstances wherein shame is involved.

Human life is certainly not valued where suicide is culturally demanded. Of course, the family and friends of an individual who commits suicide mourn that person genuinely. Yet the cultural mandate is there.

In China—probably because of overpopulation—girl babies were sometimes left out to die. Female infanticide was not uncommon and, as such, cannot be seen as part of a culture that values human life as sacred and godly.

In the modern world, there is little doubt that humanistic ethics emerged out of Judeo-Christian biblical ethics and then spread across the globe as Western nations conquered the world.

However, we must also add the democratic revolution and legal-rational authority to the spreading of the humanistic ethic. After all, the Universal Declaration of Human Rights is a law code. And its predecessor was the United States Bill of Rights, which was added to the American Constitution by the ardent Democrats at

[8] Confucius, *The Analects, Benevolence, the Golden Rule*, NY, Amazon, 2000.

the Constitutional Convention. An implicit English Bill of Rights and a French revolutionary Bill of Rights also emerged as a democracy movement—which was dormant since the time of ancient Greece and Rome but was revived during the Enlightenment period in Western Europe.

15.6 The Democracy Movement and Humanistic Ethics

"We hold these truths as self-evident, that all men are created equal (under the law)."[9]

Thomas Jefferson's words, hypocritical as they were at the time because of slavery in the United States colonies, would nonetheless become as significant as biblical ethics for establishing humanistic ethics.

The idea of "inalienable rights, as "God-given" also reinforces humanistic ethics in the sense that every individual has these inalienable rights and is therefore worthy of those rights.

Further, the idea that "consent" comes from the people and is given to the government—and can be withdrawn from the government—empowers "the people" and enhances their worth. The American Constitution, as written by James Madison, begins with "We the people…".

So the United Nations Universal Bill of Rights could not have been written and accepted without the strong tradition of democracy and legal authority among the victorious powers of World War II.

Therefore, let us move on to the next section, focusing on the global political transformation. We move on to discuss this political transformation, acknowledging that Francis Fukuyama's optimism about the "end of history" being capitalism and democracy was premature.[10]

And since Fukuyama "stood Marx on his head," as Marx had stood Hegel on his head, I must acknowledge that the socialist movement—in its ideal form before the Russian Revolution and the Stalinist corruption—was a humanistic movement. Economic justice for humans—real economic equality—was to undergird real representative democracy, after the state had "withered away" and the economic domination by rich capitalists had been removed.

We know that Marxism-Leninism led to Stalinist, murderous totalitarianism—as bad as that of Nazism.

However, the United Nations Bill of Universal Human Rights would not have included the rights to economic opportunity and equal education for all people without the socialist movement.

Having acknowledged our debt to socialism as part of the secular humanism that was to emerge, let us also acknowledge that Stalinist totalitarianism is still with us in China, North Korea, Cuba, and now Venezuela.

---

[9] The American Declaration of Independence.

[10] Francis Fukuyama, *The End of History*.

Without electoral democracy and legal authority, humanism—true caring about every individual life—cannot survive.

Therefore, let us look at this most difficult global transformation.

First, however, before analyzing the political changes, let us evaluate the impact of the social and cultural changes.

Chapter 16
Emile Durkheim's Theory of Social Change and Anomie: The Impact of Social and Cultural Changes on the Emerging Global Society

16.1 Durkheim's Theory of Anomie: Violence, Deviance, and Creativity[1]

In his book *Suicide*, Durkheim noted that during periods of rapid social change, suicide rates go up.

Why?

Durkheim theorized that during periods of rapid social change, the traditional norms and values that had guided people's social interactions declined and are no longer relevant to the new social reality.

However, the new norms and values are not yet fully accepted.

Therefore, during periods of rapid social change, there is a loss of norms and values.

This loss of norms and values produces moral confusion—what is right, and what is wrong? People are not sure there is a moral malaise.

Furthermore, during periods of rapid social change, rates of deviance, crime, violence, and political extremism go up. On the positive side, so, too, does creativity expand.

Freed from the rigidity of social norms, freethinking—innovative thinking—in every field emerges. In the arts, in the sciences, in technology, novel experimentation occurs.

Unfortunately, along with this creativity, political extremism, violence, crime, and deviance also explode—also because people are freed from their normative behavior.

Durkheim uses the Greek term anomie to characterize—literally—the breakdown of order. Nomos is the Greek word for order, so anomie means disorder.

---

[1] Emile Durkheim, *Suicide* (in the section of Anomic Suicide, Durkheim explains his theory of anomie), NY, Free Press, 1950.

R. M. Glassman, *The Great Global Transformation*, Contributions to Political Science, https://doi.org/10.1007/978-3-031-90566-7_16

During periods of social disorder (anomie), with the resulting loss of norms and moral confusion, not only suicide but also the rates of homicide and random acts of violence go up. These acts are sometimes politically targeted while at other times purely random in their target.

Rates of deviance also skyrocket: drug addiction and alcoholism rise, divorce rates go up, and rates of homosexuality and lesbianism increase. Whatever the cause of homosexuality and lesbianism is—and we do not actually have scientific data on this as yet—they were considered deviant by traditional normative standards, but they are now considered normal by new normative standards. Nonetheless, the rates go up during periods of rapid social change and anomie as modern societies emerge globally.

In terms of drug addiction, whatever drugs are in use and available, the rates of abuse using such drugs increase.

And, of course, if you add the availability of guns—as in contemporary America—then the homicide rate skyrockets to previously unimaginable rates of carnage.

Political extremism becomes more dangerous with the introduction of guns as well. And political extremism emerges because half of society will still cling to old traditional norms and values, while the other half will champion the new norms and values.

Issues such as abortion, gay marriage, divorce, marijuana use, transgender medical procedures, drag queens shows, women in combat military roles, and more will divide a modern nation into extremist political movements. Victor Orbán and Donald Trump rallied their followers around the traditional norms and values, while figures like Gavin Newsom—the Governor of California—or Angela Merkel of Germany (now retired) rallied their followers around the new norms and values.

Political extremism is ripping modern societies apart.

Today, in the twenty-first century, Durkheim's theory is more relevant than ever, for *every basic institution of society* is going through a process of rapid social change: gender, marriage, family, ethnic identity, religion, economy, and polity—all are underlying dramatic social change.

Therefore, anomie and social disorganization predominate. And, therefore, suicide, homicide, divorce, drug and alcohol addiction, family breakup, political extremism, and moral confusion are all occurring in the modernizing societies of the twenty-first century.

Remarkably, so is creativity—especially technological creativity and innovation.

The twenty-first century is characterized by the emergence and adoption of new technologies that are changing our lives.

The computer, the smartphone, the Internet, and the new social media platforms—they are changing everything. Are they wonderful? Are they terrible? No one is sure. Thus, these newly created technologies are engendering even more moral confusion. Is Facebook wonderful or terrible? What about X (formerly Twitter) and TikTok? Will these new platforms enhance free speech and democracy or destroy them?

It is too soon to evaluate their impact. Right now, these new technologies are producing more political extremism, more mass murders, more suicides, more uncontrolled sexuality, and, yes, more free speech as well.

Because the pace of technological change is so rapid, it increases social disorganization, anomie, and moral confusion. Rapid social change is supercharged in this new Internet age. People carry their smartphones—small computers are what they are—and look at them and attend to them all day and all night. Modern individuals will interact with their smartphone rather than the person they know sitting next to them. This is becoming more normative than talking to a person live.

To sum up, during periods of rapid social change—and we are living in a period of global social change—a condition of social disorganization emerges, which Durkheim has called anomie—loss of order, loss of norms, and moral malaise.

16.2 Every Basic Institution Is Changing

In the twenty-first century, every basic institution of society is undergoing a dramatic change. Gender, marriage, family, ethnic identity, religion, economy, and polity—all are undergoing dramatic changes.

We have discussed these changes, but let us do a recap on these changes in order to deepen our understanding of their impact.

16.2.1 Gender

The most basic division of the human species is gender: male and female are biological givens, right? Not anymore. Today, the very definition of gender is obscure. What is male? What is female? Both sexes do all the same roles; both sexes must be socially equal.

No, men cannot produce babies and cannot breast-nurture them. However, babies may be grown in the laboratory, and baby formula already exists.

So equal have the genders become that some people call themselves nonbinary. Does this mean that they are both sexes? Neither sex? What exactly does nonbinary mean?

On the positive side, 50,000 people ran in the New York City Marathon, and half of them were women. Women can run marathons, pole vault, shoot a gun in the military, and do so much more.

So are there any gender distinctions that make sense socially?

Differences are being debated: right brain or left brain—are these differences emphasized in women and men? Men commit 95 percent of all murders—testosterone casualty?

The whole question of gender is under discussion globally as gender differences are minimized in the economic, political, and social spheres.

The French used to say, "*Vive la difference*," as romance and sex were a major part of their cultural complex. Now, however, globally, it is said, "*Vive le sameness*," as gender differences are minimized.

This is as dramatic a social change as we can have in human society.

If the genders are the same, how shall they relate to each other in the workplace, in the political sphere, in the military, in the bedroom?

These interactions are slowly being worked out. But until they are fully worked out, normative and moral confusion will exist. Therefore, gender interactions may exhibit deviant, violent, and creative behaviors.

Workplace norms are becoming established, as are political norms, but military and sexual norms are still in flux and in crisis. Rape in the military is still a real issue. While men's role in initiating sexual contact is viewed ambivalently by women, who want to control the process, men are not sure of what is expected of them—are the Don Juans potential rapists? Should they be passive or aggressive?

Male-female relationships are in flux globally, and each cultural.

16.2.2 Marriage

Marriage is culturally universal as anthropologists have told us that every society has one sort of marriage institution or another.[2]

Hunting-gathering societies—the primeval *Homo sapiens* societies—exhibited pairing marriage: a monogamous couple that was married off at puberty. This pairing couple was surrounded by their close-knit band. The couple was married young. Since there was no contraception, the women would be pregnant often. Since they died young—the average age of death was 30 years old—divorce was hardly an issue, although it did occur.[3]

The invention of agriculture allowed humans to live in a more sedentary village settlement pattern and to live longer. Grandparents survived, and the extended family, or clan, emerged.

The clan still maintained monogamous pairing marriages, but now, they were embedded within an extended family unit rather than a band. They were surrounded by grandparents, aunts, uncles, cousins, etc.

Women seem to have invented agriculture because women gathered vegetables and grains, and while preparing them, they eventually noticed that they sprouted or grew from seeds.

Most early agriculture societies—which anthropologists call horticultural societies—exhibited matrilineal clans. That is, the husband moved into the wife's clan

[2] Ruth Benedict, Patterns of Culture, NY, Collier Books, 1952; Linton, Boaz.

[3] John Marshall, *The Bushmen of the Kalahari Desert.*

upon marriage. And the wife's clan—the matriclan—made up the unit of workers who engaged in horticultural production.[4]

Horticulture was women's work; the men went off hunting, or, later, the men engaged in animal herding.

Among American Indians (Indigenous people) in North America, the women produced corn, beans, squash, and more, and it was taboo for men to engage in gardening—though they helped in harvesting.

In matriclan societies, women's status was high—they had the vote on the clan council, and they were critical economically.[5]

However, men were the warriors, and the clan elders who were elected were always men.

Women, however, had a great deal of influence and, in some societies, had sexual freedom because in matrilineal clans, any child born to a woman was a member of her clan. The children took the name of the wife's clan. In fact, there were some societies, such as those of Polynesia, where polyandry existed.

Polyandry consists of one wife and many husbands. Polynesian women were famous among sailors from England for claiming them as husbands and having sex with them.

However, polyandry reduces the population—one woman can only be pregnant for 9 months, whether she has one husband or many husbands. On islands, keeping the population down is important. Elsewhere, it is not a good thing because a neighboring society would have more warriors and could conquer your society.

As agricultural techniques progressed, animal herding became possible because there was enough water and food to keep small animals.

Once discovered, animal herding expanded to keeping larger animals—from sheep and goats to cattle and horses.

In societies that made animal herding their central economic factor, polygamous marriages emerged, wherein one husband had numerous wives. These societies exhibited patrilineal clans. The wives married into her husband's clan, and the children took the name of the husband's clan.[6]

One man can impregnate all of his wives, so population expansion can occur in these herding societies.

Polygamous marriages encouraged male dominance, so women's status declined. And since these herding societies with their patriclans roamed with their animal herds, they were very warlike and conquered many village peoples.

The major change from matriclans occurred from an economic cause. That is, all across the world, where great rivers or lakes provided regular flooding, mass-scale grain production engendered civilization complexes in which both men and women engaged in agricultural production.

[4]Trigger, Bruce, *The Huron Farmers of the North*. New York: Holt, Rinehart and Winston, 1969.

[5]*Ibid.*, Lewis Henry Morgan, *Ancient Society*, NY. Amazon, 2012 (1877). The Iroquois.

[6]The Biblical Jews are Arabs exhibiting patrilineal clans and polygamy.

This, along with the increasing military threat of marauding herding societies, eventuated in a marriage pattern with patrilineal clans. But polygamy was only for the rich or aristocratic families. The majority of the villages—peasants and craftsmen—had only one wife.

Still, the wife took the husband's clan name, and the clans were patrilineal by and large.

Patrilineal clans with one wife for most husbands—but with the possibility of polygamy and the subsequent lowered status of women—persisted into the near modern world. It was the Industrial Revolution—and Christianity—that altered the marriage pattern.

The crowding of the industrial cities' working-class districts made clan residence impossible. The extended family began to break up.

The new family unit was the stem family: a pairing couple, their many children, and near residence of the grandparents—both sets—as well as uncles, aunts, and cousins. They did not all live together, but stem family relationships predominated, along with some friendship relationships.

Monogamous marriages with male dominance and patriclan holdovers became the norm.

Christianity reinforced this marital pattern, and Judaism—in its diaspora version—also reinforced this pattern, eschewing the polygamy exhibited by biblical forebears.

As industrialization and urbanization spread globally, so did the stem family pattern. The clan was a thing of the past, and matrilineal clans were long forgotten except in North America and Polynesia. The stem families, remember, were male dominant.

16.2.3 Marriage in the Modern World

Women's liberation in the twentieth and twenty-first centuries has completely altered marriage patterns (and the family pattern).

In terms of marriage, partnership marriage is the new normative pattern.

In partnership marriages, all marital roles are shared. The husband and the wife both work, both work out at the gym, both shop, both cook, both care for the children, both want sexual satisfaction, and both have friends.

This is the nuclear family in its bare outline; there is nobody but the partnership couple and their children—one or two at most. The grandparents do babysit—*if* they live nearby. If they have retired in the sunbelt or live in a rural village, they are not part of the nuclear family unit. If they live nearby, they are important, however.

Partnership marriage, as I have mentioned, was first suggested by Aspasia in Golden Age Athens. However, it did not catch on—not until now.

What is the problem?

Partnership marriages are very difficult to maintain. There is no role integration. All roles are done by both partners—but who does which role more often? Some men cook, while some do not; some women cook, but others do not. Some men are nurturers with children; many men are not. Many women are nurturers with children; some are not.

When the dual-career couple comes home from work—both tired—who picks up the children from nursery school or school, who cooks, who cleans, who shops, who changes the diapers when the babies are young, who feeds the children, and who puts them to bed?

All of this has to be worked out. And with little support from family or friends, these roles can be overwhelming. Romance and sex become difficult when the dual-career partnership couple becomes exhausted from work and family obligations. And today's work world is very demanding—middle-class jobs demand enormous commitments of time and energy.

Thus, given the stresses of career and marriage, the divorce rate has skyrocketed.

16.2.4 Divorce, Remarriage, and the Merged Family in the Modern World

I have already highlighted the high divorce rate that emerged with women's liberation—first in the United States during the 1970s and 1980s, then globally. The divorce rate went up as high as 50 percent in the USA at the height of the women's movement in the 1980s.

Now, the divorce rate is around 40 percent in 2023 in the USA—still incredibly high—and it is rising in the EU, China, Eastern Europe, Russia, and other areas wherein women's liberation is occurring.

The high divorce rate is one of the unintended effects of the women's movement. And a high divorce rate does destabilize society.

What is keeping modern societies together is the high remarriage rate. Again, as mentioned, remarriage rates are high—in the USA and globally. And these second marriages tend to be stable. Therefore, marriage, as an institution, has remained central and universal in modern society. In fact, modern couples have trended back toward very traditional weddings—big, expensive affairs with bridal dresses and all the other accoutrements of traditional marriage.

Divorce still occurs, however, but so, too, does remarriage.

With remarriage comes merged families—with stepsiblings and stepparents. This is a new pattern of family, and it seems to be working out effectively globally.

Since this is a new family pattern, let us look at the family as a universal institution in the world, for it, too, is changing dramatically.

16.2.5 The Family

In analyzing marriage, I have already described the transition of the family institution sociohistorically.

We described the pairing family among hunter-gatherers and the extended family, or clan, among agriculturalists and animal herders. We described matrilineal clans and patrilineal clans.

We then described the breakup of the clan under the dual impact of industrialization and urbanization, the stem family emerging transitionally, and then the nuclear family emerging.

The nuclear family of the twentieth century consisted of the pairing couple, with one or two children, plus some contact with the grandparents, aunts, uncles, and cousins on both sides. But the couple and their children live alone, separated from the extended family.

The nuclear family couple can be isolated from the extended family if they move to a new city—this is a global phenomenon. They develop friendships, but their contact with the extended family is minimal.

The nuclear couple needs government support: they need daycare, nursery schools, paid nannies, public or private schools, and after-school programs—sports, the arts, academic enrichment, and more.

The nuclear family is fragile and cannot survive without this kind of government support institutions.

As analyzed, the high divorce rate further weakens the nuclear family. And even though the remarriage rate is high, the number of single mothers raising their children alone has risen dramatically. Single fathers raising their children exist, but single mothers far outnumber them.

So, along with the nuclear family, reconstituted families—that is, merged families—now exist, and, unfortunately, so, too, do single-mothers-plus-children families. The latter is not a stable or acceptable form of family—it is deviant, and it leads to more deviance in the children, that is, drug addiction, alcoholism, school failure, criminality, and more.

So the family in the modern global world is in jeopardy, with stable institutions desperately needed to shore it up.

16.2.6 Ethnic Identity

As we have made central, a world culture is emerging. Under the influence of the mass media of entertainment—movies, television, Internet platforms, email, social media platforms (e.g., Facebook, X, TikTok), etc.—and under the influence of scientific university education, a world culture is emerging.

In this world culture, a Japanese, Chinese, German, French, American, Canadian, etc., individual may have more in common with their counterpart in a university or high-tech corporation than with someone of their own country still living in the countryside.

However, ethnic identity is a universal human phenomenon. So giving up one's ethnic cultural identity is difficult and can lead to moral confusion. Look at the situation in Palestine in 2023 after the Hamas terror attack on Israeli civilians. All over the world, wherever Jews lived in some numbers, those Jews felt that their lives were threatened. Remembrances of the Holocaust emerged among them, and their ethnic support of the Israeli Jews surged forth.

So, too, with the Arabs living all around the globe when the Israelis counterattacked and started bombing civilian targets as "collateral damage."

Ethnic identity is a powerful phenomenon that emerges especially when a group feels threatened.

I have mentioned the Hungarians—they felt threatened when thousands of Syrians flooded through their country. Even though the Syrians were headed for Germany, the Hungarians felt that their very existence as a unique ethnic group was in jeopardy.

The threat to ethnic identity has engendered extremist behavior whenever it has occurred. One could argue that the Trump phenomenon in the USA has been, at the least, partially fueled by the White Anglo-Saxon Protestant (WASP) ethnic group feeling displaced by Blacks, Hispanics, and Jews. Trump asserts this in most of his speeches. Immigrants and Blacks—they are stealing your country, he tells them. When Trump lost in 2020, the WASP Americans did think the election was stolen, for they were no longer in the majority.

Thus, all across the globe, ethnic groups who feel threatened have turned to extremist politics and extremist religious movements to reassert their identity—it is a tribal identity revival. Religious revivals in Turkey and India, for instance, illustrate this phenomenon.

Yet the world culture, the global culture, the Internet and mass media culture, and the scientific university culture are also becoming global phenomena.

16.2.7 Religion

World religion, like ethnic identity, is exhibiting a revival. The reason a revival is needed is because the rational-scientific worldview is becoming the new Zeitgeist—the dominant worldview.

As I have described, modern individuals—globally—look to the heavens and see galaxies and the event horizons of black holes. They see space stations and satellites. They do not see the sky god—not Zeus, Ahura Mazda, Yahweh, Christ, or Allah.

When sick, the global citizen goes to a doctor, not a priest, and takes antibiotics, not folk cures.

Given the miracles of science and its threats—such as nuclear bombs that could wipe out human civilization completely—many believed that religious theology has declined.

However, as I have insisted, science is amoral—it has no ethics attached to it. Scientists will make penicillin and will also make H-bombs.

So in terms of ethics, there has been a revival of traditional world religions and also the emergence of secular humanism—that is, a strict humanistic moral code without the need of a father god or a creator god or any other kind of god.

Further, as Durkheim has made central in his book *The Elementary Forms of the Religious Life*,[7] religious rituals make people feel better; they create group participation and group solidarity—therefore helping people feel more secure, less anxious, and less existentially threatened. Religious rituals make people feel less alone in the universe, less confused about death, and more certain about life.

So even though religious rituals themselves are meaningless and are often contradictory—for example, the Jews cover their heads in synagogues, while Christians remove their hat—just doing the ritual together with all the other congregants makes human beings feel good.

Thus, the revival of world religions persists, even though the rational-scientific worldview is becoming the universal, global Zeitgeist.

16.3 Conclusions on Durkheim's Theory

To sum up: having discussed the breakdown of all the basic institutions of society under the impact of the various movements for social change occurring globally, and having asserted that the breakdown of these basic institutions leads to anomie—the loss of norms and values, and the subsequent skyrocketing of rates of deviance, crime, violence, political extremism, and creativity—all of which are making modern life so difficult.

We conclude that the great global transformation will continue to occur and will eventually change the world.

However, during this period of rapid social change, anomie will occur and social disorganization will destabilize modern societies.

[7] Emile Durkheim, *The Elementary Forms of Religious Life*, NY, Free Press, 1952.

Part V
The Political Transformation to Electoral Democracy and Legal-Rational Authority

Chapter 17
The "Third Wave" of Democracy

17.1 The Third Wave of Democracy and Reactions Against It

Political scientists, such as Huntington[1] and Fukuyama,[2] use the term "the third wave" to refer to the wave of democracy that occurred when the Soviet Union collapsed. This third wave also included the emergence of democracy in Spain, South Korea, Singapore, Hong Kong, and Taiwan.

If these nations exhibited the third wave of democracy from the 1970s to the present, then what were the first and second waves of democracy?

17.2 The First and Second Waves of Democracy: The Dutch Republic, the USA, and the British, Then Germany, Italy, and Japan After World War II

The first wave that political scientists identified was the democratic revolutions that began in the sixteenth century with the Dutch Republic and the Swiss Confederation; continued with Cromwell's Democratic Revolution in England; peaked with the American Revolution with its remarkable Declaration of Independence, Constitution, and Bill of Rights; and then crashed with the violence of the French Revolution.[3]

After this first wave of modern democracy, reaction set in Europe, with monarchy and aristocracy making a comeback in Germany, Austria-Hungary, most of Eastern Europe, Russia, and even Great Britain—though the restored monarchy was limited and an oligarchic parliament ruled after 1688.

---

[1] Samuel P. Huntington, *Culture Against Democracy*, Amazon, 2000.

[2] Francis Fukuyama, *The End of History*.

[3] Ronald M. Glassman, *The Origins of Democracy in Tribes, City-States, and Nation-States*, 2017.

R. M. Glassman, *The Great Global Transformation*, Contributions to Political Science, https://doi.org/10.1007/978-3-031-90566-7_17

From 1812—the era of Napoleon and his conquests—to World War I, the reaction against democracy prevailed, though the Dutch, Swiss, and Americans maintained their democracies strongly. America was wracked by a terrible Civil War but extended its democracy westward to the frontier and the Pacific Ocean, though not yet to the South—and, of course, committing near genocide against the Indigenous Peoples.

The "second wave" of democracy did not occur until after World War II.

The victory of the United States, Great Britain, and France against Germany allowed the Allied Powers to force democracy on the Axis Powers, namely, Germany, Italy, and Japan.

Now, Germany and Italy have had parliamentary democratic governments before they were overwhelmed by the fascist dictatorships of Mussolini and Hitler. Japan had no tradition or history or intellectual background of democracy.

Yet, and this was remarkable, the United States, led by General Douglas MacArthur, helped the Japanese establish democracy and successfully institutionalize it.

In the case of Germany, Italy, and Japan, the second wave of democracy was forced on them by the victorious Allied Powers. But what about Russia?

Russia was a member of the Allied Powers. Without Russia, victory over the Germans would have been much more difficult. The Russians took terrible casualties fighting the Germans. When the war ended, Russia occupied Eastern Europe, including Eastern Germany (Prussia).

Russia, of course, had a communist revolution—and an idealistic revolution, which was hijacked by Stalin. Stalin took over the "temporary dictatorship" of the Communist Party and turned the Marxist-Leninist idealist experiment into a totalitarian, murderous regime.

When the war ended, the United States, England, and France could not enforce their will on Russia. The Russian army was entrenched in Eastern Europe, such that the Allied Powers could not enforce an institutionalized democracy in the Eastern European countries, much less Russia itself.

Once the Russians gain the atomic bomb and advanced missile technology, the Russians were able to dominate Eastern Europe, the steppe lands, and the other "Soviet" republics.

So the "second wave" ended with Germany (West Germany), Italy, and Japan exhibiting successful democratic governments, while Russia, Eastern Europe, and the steppe republics remained under the Russian dictatorial control.

The "third wave" could not begin until Stalinist Russia collapsed. Or could it start sooner and unexpectedly?

17.3 The Third Wave

17.3.1 Spain and Democracy

Spain, Portugal, Germany, and Italy had a moment of parliamentary democracy in the 1920s after World War I. The Spanish parliamentary democracy was overthrown after the Spanish Civil War left the fascists victorious. Francisco Franco copied Benito Mussolini closely, embarking on a program of industrialization and dominating Spain dictatorially with terror and violence.

When World War II ended, Spain, which had not participated in the war, remained fascist. However, when Europe was rebuilt with the help of the American-led Marshall Plan, Spain participated in the revived industrial-capitalist economy established by the newly founded European Union (EU).

Spain joined the EU economically but not politically. Franco, though ruling dictatorially, encouraged the development of free market capitalism in Spain. Again, Spain copied Italy in this economic process. But Spain was also being influenced by both France and Germany.

When Franco died, in the mid-1970s, the Spanish economy was a well-developed, successful industrial-capitalist economy, and it was linked with the EU. Spain's economy was better than that of the UK.

Being closely integrated into the EU economically, with the death of Franco, Spain surprised the world by establishing a parliamentary democracy. King Juan Carlos, who had opposed fascism unsuccessfully, now strongly supported democracy and was rewarded by being allowed to hold his kingly office as a "limited monarchy," similar to that of Great Britain.

The limited monarchy of Juan Carlos helped legitimize democracy among the previously fascist-oriented Spaniards. And so Spain—whose culture was considered incompatible with democracy—went democratic and has astounded historians by remaining stable and even enthusiastic about democracy.

The case of Spain is critical because political theorists, such as Samuel Huntington, had held that certain cultures just could not become democratic. He was referring to Asian culture generally, but Spanish intellectuals believed that Spanish culture could not support democracy—Spanish culture is characterized by bullfighting, Don Juan masculinity, and blood sport violence. It should be mentioned that German militaristic culture was also condemned as incompatible with democracy. Even before Hitler, the Kaiser (King) and his feudal-oriented aristocratic officer corps denounced democracy as weak and ineffective.

So both Germany and Spain were considered to have cultures incompatible with democracy, yet both nations have exhibited stable, democratic governments for half a century now.

17.3.2 The Four Asian Tigers Go Democratic

With the warning of theorists, such as Huntington, that Asian culture would prevent the emergence of democracy, the explosion of the "Four Tigers" onto the scene as both democratic nations and capitalist economic powerhouses astounded the Western world. Singapore, Hong Kong, Taiwan, and South Korea were taking off economically and politically.

Of course, Singapore and Hong Kong had been part of the British Commonwealth. And Taiwan and South Korea were under American influence after World War II and the Korean War. Still, they were "Asian" cultures, were they not?

Huntington and other Western political scientists were surprised by the democratic success of these nations. The idea of a "third wave" of democracy emerged from the success of the "Four Tigers."

Now, Singapore is not fully democratic—the leaders do exhibit authoritarian tendencies. And Hong Kong is now being overwhelmed by Xi's totalitarian China. However, Singapore is moving in a democratic direction, and Hong Kong was fully—and proudly—democratic before the Chinese takeover.

Both Singapore and Hong Kong show us that British political and intellectual culture has had a powerful effect in establishing the ideas of "government by law" and parliamentary electoral processes of governance. We shall discuss this further when we discuss India and the other British Commonwealth nations.

Here, let us establish that "Asian" culture—which has no tradition of democracy—can support a democratic form of government under certain circumstances. In the case of Singapore and Hong Kong—both Cantonese-speaking Chinese societies known for their business orientation and success—the long British colonial period and the success of British education created a new cultural, educational, and economic subculture that is supportive of democracy and legal authority.

In Taiwan and South Korea, American political influence and Japanese economic influence created a new subculture supportive of capitalism and democracy.

The Japanese occupied Korea and Taiwan before World War II, and their influence was quite profound. They were both hated and admired. They were hated for their domination and sadistic militarism but were admired for their economic efficiency and industrialization. The Japanese had created an industrial-capitalist economy that almost helped them conquer all of Asia. Therefore, following the Japanese' lead economically was seen as forward-looking.

Since the Japanese were hated for their dictatorial domination, Japanese politics were rejected.

Taiwan, of course, was taken over by the Chinese Kuomintang under Chang Kai-shek, after the American-backed Chinese Party lost the Civil War to Mao Zedong and his Russian-backed Communists in 1948.

At first, the Kuomintang ruled the native Taiwanese rather dictatorially. However, after Chang's death, and with strong American support, Taiwan established a fully democratic government—with legal authority and free elections.

Today, Taiwan boasts a democratic and stable government, along with a very entrepreneurial capitalist economy. For a while during the 2000s, every carbon fiber bicycle frame was made in Taiwan. And the best microchips in the world are manufactured in Taiwan.

Korea was also caught in the world war between communism and capitalist democracy.

After the Korean War ended in 1953, South Korea came under American influence, while North Korea came under Russian and Chinese communist influence.

In South Korea, at first, a dictatorship emerged. The economy was not yet developed—Korea was agricultural—and politics was almost "dynastic"—certain families dominated the political process.

From the 1960s to the 2000s, the Korean economy took off. Copying the unusual Japanese zaibatsu system—a system of giant conglomerate corporations dominating basic industries—the Korean economy exploded onto the global capitalist scene.

The Koreans call the zaibatsu "Chaebols." Companies such as Samsung and Hyundai have copied the Japanese style of industrial production and successfully compete in the world market. The Koreans have excelled in technology products and innovation and lead the world in electronics.

With the incredible success of the Korean−/Japanese-style economy, pressure for a more modern form of polity to go with it emerged, both from the new middle class of college-educated Koreans and from the American government—remember that the USA still occupies South Korea militarily because of the threat of North Korean invasions.

Under American pressure and with the support of the growing middle class, South Korea established democratic national and local systems of government.

The aristocratic families still try to dominate leadership positions. However, new middle-class candidates and new billionaire entrepreneurs are beginning to establish a nonaristocratic pool of candidates who can better represent the new South Korea.

Most importantly, the existence of democracy in South Korea, Taiwan, Singapore, and Hong Kong shows us that Asian culture can be combined with a "third wave" culture of democracy, constitutional law, and free market capitalism.

Will Hong Kong be able to maintain its democracy, or will China override it completely? We must wait and watch.

17.3.3 India and the British Commonwealth

The British Empire rivaled the Roman Empire. In the nineteenth century, it stretched from Canada to Australia, from India to Hong Kong, from Egypt to South Africa, and more.

The key fact for us concerning the British Empire is that through British education, the English language and the institutionalization of government by law with parliamentary elections were spread.

Even though the colonized peoples hated the British for their arrogant and often racist domination, they also admired the British for their classical education and their sense of lawful political action.

We have discussed how Hong Kong and Singapore surprised Western political scientists by establishing functioning parliamentary democracies grounded in constitutional law. India, however, is an even more remarkable case, given its enormous population, its terrible poverty, and its Hindu (and Muslim) religious traditions.

Because India has more than one regional language, English became the de facto national language. And because English became everyone’s second language, British education—in English—became very influential culturally in India.

Of course, India had a traditional culture that venerated the Hindu Brahman priests as the highest “caste” of society—the educated priesthood was more highly venerated than the warrior caste or the business caste. This veneration of the educated elite carried over into the veneration of those with a British education. Mathematics—which had been part of the Indian culture (we use Indian numerals and call them “Arabic” numerals because Arabic-speaking intellectuals replaced Greco-Roman numerals with these Indian numerals)—science, history, literature, and the whole of the British classical educational sequence were actively absorbed by the Indian intellectuals.

Along with this remarkable absorption of British education came a desire to copy the British politically—the Indians wanted to drive the British out in order to advance their own parliamentary democracy and establish their own legal authority.

With the charismatic leadership of Gandhi, who encouraged nonviolent resistance, the British were eventually driven out. And, remarkably, the overpopulated, impoverished nation of India successfully established a British-style parliamentary system.

So India became part of the “third wave” of democracies emerging after World War II. Tragically, Pakistan was split off from India, and this Muslim nation—also overpopulated and poor—has had an unstable government—sometimes democratic and sometimes autocratic, leaning toward democratic processes but wracked with violent episodes.

Regarding India, we shall discuss the new Hindu Naturalist Party and its leader, Narendra Modi—will India remain democratic? In terms of the third wave, it must be emphasized that when India became independent in the 1950s and when it established democracy and legal authority, it gave impetus to optimism about the future of democracy in the world.

Australia, New Zealand, and Canada—all British commonwealth nations—were already legal-democratic states. But since these nations were settled by the British people, it was not surprising that they established British political institutions.

What about South Africa?

Many Americans think of South Africa as a British colony. However, it was a Dutch colony until the British defeated the Dutch South Africans in the Boer War.

Though defeated, the Dutch fled north and established a new colony with new cities: Johannesburg and Praetoria. These Dutch farmers then encountered the Zulu Empire. Calling themselves “Afrikaners” and armed with guns and cannons, they subdued the Zulus and other "Nguni" kingdoms and founded a new nation based on Dutch capitalist corporations, modernized farming, and African (Nguni-Zulu) labor.

The British were technically still in control, with their city—Cape Town—being the major port of South Africa. When the British discovered diamonds, gold, and other precious metals, South Africa became rich—that is, the British and the Dutch South Africans became rich, while the Africans were exploited as underpaid miners doing dangerous and dirty work.

Unfortunately, the Dutch Afrikaners became caught up in Nazi-style racism. They created a racially divided society. "Apartheid"—apartness—was their mantra. Apartness was not only racially maintained but also economically enforced. The Whites got rich, while the Blacks remained poor. The Whites were educated, whereas the Blacks were denied education.

So South Africa did *not* become part of the third wave of democracy until the United States, the United Nations, and the British isolated the South African Dutch economically and politically.

Finally, in the 1980s, Nelson Mandela, the leader of the Black South Africans was released from jail, and Black South Africans were allowed to vote. They won the election, Mandela became the Prime Minister, and South Africa began its difficult metamorphosis toward a democratic and racially equal society.

The Dutch still control the economy and dominate society financially. The Dutch-Afrikaner Party does participate in the Parliament, and the Afrikaners are prominent as leaders in the modern sectors of society.

Education for the working-class Africans is still lagging far behind its goals. But enough Black Africans go to college such that an emerging middle class is allowing educated Blacks to begin to occupy important positions in society.

South Africa is a legal democracy, but its stability is still undergirded by the Dutch and British South Africans. When the Black middle class becomes larger and better educated, hopefully democracy will be stabilized by them as well.

Other British Commonwealth nations, such as Kenya and Nigeria, have established democracies but are struggling mightily with tribal conflicts, religious conflicts (Islam versus Christianity), poverty, and slow economic development. Still, Kenya and Nigeria do exhibit functioning democracies even though they are barely stable and suffer from nepotistic economic corruption by the ruling elites.

17.4 The Collapse of the Soviet Union and the Third Wave of Democracies

The collapse of the Soviet Union in the 1980s caught the world by surprise. When President Reagan stood near the Berlin wall and said, "Mr. Gorbachev, tear down this wall!" nobody—including Reagan—believed that Mr. Gorbachev would allow the wall to be torn down.

What happened? Stalinist communism failed economically to keep up with high-technology industrial capitalism, and the Communist state—instead of "withering away," as Marx had idealistically predicted—had become a totalitarian monstrosity.

The older leaders of the Soviet Communist Party—including Brezhnev—died of natural causes. And a younger leader—Gorbachev—was chosen. He had traveled to Europe and seen the modernization of the economy and society firsthand. He tried to move the Soviet Union forward, economically and politically—"Perestroika and Glasnost"—restructuring the economy and allowing political and policy debates.

But "Perestroika and Glasnost" failed. The Communist bureaucracy was entrenched and obstructive.

Gorbachev decided to take the drastic step of disbanding the Communist Party. The Communist Party leaders who disagreed captured Gorbachev and were going to kill him and his wife, but they relented eventually because they knew there had to be change in order to modernize.

They released Gorbachev, and he did disband the Communist Party. But then, suddenly, the Soviet republics, which did not want to be dominated by Russia, withdrew and declared their independence.

Gorbachev did not expect this—he was unprepared for the breakup of the Soviet Union, but he allowed it to begin.

Thus, Armenia, Georgia, and the steppe republics—from Kazakhstan to Mongolia—and the Eastern European countries, including Ukraine, Estonia, Latvia, Lithuania, Poland, the Czech Republic, Slovakia, Romania, Hungary, and more, all declared independence.

Then Yugoslavia broke up, and after a horrifically murderous civil war, Serbia, Croatia, Slovenia, Bosnia Herzegovina, Montenegro, Kosovo, and North Macedonia all became independent nations. Bulgaria and Albania also became independent countries.

The third wave was going to receive a host of new democracies that had all been dominated by Communist Russia. There were so many new nations, and many of them were democratic.

We shall come back to Russia. First, it must be understood that the third wave was genuinely enhanced by nations such as the Czech Republic. Even though Slovakia broke away, both the Czechs and the Slovaks established democratic and lawful regimes. They are still stable.

Ukraine tried but became caught up in the Russian web—I shall come back to Ukraine when discussing Russia.

The Baltic republics of Estonia, Latvia, and Lithuania have established stable democratic regimes—terrified of Russian interference, they have still maintained their democratic stability.

Romania, having thrown off its dictatorial leader, is shaky but democratic—economic development is slow there.

Poland and Hungary had established democratic regimes but, after years of Russian domination, are struggling to establish their own cultural identity. The massive immigration from Syria—headed for Germany, not Poland or Hungary—set off a kind of tribalistic identity politics, which is threatening democracy but has not yet destroyed it. I will discuss this further soon.

All the former Yugoslavia countries, led by Serbia and Croatia, have established democracies, and so far, they are stable. The Civil War left deep scars, but the politics is beginning to stabilize. Bosnia-Herzegovina and Kosovo are still disputed territories, and Christians versus Muslim religion still triggers historical memories of Turkish domination. So all is not well in the former Yugoslavia.

The third wave of democracies in Eastern Europe was remarkable, though still a work in progress.

Add to this Eastern European democratic wave the stabilization of democracy in Greece—which had gone through a civil war after World War II—and democracy in Europe began to look more and more expansive. Greece, after all, is the birthplace of democracy—the nation that made democracy famous. If Athenian democracy was the model of democracy remembered historically by Renaissance and Enlightenment Europe, then the reestablishment of democracy in modern Greece, with its capital in Athens, brought the world full circle back to a time when democracy triumphed in the world.

And the third wave continued to expand: Latin America was going democratic. After centuries of dictatorship, democracy was being established.

17.5 Latin America and the Third Wave of Democracy

Mexico, Brazil, Argentina, and Venezuela began to establish democratic governments from the 1960s onward.

Yes, Cuba went communist, and Columbia went violent and anarchic, but Mexico, Brazil, Argentina, and Venezuela threw off the dictatorships and began the march toward constitutional law and democracy.

These nations had been dominated by the Spanish conquistadors, who had established an aristocratic-dictatorial domination over the Indigenous peoples. The people call the Spanish domination "La Oligarchia." Spain itself was still under Franco's fascistic dictatorship.

Rapid economic development from the 1960s onward generated an expanding middle class—educated, employed in white-collar and professional jobs, and a mixed race in Mexico, Brazil, and Venezuela but European in Argentina (Spanish, Italian, German, Jews from Europe)—this middle class demanded both a modern industrial capitalist economy and political democracy.

With the economies expanding under American and EU influence (and now Chinese influence), the middle class became solidly entrenched, and democratic politics flourished.

Latin America, which had always been characterized by corrupt, violent dictatorships, was joining the third wave and generating democracies, which were gaining acceptance throughout the region.

Of course, we shall discuss Venezuela's regression to dictatorships shortly.

Venezuela aside, the democracies of Mexico, Brazil, and Argentina—Latin America's largest nations—provided tremendous enthusiasm to those political theorists who were skeptical about democracies' expansion.

Political theorists, such as Francis Fukuyama, even predicted that "the end of history" was the inevitable surge toward capitalism and democracy exhibited globally.

Of course, now Fukuyama has changed his mind as the globe is swept up in a new wave of tyranny—from illiberal democracy in Eastern Europe to technological totalitarianism in Xi's China.

Chapter 18
The New Wave of Dictatorship Begins to Displace the Third Wave of Democracy

18.1 Russia: The Putin Dictatorship with Vestiges of Democracy

It all begins in Russia. When the Soviet Union broke up and Russia suddenly found itself to be an independent nation-state, instead of the dominant partner in the Soviet Union, Russia had to establish its own national government and borders.

For just a "moment" in its history, Russia established a democratic government. Encouraged by the United States—which had suddenly "won the Cold War" against communism, the Russians established a written constitution based on American, British, and European constitutions. Political parties were allowed to emerge, and candidates ran for parliamentary office and the presidency.

Boris Yeltsin won the first election with a parliamentary majority that supported him. The United States was overjoyed and supported Yeltsin enthusiastically.

At that moment in history, it was thought that the Russians would finally institutionalize a legal-democratic form of government and that Russia would develop a capitalist economy.

In terms of the economy, Russia had the science, engineering, and university systems to support the development of high-tech industrial capitalism. Russia also had unlimited national resources in its vast Siberian and steppe land regions.

There was, however, no tradition of entrepreneurialism or independent business enterprise in Russia. Rather, the bureaucrats, selected from the Communist Party, had always run Russia's state-controlled economy. Unlike China, where the entrepreneurial business tradition was well developed in the coastal regions and in Southeast Asian market cities, Russia had no such business tradition in the era of the czars and feudal barons—and, of course, any such developments were brutally stamped out by Stalin after Lenin and Trotsky's deaths.

R. M. Glassman, *The Great Global Transformation*, Contributions to Political Science, https://doi.org/10.1007/978-3-031-90566-7_18

So who would gain control of the Russian state-run economy, and what economic policies would they pursue? To answer this economic question, we must return to that moment of democratic politics.

Boris Yeltsin, unfortunately, was an alcoholic—a problem that plagues Russia as its main social issue. Yeltsin was embarrassing Russia to the world by appearing at international and national meetings drunk and staggering around.

He chose to retire from politics and was succeeded by Vladimir Putin. Putin was young, handsome, and charismatic. He pledged to restore Russia's standing in the world—no more drunken and weak leadership; no more kow-towing to the Americans, who had gained a good deal of influence among democratic politicians.

When Putin told the Russians that he would restore their power and extend their borders and regain the glory of the Soviet Union, the Russian people loved it. They elected Putin with a large majority.

Why did Putin's message resonate with the Russian electorate? This is because when the Soviet Union broke up, Russia was suddenly left greatly weakened and without sensible borders.

For instance, Russia's Black Sea naval fleet was largely based in Odesa, a great port city founded by Catherine the Great in the early 1800s. But Odessa was now part of Ukraine, which desired independence from Russia. What to do about the fleet?

The rest of the Black Sea fleet was housed at the port in Crimea, but this, too, had become part of Ukraine. Most Russians believed that Ukraine was part of Russia, but after the Chernobyl nuclear disaster, the Ukrainians—outraged by the Russian mishandling of this disaster and harboring a historical desire to break from Moscow's control and join Poland and Slavic Europe in a Western European orientation to the world—desired a full break from Russia.

Putin invaded Crimea and annexed it to Russia; he built new port facilities for the fleet and connected Crimea to Russia by bridges and waterways. He then ordered the invasion of Eastern Ukraine—which has a Russian-speaking majority—and Russia's military forces have since dominated this region.

Putin attacked the Georgians and Chechens, reattaching them to Russia while allowing Georgia nominal independence.

The Russian electorate loved it, and they backed Putin electorally. This emboldened Putin to reassert Russia's geopolitical expansionary military influence. Russia—with President Trump's blessing—took military control over Syria, backing the Assad dictatorship with Russian soldiers, tanks, and airplanes. He made an alliance with Turkey, supplying the would-be dictator *Erdoğan* with advanced military equipment.

Putin aggressively intervened in Western European politics—and even that of the UK—by using high-technology cyber propaganda. Brexit from the EU was fueled by Russian cyber misinformation, while right-wing political moments, such as that of the Le Pen Party in France, were supported financially and through cyber misinformation.

In his ultimate revenge, Putin engaged in very sophisticated cyber influences on the American elections, succeeding monumentally by helping Donald Trump—the only pro-Russian American political candidate—succeed to the presidency of the United States.

Now, Putin could have done all of this as a democratically elected President of Russia. However, that was not who Putin was, nor was it who he wanted to be.

Putin tolerated the constitutional constraints on his power and tenure for a while. He cleverly ran his friend Medvedev as President and ruled from the shadows. But when Medvedev's term was over, Putin showed his true colors and forced an override of the constitutional limitation on his power and tenure. The Constitution was changed so that Putin could hold the presidency for life.

Significantly for the future of Russia, Putin allowed the constitutional provisions for parliamentary elections to remain intact.

Of course, he poisons his opposition leaders and manipulates the elections so that he always wins. Still, the opposition continues to bravely resist and speak out against Putin's dictatorship and for democracy. Nonetheless, Putin is popular among rural farmers and industrial workers, and he has given enough cleverly instituted consumer products to the expanding middle class.

Upscale restaurants abound in the big cities; fashionable clothing is available from Italy, France, and the USA; and cars made in Germany and the Czech Republic clog the Russian avenues—a modern European lifestyle has brought Putin's popularity even among college-educated middle classes in the big cities.

But how has Putin paid for this upscale lifestyle if Russia has not developed a modern economy?

Answer: Russia supplies Europe with oil and natural gas through pipelines that go directly into Eastern and Western Europe—into Germany and beyond.

Who runs this raw material economy?

To answer this question, we must analyze who Putin really is and what his political background actually was.

Putin, unfortunately for the political history of Russia, was a KGB agent stationed in East Germany. He was all for dictatorship, terror, and unlimited power. He famously remarked: "The worst thing that ever happened to Russia was the collapse of the Soviet Union." He vowed to restore its geopolitical and military power.

When he became President—legally elected with an electoral majority—he immediately set about to gain control over the raw material economy and the military weapon production economy.

How did he gain such control? Putin appointed his trusted friends and former KGB operatives to manage and control both the new materials and the military economy. These men have since been called "oligarchs" because Putin rewarded them by allowing them to amass great personal wealth as long as they were successful in managing the economic production of raw materials and advanced military weaponry.

These men are *not* oligarchs in the capitalist sense. They are not operating capitalist, free-market businesses. They are managing a raw material market and are managing it quite well while skimming off billions for themselves.

Scandalously, they have been encouraged to "launder" this money by investing in global real estate and corrupting German and Swiss bankers by paying them to "launder" the money.

Only a small portion of the money from the raw material market goes into Russian infrastructure—just enough to buy off the middle class in the big cities. Yet the Russian countryside remains quite embarrassingly backward.

What about the military economy and its offshoot, the space economy?

The Russian Communist economy had failed to produce consumer products and had failed to help create a high-tech computer revolution. However, Russian universities churn out excellent scientists and engineers. Under the Soviets, these scientists and engineers were directed to invent and produce military equipment and space rockets.

Putin directed these scientists and engineers to incorporate the new computers, cyber-technology, and high-tech products into their military and space industries. This was successfully accomplished such that, today, the Russians are developing new and frightening military weaponry and computer-hacking techniques that compound the world and a space program that is so advanced that even the Americans cooperate with the Russians in running and maintaining the International Space Station.

Recently, a Putin-touted missile system that is run with a nuclear engine and armed with nuclear warheads and capable of flying under radar detection *exploded* in a terrible accident. Before it exploded, it had terrorized the Americans and Europeans so much that they are still trying to catch up with this potential military technology.

To sum up, then, Russia's economy never went capitalist—it remained a peculiar "Third World" raw material economy. And its military and space sectors are highly modern but also not capitalist—that is, not efficiency oriented or profitable but rather state directed and scientifically advanced and very expensive. Finally, instead of expanding computerized production and inventing new high-tech products, Russia's computer "geniuses" are directed toward hacking operations designed to disrupt Western democratic processes, confuse the cyber world, and steal technology from American and European companies.

Politically, Putin has pioneered a new form of tyranny that political scientists are calling "illiberal democracy." Why do they use the term democracy if this is a dictatorship? This is because Putin and his oligarchic friends have allowed parliamentary elections to continue, opposition parties to exist, opposition leaders to speak at rallies, and some newspapers and television news people to be critical. The democratic and lawful constitutional guidelines still exist by and large.

Of course, if the criticism becomes too strong, the news person may be killed or the opposition leader poisoned—with the Russian "signature" high-tech nuclear poison—and the election will be rigged or discounted if they go against the leader, Putin.

So it is dictatorship, but the trappings of democracy remain intact, which could be a good thing in the long run—or not…

18.2 Hungary, Poland, and Illiberal Democracy

18.2.1 Hungary and Orban's Dictatorship

In our discussion of the social and cultural transformation of the global world, we emphasized the reaction to global citizenship and world culture as a return to "tribalism."

Nationalism, populism, and a powerful revival of tribalism have generated a new wave of charismatic dictatorships. These dictatorships have emerged in nation-states, which had established legal-democratic institutions but wherein these institutions did not have a long history of legitimation.

Both Hungary and Poland fought hard to shake off Russian domination, and both desired to join the EU.

But though Hungary and Poland were happy to participate in the economic union of Europe, their own economies were not at the level of Germany, France, or northern Italy.

Economic development occurred, but economic opportunity lagged in Hungary and Poland. This slow economic development characterized most of Eastern European countries, but it did not become politically problematical until Muslim immigration from Syria flooded Europe suddenly.

Now, ironically, the Muslim Syrians did not want to go to Hungary, Poland, or any other Eastern European country. They were headed for Germany or the United Kingdom, where they believed there would be jobs for them in the manufacturing sectors of the economy.

However, they had to pass through Greece, the South Slavic lands, and then Hungary in order to get to Germany. This mass migration of displaced Syrian Muslims set off a panic in Hungary. Even though the Syrians made it clear that they did not want to stay in Hungary, the Hungarians reacted with panic, as if their tribal identity was being overwhelmed by another tribal group.

The Hungarians had a history of almost being wiped out by the Mongols, then being dominated by the Germans and Austrians, then being overrun by the Turks, and finally being protected within the Austria-Hungarian Empire, only to be overrun and dominated by the Russians. And in 1956, when the Hungarians revolted against the Russians, no nation came to the rescue, and the Russians clamped down on them harder.

So the Hungarians felt abandoned and alone, unable to establish their independence and unable to secure their national identity.

Having gained their independence when the Soviet Union suddenly broke apart, the Hungarians joyfully joined the EU. But they were treated like a poor cousin—economic development lagged, while their political influence was weak.

When George Soros—the billionaire Hungarian Jew who had grown up in Hungary but made his fortune in New York on Wall Street—lavished money on Hungary—establishing a phone network and a university with scholarships for Hungarian students—the Hungarians saw it as "charity." They believed it demeaned them because Soros was a Jew, not a Hungarian Magyar. The Jews of Hungary had been famous for their intellectual and economic success—as they were in Austria and Germany—but the Hungarians had been negatively stigmatized as "The people who had not won a battle for a thousand years" and the people whose "peasants could not plow in a straight line."

So instead of being grateful to Soros, they hated him. But there were few Jews still living in Hungary, and so even though antisemitism was regenerated by Soros' contributions, it was not until Muslim Syrians flooded across Hungary that tribalism was truly generated.

Viktor Orbán, seizing on the tribal revival, emphasized Magyar heritage—culture, language, and the Catholic Christian religion.

Along with this tribal revival and the Christian revival, Orbán emphasized traditional Christian family values and spoke out against gay liberation and women's liberation.

He exhibited the same kind of macho masculinity that Putin had succeeded with in Russia. And just as Putin had revived the Russian Orthodox Church after its suppression under communism, Orbán did the same with the Hungarian Catholic Church.

Finally, why did the anti-Muslim hysteria work politically in Hungary? The reason is that the Turks had twice invaded Yugoslavia and Hungary. And twice the Hungarians had fought heroically against the Turks, helping stop Islam from dominating Christian Europe.

Thus, even though the Muslim Syrians were not staying in Hungary, the fact that they wanted to stay in Germany really bothered the Hungarians.

Hence, Viktor Orbán was able to win the popular vote and to become President. But once elected, he, like Putin, sought to undermine democratic institutions and rule dictatorially. As in Russia, the Constitution remained in place but was altered to accommodate Orbán as he expanded his power and tenure. Further, and this would be typical for "illiberal democracies," he gained control of the mass media: television, news, newspapers, and Internet blogs. He is censoring all of these mass media and using them to enhance his support and fill the populace with propaganda, favoring him and demonizing the PC left, George Soros, and the Jews and Muslim-Syrian migrants.

If the Syrian Civil War is somehow ended and the Syrians are allowed to return, will this weaken Orbán?

Once dictators take charge and gain control over the military, police, and media, it is difficult to overthrow them. Right now, the Hungarians love Orbán and are trying to reestablish their cultural identity and national pride.

The hope for democracy lies with the young people. In the summer of 2019, in the main square of Budapest, young Hungarians held a gay pride rally with rainbow flags and European unity signs. They defied Orbán and demanded a return to a European identity following the democratic and humanistic laws of the EU.

So the future of democracy and law are unclear in Hungary, but there is still hope for the future revival of democracy, law, and humanism.

18.2.2 Poland and the Illiberal Democracy—With a Happy Ending

Poland also has a depressing military history—always under invasion from the Germans or Russians and not powerful enough to hold them off. Once in their history, the joint forces of Ukraine and Poland defeated the Germans. But they were not able to maintain their independence, and eventually, Poland was divided between Germany and Russia.

Invaded by Germany in World War II and then occupied by Russia after World War II, Poland did not become independent until the 1980s.

Poland led the movement for the liberation of Eastern Europe from Russian domination. The "Polish Pope"—John Paul—helped lead the "solidarity "movement against the Russian occupation. Therefore, when Gorbachev finally pulled Russian troops out of Eastern Europe, it was natural for there to be a Catholic Church revival in Poland.

The Catholic Church provided a bridge to Western Europe. But since the days of the Protestant Reformation, Northern Europe had developed a different Christian tradition. Still, with the leadership of the Polish Pope and the political leadership of the solidarity movement, Poland sought to enter modern Europe.

A democratic government was established and was enthusiastically supported in Poland. The problem was economic development. As in much of Eastern Europe, it was slow. And the question of Polish national identity was real: had the Polish people been antisemitic? Had the Polish Communist Party been too subservient to Stalin?

Also, the tragic loss of the Polish aristocracy with the wholesale murder of the Polish officer corps by Stalin and the outset of World War II had left Poland bereft of its intellectual and military leadership.

So a tragic history with a few heroes left Poland searching for its own identity. Yes, there had been Polish military heroes, and, yes, there had been Copernicus and Chopin, but what about modern Poland?

The Jewish issue arose again as I have described in an earlier section because the Israeli government began to organize trips to Poland for Israeli and American Jews. They visited both the "Shtetls"—ghetto villages where the Jews had come from—and Auschwitz—the most infamous concentration camp where thousands of Jews had been put to death.

The Polish people did not want to be blamed for the horrors of Auschwitz. They wanted it to be made clear that it was the Germans—the Nazis—who did it. But with all these Jewish visitors coming to Poland and finding the ghettos empty and Auschwitz still standing, it seemed to implicate the Polish people in the Holocaust against the Jews.

When an airplane accident killed the Prime Minister and members of his cabinet—ironically attempting to visit the graves of the murdered Polish officers in rural Russia—a new party came to the fore: the Order and Justice Party.

This party emphasized Polish “tribal “identity, Polish, history, and Polish culture. It vehemently rejected the stigmatization of the Polish people as anti-Semitic or pro-Nazi. It demanded that Jewish tourists stop coming and stop linking Poland with the German concentration camps.

When it was discovered that the Polish news media—television news—was being supported and advised by an American broadcasting company, they demanded to establish their own network news—Polish owned and Polish directed.

As in Hungary, the leaders of the newly elected Order and Justice Party began to usurp dictatorial powers, including the control of the news media, newspapers, and Internet blogs. EU rules and regulations were followed economically but politically, Poland wanted its independence.

Whether this dictatorial trend will continue in Poland or whether legal democracy will be reconfirmed in the near future is unclear. The Muslim-Syrian immigration, though it did not enter Poland, helped trigger the paranoia about Polish tribal identity, as it did in Hungary. However—and this just occurred in October 2023—the Order and Justice Party was defeated. Seventy-five percent of the vote went to parties insisting on democracy.

It seems that the Ukrainian War—the Russian invasion of Ukraine—frightened the Polish people back into the democratic fold of the EU and the United States.

This is a hopeful sign for democracy in the world—not only in Poland but also all across the globe.

We shall wait and hope that this will create a trend away from illiberal democracy and back toward real legal-democratic authority.

To conclude on Eastern Europe, though the Czech Republic is economically successful, most of the Eastern European countries are experiencing slow economic development. Will Hungarian-Polish style dictatorship emerge in some of these nations? So far, Romania, Slovakia, and the former Yugoslavia nations are retaining democratic institutions; so, too, are the Baltic republics. However, Eastern Europe is shaky.

The good news is that the EU is strongly supporting the economic development of the entire region. And if such development is successful, perhaps as in Spain, democratic institutions will eventually become stabilized and legitimized.

18.3 Turkey and Erdoğan’s Religious Revival and Political Party

Atatürk, the founder and first leader of Modern Turkey, had followed the Western tradition of separating church and state—Caesaropapism, as Max Weber called it, and the separation of church and state, as the American Constitution established it.

Atatürk, who grew up in Thessaloniki, a city of Greek Christians, Sephardic Jews, and Turkish Muslims, established a Turkish Constitution, guaranteeing religious freedom and separating church and state. He went so far as to convert Hagia

Sofia, the first grand Christian Church dating back to the days of Justinian and Theodora in the fifth century AD and which had been turned into a Muslim mosque by Suleiman the Magnificent in 1453 AD—into a museum. Neither the church, the Noor mosque, nor Hagia Sofia had been put forth by Atatürk as a symbol of the New Turkey, where religious freedom was guaranteed and the church and state were separated.

Enter Erdoğan.

In the 1980s and 1990s, Erdoğan organized less educated working-class Turks into a Muslim-Naturalist Party. The church and state were united—Islam and Turkish nationalism were joined together. This was exactly what Atatürk had tried to prevent.

Atatürk wanted Turkey to copy the West, for the West had become dominant through science and industrial production. Erdoğan originally wanted Western recognition but soon turned away from this path.

Failing to gain entrance into the European Economic Union, Erdoğan became increasingly nationalistic, turning Turkey away from the West and toward Islamic religious fanaticism.

Now, Turkey is divided politically. The western portion of Turkey is European oriented—this includes Istanbul, Izmir, and the Aegean coastal resort areas. The eastern sector, however, is Islamic oriented. This includes the capital, Ankara, and the rural steppe lands. Also, in eastern Turkey, the Kurds—a Muslim people of Persian origin who want their own state, separate from Turkey—make up about one-third of the population. This generates strong nationalism among the eastern Turks, who do not want the Kurds to gain an independent state.

Thousands of eastern Turks have moved to Istanbul in search of jobs. And they bring with them their Turkish nationalism and Islamic fanaticism.

Erdoğan wins elections by appealing to this Islamic nationalist sector of the electorate. His political party is an Islamic party, and he has purposely violated Atatürk's attempt to separate church and state.

Elections in Turkey have been close—Erdoğan wins by a small margin. Unfortunately, this frustrated the European-oriented political parties based in Istanbul and the Aegean coast.

A group of army officers—harking back to Atatürk's Constitution—demanded the separation of church and state. When Erdoğan refused and encouraged the Islamic radicals to participate in his political party and support his reelection, the army officers attempted a coup.

The coup was almost successful, and Erdoğan blamed a former colleague of his, an Islamic Imam, who had encouraged an Islamic revival in Turkey, for instigating the army officers' coup. This Imam was actually living in the USA because he was angry with Erdoğan. And so Erdoğan not only blamed him for the coup attempt, but he blamed the United States as well.

Having arrested the army officers, Erdoğan then arrested all the newspaper people and university teachers whom he believed favored the coup. This crackdown was unlawful and antidemocratic, and it also led Erdoğan away from the West. He was furious with America and formed an alliance with Russia. He broke with the

North Atlantic Treaty Organization (NATO) and began getting weaponry from Russia. And emboldened by Russia, Turkey intervened in northern Syria and Iraq, pushing the Kurds out and allowing the Arabic-speaking Syrians and Iraqis to gain control of these territories.

In short, Turkey became a dictatorship, with its political base rooted in the Islamic political party, and its foreign policy became aggressively aligned with Russia and hostile to America and Europe.

Turkey's economy, however, is integrated with Europe and America, so Erdoğan is limited by this.

And the pro-Western anti-Erdoğan sector of the population makes up a large electoral group.

Still, Turkey became part of the new wave of dictatorships spreading across the globe. And the mixing of religion and nationalism became a political model for other nations—most notably India, where Modi has come to power with a Hindu-based party. Modi is not a dictator, but the fear is that he could become one.

Finally, in terms of "illiberal democracy," the Philippines is moving in this anti-democratic direction as well. Hopefully, this will not be a permanent situation in the Philippines, but this trend was popular. A democratic revival is occurring as of 2024–2025.

18.4 Venezuela and the Resurgence of Left-Wing Dictatorship

From the time of Rómulo Ernesto Betancourt onward, when vast oil reserves were found in Venezuela, the oil revenue was used to generate the modernization of the cities and the establishment of a consumer economy.

After centuries of military dictatorships, Venezuela had gone democratic. And democracy was stable as the economy generated an upscale middle-class lifestyle. Venezuela did not develop a manufacturing economy but rather use oil money to import consumer goods, build fancy stores, and create a modern infrastructure of roads, cars, trucks, electrification, etc.

The new wealth of an upscale lifestyle was spreading rapidly, and Venezuela seemed like a model of democratic stability and economic success.

It was barely noticed that the entire backcountry—inhabited by Native Americans—had been neglected.

With the introduction of modern medicine and sanitation in the cities, the Native Americans moved in searching for jobs, dazzled by the upscale lifestyle. The widespread availability of modern medicine led—unexpectedly—to a population explosion among the Native Americans now living in the cities. The more the population expanded, the poorer they became.

These Native American poor could not be absorbed fast enough to alleviate their deteriorating conditions.

Seeing a base for political power in this impoverished population, Hugo Chavez organized them into a voting bloc. Given their expanding numbers, he won a surprise victory and became President.

As soon as he was elected, he recruited thousands of poor Venezuelans into the military. Using oil money, he paid them well, fed them, and armed them. He was creating the power from which to become a dictator of Venezuela.

Chavez, however, won another election, and seeing that the prosperous middle class—and US oil companies—were becoming worried and turning against him, he made an alliance with Castro's Cuba. They helped train his military and turned him against America. But oil was the source of Venezuela's wealth, and the oil companies were American run. Venezuela's oil revenue was cut, and the economy began to collapse.

Hugo Chavez was a charismatic figure to his Native American poor supporters. But he suddenly died of cancer. His second in command, Maduro, is not charismatic—he is not even competent. Venezuela collapsed economically and dissolved into a near civil war politically.

Maduro rules through his military, and this military has become increasingly corrupt.

No one predicted that Venezuela's democracy would collapse or that its economy would fall apart.

Aristotle, in ancient Greece, had warned that, "Where the poor gain majority control in the democracy, the state is speedily ruined," for, as Aristotle warned, the poor take the wealth of society for themselves but, not knowing how to use it, eat it up and then have to ask for more. "Giving money to the poor is like pouring water in a leaky jar," said Aristotle. Then, out of humane considerations, he asserted that the way to help the poor is to provide them with jobs—in craft workshops or on cash-crop estates—and make sure they have a modicum of education. Then they can be absorbed into the middle class, thus stabilizing democracy.

This latter did not happen fast enough in Venezuela. And the poor, taking money from the oil economy and then continuously asking for more, ruined the economy. Nothing was put into the infrastructure or retail consumer sectors, such that the whole of the economy collapsed.

Maduro now rules as a military dictator, presiding over a ruined economy.

The worry is that Peru, Bolivia, Paraguay, and other poor nations (including those of Central America) could go the way of Venezuela—all of them have a majority poor who are uneducated and disconnected from modern economic and political life. And all these nations have overpopulated poor exploding from the introduction of modern medicine and sanitation.

18.5 China and the Future of Democracy in the World

18.5.1 Mao: From Marxism-Leninism to the Capitalist Road

China, as is so well known, has a millennia-long history of political despotism. The emperorship was established before the birth of Christ. Egypt and Mesopotamia date back much earlier than Chinese unification and emperorships, but they collapsed after the Greco-Roman conquests, while China retained its emperorships into the twentieth-century colonial period.

The United States had high hopes for China before World War II. Sun Yat-sen, then Chiang Kai-shek, seemed to be leading China toward democracy and capitalist industrialism. *Mao Zedong* and his communist cadres were soundly defeated and driven deep into the western area of China.

The Japanese invasion, however, prevented Chang Kai-Shek from pursuing Mao and the communists.

Unknown to the Americans, the Russians were arming and training Mao's army during World War II. When the war ended and Japan withdrew, the Americans believed that Chang and his American-oriented political party—the *Kuomintang—would easily* defeat Mao and his communists a second time. But Mao had a well-trained army, Russian weaponry, and a huge following among the peasantry. Chang, on the other hand, had developed a bad reputation—he was accused of cruelty and fascistic leanings.

Mao surprised the Western world and won the Civil War. From 1949 onward, China became communist.

Now, traditional China has had a humanistic political ethic derived from Confucius. The Emperor was supposed to be "benevolent" and take care of his people the way a father takes care of his family. And Confucius believed that a well-educated strata of government officials—the Mandarins, chosen by examination in a meritocratic manner—would ensure that the Emperors, indeed, ruled benevolently, for if the Emperor was tyrannical or incompetent, he would lose "the mandate from heaven" and could be overthrown.

This meritocratic bureaucracy helped rule China well and, some of the time, even benevolently. However, Confucius' system was flawed in that the Emperor possessed the military power and the "office charisma"—they were God's ruling with the mandate from heaven—to overrule the educated Mandarins. And this they often did. The Emperors were more often murderous tyrants than benevolent rulers.

Mao, espousing Marxism-Leninism, ruled benevolently for the first 10 years or so.

Through the Marxist-Leninist model exhibited by Stalin's Russia, Mao established an infrastructure, promoted industrialization, and developed an educational system for China. This was a difficult and heroic feat. We should not minimize what Mao achieved. China was rural agrarian, and Mao did industrialize and urbanize China in a modernist direction.

But, as Lord Acton warned, "Power corrupts; absolute power corrupts absolutely."

Mao became a tyrant. He pushed the Chinese population to exhaustion during his "Great Leap Forward." Mao tried to organize China into the corvée work teams that had built the Great Wall. But modern industrial economies do not get built that way. The Great Leap Forward was a failure—unfortunately, it led to the death of millions of Chinese from starvation and overwork.

Mao gave it up and retired to a Buddhist monastery. Unfortunately, he emerged with another plan for mass mobilization, which would fail.

This time it was "the Cultural Revolution," in which Mao empowered the young people of China to go around and destroy all things Confucius and all things Western. The young people—wearing armbands and headbands—burned books, beat up teachers, smashed violins, and basically accomplished nothing but chaos.

Mao retired again, and this time, he would soon die. But before he died, he recalled Deng Xiaoping and *Chou En-lai* and told them they could embark on "the capitalist road."

The Communist Party retained control over the army, the police, and the political bureaucracy. Yet they began to encourage the foundation of a capitalist, entrepreneurial, business-oriented, and profit-driven capitalist economy.

Industrial production was shifted away from bureaucratic Communist Party control—at least some of it—and placed on an efficiency-oriented system, run by corporate managers utilizing capitalist measures of production, pricing, and profit.

Further, consumer-oriented capitalist enterprises were allowed to emerge and were encouraged to flourish. The uniform Mao-style clothing gave way to imitation designer clothing—men's and women's fashions diverged. Consumer goods exploded onto the scene with the Chinese middle class, upper middle class, and millionaire classes emerging and embracing these new consumer products "conspicuously," to quote Veblen.

The Chinese capitalist economy has been one of the most successful and dynamic achievements in the modern world. The Chinese are good at business, venerate education, and excel in mathematics and science. Therefore, an industrial-scientific-technocratic economy emerged quickly, and it was put on a business efficacy footing.

Western capitalist nations were invited to join the Chinese economy as part of a system of joint ventures. American and European companies expanded in China because China's workers were paid less, and the Chinese market of a billion people presented an amazing opportunity for the sale of Western goods.

The incredible success of the Chinese capitalist economy and its integration into the global capitalist economic system led Western observers to hold out some optimism about Chinese political future.

Cautiously, some Western political scientists predicted that the new capitalist economy would lead China down the democratic road. Others, like Samuel Huntington, believed Chinese culture was too inconsistent with democracy for it to emerge.

When Xi Jinping—who had been the Mayor of Shanghai during Shanghai's capitalist success and its competition with Hong Kong for super-modernization—was chosen Premier of the Chinese Communist Party and went to Beijing, foreign observers believed Xi would be a modernizer, a forward thinker, and a leader who would encourage not only capitalism but also the democratization process in China. They could not have been more wrong.

18.5.2 Xi Jinping and Totalitarianism in China

Xi, having lived through the collapse of the Soviet Union and realizing that China's empire could collapse as well—with Tibet and the Uyghurs declaring their independence and encouraging other ethnic regions to do so—embarked on a program of geopolitical expansion, like Putin's Russia.

China has embarked on an ambitious campaign to expand its borders along the old "Silk Road" and into the South China Sea. It has built huge modern container ports in Greece, Italy, and South America to ship its goods through to global markets.

And China is expanding its military and space programs—just like Russia—creating a gigantic, well-trained, and well-supplied army, easily recruited from its billion-strong population. And, like Russia, China's scientists and engineers have been pushed to focus on military weaponry and space technology.

These aggressive geopolitical and military programs have been as successful as China's consumer capitalist economy. But Xi, frightened that China could break up from its outside ethnic groups, is equally nervous about China's internal growing, well-educated, and freethinking middle class.

The new middle class in China is developing an upscale lifestyle of condominiums, tennis courts, sports stadiums, upscale malls, fancy designer clothing, luxury cars, and more.

Fearing that this new middle class will desire political participation and the elimination of the old Communist Party, Xi is engaged in an unprecedented program of technological totalitarianism.

I say "unprecedented," but of course, it has had precedent in Nazi Germany, Fascist Italy, and Stalinist Russia.

What is unprecedented is that Xi has access to modern technology unavailable to these earlier totalitarian regimes.

Xi has surveillance cameras on all streets and malls and inside buildings. He has cell-phone surveillance capability. He has computer surveillance systems. The modern, high-technology economy has produced the most wonderful global systems—mass media of communications never before imagined even in science fiction. The Internet is marvelous; Google Maps and Wikipedia information are astounding—almost like magic. The most obscure source can be found—just "Google it."

Unfortunately, this high-technology global communication network can, and is, being used by totalitarian regimes.

With the vast, loyal, and well-cared-for army and a tough, sometimes sadistic and omnipresent, police force, Xi has the Chinese population terrified to oppose him and his Communist colleagues. The police swoop down on anyone engaging in activities in opposition to the regime—they are arrested, interrogated, and often jailed and mistreated in jail.

Given Xi's police and military power as well as the tremendous success of China's economy, the Chinese middle class has been forced into political silence and contentment with economic success.

As long as China and Russia remain despotic, the global democracy movement cannot fully succeed. And with China supporting North Korea, totalitarianism will remain a potential model for nations developing the high-technology economy.

Given this new wave of tyranny, is there any hope for the future of democracy?

18.6 Why a Democratic Future Is Still Possible Globally

Though Germany and Japan were forced to adopt democracy after they lost World War II, there have been instances of transitions from dictatorship to democracy that occurred peacefully—that is, without it being forced upon a nation by the victors in a war.

Spain and Russia stand out in the modern world because Spain made the transition from fascist dictatorship to legal-rational democracy without outside invasion, while Russia made the transition from communist totalitarianism to legal-rational democracy. However, whereas Spain has established a solid capitalist-industrial economy—linked closely to the EU—and a strong, stable democracy, Russia has not been able to establish either of the two. The Russian economy is not a capitalist-industrial economy; it is a raw material economy administered by "oligarchs"—wealthy, violent quasi-mafiosa rather than law-abiding businessmen—and Russia's democracy was hijacked by Vladimir Putin, who has created a dictatorship with rigged elections and the suppression of opposition candidates.

Why mention Russia in the same category as Spain? This is because in both nations, a seemingly invincible totalitarian government was peacefully overturned because of the basic socioeconomic alteration of society. Even though Russian democracy has not become stable, Stalinist totalitarianism did decline. Putin, as bad as he is, is a mildly repressive dictator, not a full-fledged totalitarian.

Therefore, China could change—even though it looks like it cannot.

What are the conditions that could lead to a sociopolitical change in China and other dictatorial regimes?

We have seen the transition from traditional authority—kingship and aristocracy—to legal-rational authority—electoral democracy with constitutional limitations of power and tenure.

Now, will we see a transition from fascists, communists, and dictatorships to legal-rational democracy?

18.7 President Trump in 2025 Pushes Back Against the Social Changes in Gender and Race: Is American Democracy in Jeopardy?

In a flurry of presidential proclamations, Trump has sought to roll back the transformations of gender and race that had been occurring in the twenty-first century.

He banned transgender women from women's athletics because they had been men and, therefore, had an unfair biological advantage. In this, he was actually consistent with the World Olympic Committee, which had done the same.

The National Collegiate Athletic Association (NCAA) must now comply.

Trump then banned all medical treatments for children under the age of 19 who wanted to become transgender—they call it "gender-affirming "medical treatment. Its opponents call it "sex-change "medical treatments.

Again, in this, Trump is consistent with the new laws just passed in 2024 in Norway, Sweden, and the United Kingdom.

Notice, however, that in all three countries, plus the USA under Trump, an individual can still choose to be transgender after the age of 19. So transgender individuals will continue to choose to do so in many modern nations.

However, Trump has insisted, in another presidential decree, that there are only two genders: male and female—no more "nonbinary "or "transgender. "An individual is either a male or a female.

The Christian fundamentalists love this, as do the Orthodox Jews. However, gays and lesbians still exist, and as of 2025, the fundamentalist Christians and Orthodox Jews acknowledge their existence and their civil rights but do not accept gay marriages, lesbian marriages, or the child raising that often goes with such marriages. As for Trump, he has not spoken against gay or lesbian marriages.

The whole subject of homosexuality—LGBTQ+—is contentious worldwide. But while the democracies are open-minded on this issue, Putin's dictatorship is hostile to it. So, too, is Victor Orban's dictatorship in Hungary. And wherever religious parties become prominent, they reject LGBTQ+ activities or demonstrations. So Modi in India, Erdoğan in Turkey, and all Muslim countries are hostile to LGBTQ+ movements. So far, Xi Jinping in China has been silent on this issue. However, many LGBTQ+ people flee China and live in the USA or Canada if they can. Ang Lee, the great Hollywood director, describes the Chinese dilemma in his 1993 movie *The Wedding Banquet*.

18.7.1 Trump and Women's Liberation

Trump cannot roll back the remarkable gains that women have made in America and the world. But he has sought to restrict women's role in the military to noncombatant roles. The American military has resisted his ideas. Transgender people, however, have been forced out of the military, nor will the military pay for their gender-affirming medical treatments anymore.

In abolishing diversity, equity, and inclusion (DEI) programs in the government, universities, and corporations, Trump may be impeding women's progress, for DEI programs pressure these institutions to hire women—along with Blacks—and not just hire White men. The DEI programs led to a very positive increase in the number of women attaining leadership positions, which had been previously denied to them for many years.

Because women excel at college, many qualified women were available for leadership positions in most fields of endeavor. The only fields that women have not yet excelled in are mathematics, physics, chemistry, engineering, and computer technology. But women had never been encouraged to go into these fields. Now, in 2025, since women are being encouraged to go on in the "hard sciences," they may begin to excel in these fields. Women are already in medicine and biology, so we shall see whether there are gender differences or not in other scientific fields.

To return to Trump, he, as a person, has exhibited aggressive masculinity in his sexual connections to women. Women hate this, and the "Me Too "movement encourages women to speak out against any man who sexually harasses them. But young men and working-class men oppose the "Me Too" movement and insist that men have always been encouraged to be aggressive toward women—they insist that this is a cultural phenomenon; they love it, and Trump represents it. All of his wives were (and are) beautiful—he surrounds himself with gorgeous women—and he rewards them with political positions of power. He rejects all the lawsuits against him as politically motivated. Many men love that he had a fling with Stormy Daniels, a porn star.

So in "the war between the sexes," which has been quite nasty in the twenty-first century, Trump reinforces men's cultural right to aggressive sexuality.

This sexual conflict has even emerged recently in France and Spain, where "Don Juanism" has always been accepted by women. A "Me Too" movement has emerged in both these nations. And Trump's emergence in the USA has stimulated the debate there.

18.7.2 Is Trump a Racist? He Pushes Back Hard Against Black Achievement

Not only has Trump revoked DEI—diversity, equity, and inclusion—but he also eliminated Martin Luther King Jr. Day as a national holiday as well as Juneteenth and Black History Month. All have been rejected by Trump in presidential decrees.

If Trump had just revoked the DEI programs, one could have said, as he did, that it was just a return to *meritocracy*—all hiring would be done on merit alone, not on racial or gender guidelines. But why revoke Martin Luther King Jr. Day as a national holiday? Have not Black people been part of America's history?

If slavery, the Ku Klux Klan (KKK) and its lynchings, and Jim Crow segregation have been part of America's history, then Martin Luther King Jr. Day should surely be a national holiday.

Further, Trump is talking about putting statues back up that have been taken down. Does he mean Robert E. Lee? One can make a case that statues of Christopher Columbus should be put back up—along with statues of Indigenous peoples—because Columbus did change the world for the better in the long run. He did bring the Renaissance knowledge to the New World. It was terrible for the Indigenous people, but the Aztecs were terrible as well, and eventually Western civilization, with religious humanism, prevailed.

Robert E. Lee, on the other hand, fought to the death for slavery. What could be good about this?

So Trump is exhibiting racist tendencies, and so is his man, Elon Musk, who has backed right-wing neo-Nazi parties in Germany.

Now, let us discuss Trump's revocation of DEI organizations in all spheres of the American experience.

18.7.3 Diversity, Equity, and Inclusion (DEI)

After centuries of exclusion, Black Americans wanted a mechanism that would ensure their inclusion at universities, corporations, and government agencies.

As an example of exclusion, Woodrow Wilson, when he was the president of Princeton University, made sure that all Blacks who applied would be denied entrance—even if they qualified. Then when Woodrow Wilson became President of the United States of America, he forcibly segregated the workforce of Washington, DC, firing all Blacks from the United States Post Office.

Needless to say, Blacks were kept out of universities, corporations, and government agencies.

Therefore, to correct this prejudicial process, affirmative action laws were passed that helped Black people gain entrance to these positions. But the progress was slow, and progressive Whites and Blacks initiated the DEI programs to ensure that there would be more quality and inclusion.

The problem has been that the DEI programs became too aggressive. It is not that hiring was more inclusive of Blacks—and women—but that the officials in these programs began to engage in "thought control"—my term. They banned all words that could be construed as "microaggression "against Blacks. For instance, the term "fieldwork" in social work and education was renamed "practicum" because fieldwork sounded like picking cotton.

Individuals using the old terminology were sometimes fired by universities and government agencies. DEI training was forced on all personnel in all major universities, corporations, and government agencies. These sessions—though inherently progressive and well intentioned—felt like Chinese "brainwashing," which the Chinese did to war captives during the Korean War.

I know this sounds very reactionary, but the DEI programs really did cross the line of constitutionality guaranteeing free speech and ethnically acceptable standards of action.

Therefore, Trump's dismantling of the DEI programs has been granted ambiguity. On the one hand, it is good that this left-wing thought control has been removed; on the other hand, discrimination against Black people—and women—may now be given a pass.

As with women's liberation, Trump's pushback on Black progress in America may slow things down, but Black upward mobility has been growing nevertheless.

18.7.4 Trump Rejects Climate Change

Trump insists that climate change experts are scaring us for no reason. He believes that we can keep using oil, natural gas, and even coal with no ill effect. "Drill, baby drill!" he keeps repeating.

The unprecedented rainstorms, such as the one that just inundated North Carolina, he blames on the Democrats! The flooding, such as had never been seen before in the Carolinas, was nothing—it was the Biden administration that mishandled the aftermath. He even blamed the Federal Emergency Management Agency (FEMA), the US agency that oversees the funding for disaster relief.

Trump blamed the Los Angeles fires—fanned by unprecedented 100-mile-an-hour winds off the Pacific Ocean—on the mismanagement of the water supply by the Los Angeles and California authorities.

He refuses to see that the warming of the oceans is creating an enormous increase in the wind and water carried by hurricane-level storms. He listens to no science, instead telling unbelievable lies about the climate changes that everybody else sees and is experiencing.

In terms of alternative energy, he criticizes windmills. He says that the windmills in the coastal waters are killing whales. Somehow, the whales are leaping 80 feet into the air and are being hit by the blades of the windmills. Windmills do kill birds, and this is a problem, but the whales are being hit by ship propellers, not windmills.

As for solar panels, he says nothing about them, but in attempting to stop the funding of the "Green New Deal"—passed under the Biden administration—he is cutting off funding for solar panel development in American factories.

No solar panels power the air conditioning at Mar-a-Lago, Trump's home in Florida. And the governor of Florida, Ron DeSantis, a Trump supporter, has also prevented the installation of solar panels in the state of Florida. Florida, "the Sunshine State, "with a bright, hot, steady stream of sunny days, could power all its air-conditioning needs with solar panel energy. And electric-charging stations for electric cars could be powered with solar panels—thus establishing carbon-free automobile driving.

But, no, Trump pulled the USA out of the Paris Climate Accord program, which funds climate change programs worldwide. And, as mentioned, he is trying to end the Green New Deal in the United States.

Slowing down the pace of carbon-free energy development is morally reprehensible and dangerous for the future of the world. But Trump does not care: "Drill baby drill!"

18.7.5 Trump Against American Democracy

Worse than the pushback on the global changes in gender and race is Trump's flagrant disregard for the American Constitution. Lawful action and democratic norms and traditions are meaningless to him.

Trump loves dictators. He idolizes Vladimir Putin and Viktor Orban and even counts Kim Jong Un of North Korea as a "friend.".

Not only does Trump call Putin from time to time, but he has had Viktor Orban of Hungary visit Mar-a-Lago numerous times. He will undoubtedly give Putin everything he wants in the settlement of the Ukrainian War.

In terms of Viktor Orban, he utilized the fear of immigrants—Muslim immigrants from Syria—and the LGBTQ+ movement to get elected in Hungary. Similarly, Trump uses the fear of Mexican and Central American immigration and the rejection of transgender medical treatments to gain his electoral victory in 2024.

Orban, once elected, engaged in a series of activities that stripped Hungary of its democracy—a series of dictatorial activities that Trump is attempting to emulate.

Orban took control of television stations, and he blocked all criticisms from newspapers. He aligned himself with the Catholic Church on all social issues regarding gender and women's liberation.

Trump has insisted that CBS, NBC, and ABC not criticize him. He says he wants "fair "coverage, but he means positive coverage. He has demanded the same from the *New York Times* and the *Washington Post*.

So far, the American TV networks and the American newspapers have not caved in to his demands. But he is trying to muzzle the news media, just as Orban did in Hungary.

Beyond Orban's "illiberal democracy," as the political scientists call it, Trump has also hung a portrait of Andrew Jackson on his Oval Office wall.

President Andrew Jackson was not only a slaveholder but also an unapologetic Indian hater. As a general, before his presidency, he led the military push to drive the Indians off their land, exiling men to Oklahoman territory and seizing their tribal lands.

When Andrew Jackson became President, he dismissed as many government officials as he could and replaced them with men loyal to him and him alone. It came to be called "the spoils system"—to the victor goes the spoils.

Those loyal to Jackson were often inept at their government jobs; they had no expertise in this, and some had little education—Jackson did not care, as long as they did what he wanted and were loyal only to him.

In later years, historians referred to "Jacksonian democracy," because Jackson kicked out the southern aristocrats and the northern wealthy elite, and put in his backward cronies as the government officials.

However, this spoils system led to so much corruption and ineptitude that after the Civil War, the Civil Service Act was passed. From then on, nonpartisan well-educated individuals were chosen meritocrally to do the bureaucratic work of the government. The President could still choose the heads of each department, and they would be loyal to the President in carrying out his policies, but the civil servants working under these department heads were competent and not corrupt throughout America's modern history.

Enter Trump. He is trying to emulate Andrew Jackson. He has attempted to fire thousands of civil servant bureaucrats and replace them with individuals loyal to him. Further, his choices for department heads have been very peculiar. It is not that they are very loyal to Trump; it is that they are incompetent—and some are deranged—such as R.F. Kennedy, Jr., and Tulsi Gabbard. Loyalty is one thing; idiocy is another. And many of Trump's choices to lead critical agencies appear to be unstable as well as incompetent.

One further antidemocratic process that Trump is engaged in must be emphasized, that is, the cutting down of government agencies—the elimination of the United States Agency for International Development (USAID) and the Department of Education, along with the attack on the Federal Bureau of Investigation (FBI), the Central Intelligence Agency (CIA), and the Pentagon.

The Republican Party has long wanted to cut off foreign aid. USAID was created by President John F. Kennedy. It brings food and medicine to developing nations. The idea was to bring a positive influence to developing nations so that they would prefer America to Russia or other dictatorial nations.

The Republicans have always thought this was ineffective, while the Democrats believe the program has been successful. Trump wants to end it completely.

As to the Department of Education, Trump and the Republicans want to abolish it because they believe that the Department of Education was pushing a "woke "or politically correct (PC) education agenda.

Trump believes they were insisting on teaching LGBTQ+ values and pro-Black and anti-White ideology as well. Trump says they were teaching "White privilege" and "Black oppression," as well as Western colonial domination of the Third World.

The Republicans see all this as racism in reverse against the Western White world. Trump wants to abolish what he sees as a "woke" curriculum and to return to the older pro-Western society curriculum, hence the abolishment of the Education Department.

Trump wants the states to decide the curriculum for the schools. The problem with this is many of the southern states—including Texas and Oklahoma—want to include Christian biblical teachings in schools, which the Constitution specifically forbids. The "separation of church and state" was one of the founding principles of the American Constitution, for in Europe, the violent wars between the Catholics and the Protestants had torn nations apart. So the American Founding Fathers sought to avoid religious strife. They, therefore, made it clear that religious teachings belong in the church—whatever church you want—freedom of religion is in the Bill of Rights, but public schools were to remain secular.

You can establish religious schools, but these must be private and shall not receive public funding.

Therefore, leaving curriculum decisions to the states is problematic on these grounds alone, notwithstanding the possible racism, sexism, and anti-LGBTQ+-ism that might emerge in various state curricula.

Then there is Trump's attack on the FBI, the CIA, and the Justice Department.

Because Trump was persecuted for tax evasion, improper campaign funding, taking classified documents, and encouraging the January 6 rioters who illegally entered the Capitol Building and tried to stop the certification of the Biden electoral victory, he, Trump, wants to punish all these FBI and justice department individuals who worked on the cases against him.

Retribution—that is what he wants. Of course, such actions are totally unconstitutional, unlawful, un-American, and un-Christian. But this has not stopped Donald Trump.

There will be lawsuits against Trump‘s actions, but the courts are slow—and the Supreme Court is ultra-conservative and pro-Trump. So the final outcome of all this retribution against the FBI and Justice Department is uncertain.

If Trump succeeds in firing hundreds of FBI agents, Justice Department lawyers, and CIA operatives, the United States would be in grave danger from foreign spies and assassins, terrorists, and criminal syndicates.

Trump does not seem to care and continues to proceed with his attempt to dismantle the law and democracy, which have made America the symbol of freedom as "the shining city on a hill": a celebration of individual freedom, material prosperity, and American power and—above all—a call for Americans to renew their optimism and believe in themselves again. This was from Ronald Reagan, who used to be the ultimate Republican President. Trump has made a mockery of Reagan‘s imagery of America.

Finally, there is Elon Musk, the richest man in the world—a Trump supporter, financier, and underling.

Musk, partnering with Trump, wants to cut the government down. He also hates USAID and the Department of Education. He is a South African who has funded neo-Nazi parties in Germany.

Trump has given Musk carte blanche to do whatever it takes to eliminate government bureaucrats and agencies he does not like. Citing fraud and waste—though there is none—he is ruthlessly cutting down these government agencies. Thousands have been fired.

Again, all this is in the courts. Will the courts uphold the American Constitution? Will they uphold the rule of law? Or will American democracy go the way of Hungarian democracy?

The world is changing. Trump is pushing back against these changes mightily. However, the transformation of the globe will continue, and I believe that American democracy will survive the Trumpian assault. And I predict that Reagan‘s vision of America as a “shining city on a hill” standing for freedom and opportunity will replace Trump‘s negative view.

America does need a controlled border, but it also does need immigrant labor—both low level on farms and high tech in Silicon Valley. And the progressive Democrats may have gone too far with their diversity, equity, and inclusion programs and their support for LGBTQ+ rights. But women will continue to attain leadership positions, LGBTQ+ people will not go back “into the closet,” and Black people will continue to make gains politically and economically.

Barack Obama was President of the United States, Margaret Thatcher was Prime Minister of the United Kingdom, and the Governor of Colorado is a gay man, married with children. The world is changing, and Trump cannot stop these changes.

Chapter 19
Max Weber's Theory of the Transition from Traditional Authority to Legal-Rational Authority, with Charismatic Leadership as a Bridge Between Them

19.1 Weber's Theory of Legitimate Domination: Divine Kingship vs. Rational Law[1]

Max Weber, in *Economy and Society*, which is brilliantly translated in a new English edition by Gunther Roth and Claus Wittich, presented his theory of "legitimate domination."

Weber describes three different kinds of legitimate authority: traditional, legal-rational, and charismatic.

Traditional authority emerged with the early civilizations and continued into near-modern times.

Traditional authority consists of a monarchy—with the king or emperor conceived of as divine or semi-divine or, at least, descended from a god, ruling, as the Chinese put it, with the mandate of heaven.

Along with the divine king, a state bureaucracy—either priestly or secular—administers the kingdom.

Contrasting with this, Weber describes the emergence of a government based not on divine kingship but rather on laws—rationally debated laws. The authority of rational laws supersedes the authority of irrational men.

As Aristotle put it, "When the law rules, god and reason rule; when a man rules, we add the character of the beast."[2]

Max Weber, *Economy and Society* (Gunther Roth and Claus Wittich, translators). NY: Bedminster Press.

---

[1] Section on Legitimate Domination in *Economy and Society* (Gunther Roth and Claus Wittich, translators). NY: Bedminster Press.

[2] Aristotle, *Politics* (on Law).

R. M. Glassman, *The Great Global Transformation*, Contributions to Political Science, https://doi.org/10.1007/978-3-031-90566-7_19

So, for Aristotle, laws are rational and moral (reason and god rule when the law rules), but when a man rules, violence, territoriality, and sexuality emerge from our alpha-male animal heritage (we add to this the character of the beast).

By quoting Aristotle, we are establishing that legal-rational authority emerged in ancient Greece from the sixth to the third centuries BC.

It declined with the fall of the Hellenistic and Roman Empires and then reemerged during the Italian Renaissance.

Then legal-rational authority reemerged in full flowering during the Enlightenment era—1500 to 1900—and it was accompanied by electoral democracy, as in Ancient Greece. Representative democracy, in large nation-states, replaced the small-scale city-state democracies of ancient Greece.

The rule of law, above the rule of men, was one of the basic principles of the Enlightenment. This principle culminated in the creation and enshrinement of "constitutions" embodying laws governing all political actions.

Weber, living in Germany and writing between 1900 and 1920, emphasized the difficulty that a nation can have in making the transition from traditional authority to legal-rational authority. This difficulty is still occurring in Russia, China, and most of the Third World nations.

Weber emphasized the difficulty because he saw it firsthand in Germany. In his lifetime, the German king—the Kaiser—and his state bureaucracy, headed by Bismarck in Prussia (Berlin), exhibited the remnants of traditional authority. While rational-legal authority and representative democracy—though existent in Germany, especially in western German states—had not yet become institutionalized or culturally accepted.

Because of the difficulty of this transition—this political transformation—Weber turned to his conception of charismatic leadership.

19.2 Charismatic Leadership and Its Rule

According to Weber, charismatic leaders created a kind of temporary authority structure. Because a people came to believe that a given leader has "the gift of grace"—charisma—they believe in him (or her, such as Joan of Arc and Cleopatra), and the charismatic leader creates a temporary unity—a temporary order—and therefore creates a temporary authority system, which can serve as a bridge between traditional authority and legal-rational authority.

As examples of charismatic leaders providing a bridge between traditional and legal-rational authority, Weber thought of Cromwell and Napoleon—both tough military heroes but both imbued with legal-rational ideas for their nations. Full-fledged democracy and the rights of man motivated these leaders as they unified their nations.

And, in the United States, which Weber visited, he saw, in the "charismatic plebiscitary presidency," the possibility of having a charismatic leader within the constraints of constitutional law.

Teddy Roosevelt was Weber's heroic figure within the "charismatic plebiscitary presidency."

Fortunately—or unfortunately—Weber died before Mussolini and Hitler emerged in Italy and Germany.

Here were two charismatic leaders, unifying their nations but not leading them to legal-rational authority. Fascism and Nazism unleashed "the character of the beast," as Aristotle put it. Violence, cruelty, and war were championed by these leaders. They were charismatic, but they created a bridge that led away from democracy and rational law.

I highlight this because throughout the developing world today, in the twenty-first century, the transition from traditional authority to legal-rational authority has proven quite difficult in many nations. And in some of them, charismatic leaders have emerged. In some cases, as with Nelson Mandela of South Africa and Lee Kuan Yew of Singapore, the charismatic leader does provide a bridge to legal-rational authority and electoral democracy. Unfortunately, in many other countries, such as China and North Korea, Mao and Kim provided a bridge to Stalinist totalitarianism. And in Argentina, Peron tried to emulate Mussolini, while a few years ago, Hugo Chavez tried to emulate Fidel Castro, who was emulating Stalin.

So the transition to legal-rational authority is, indeed, difficult, and Weber would be turning over in his grave if he had lived to see Hitler—a full-fledged, charismatic leader—lead Germany as far from legal-rational authority as human beings can get.

19.3 Nations That Have Made a Successful Transition to Legal-Rational Authority

We have already pointed out that ancient Greece was the first region to establish legal-rational authority. Aristotle wrote extensively on "law," and Plato, in his last book entitled *The Laws*, added the need for the constraining power of constitutional law, even to his ideal form of government, the philosopher guardians.

We have also determined that during the Enlightenment, the Dutch Republic, the Swiss Cantons, the English Civil War, the English limited monarchy, the American Revolution, and the French Revolution all contributed to what political scientists call "the first wave of democracies," and all established legal-rational authority.

After World War II, Germany and Japan were forced to establish legal-rational constitutions and democratic processes of government. And this process was remarkably successful.

Then we discussed the so-called third wave of democracies that occurred with the fall of the Soviet Union and the establishment of legal-rational authority in Eastern Europe and the Baltic states; the rise of the Four Asian Tigers—Singapore, Hong Kong, Taiwan, and South Korea; and the decline of fascism in Spain and the rise of legal-rational authority there.

In the twenty-first century, there has occurred a regression to authoritarian regimes.

19.4 Nations That Have Failed to Make the Transition to Legal-Rational Authority

In Russia, there was a reversion to dictatorships, with Putin vowing to restore the Soviet Union and Russian world power. China was on "the capitalist road" and looked like it might be on the democratic road as well until Xi Jinping took China back toward Maoism.

North Korea is more totalitarian than ever and still has a perverted form of traditional authority based on a family dynasty.

Turkey, Hungary, the Philippines, and almost Poland drifted back toward dictatorships.

So the transition to legal-rational authority has hit a wall of resistance globally.

19.5 Charismatic Global Movements: Fascism and Communism

Weber observed that charismatic leadership could possibly provide a bridge from traditional to legal-rational authority. However, we have seen, since Weber's death, that charismatic leaders can also lead a nation away from legal-rational authority and toward various forms of irrational, violent, and totalitarian domination.

In fact, the transition from traditional authority to legal-rational authority is so destabilizing and disruptive that, what I call, "charismatic movements" have emerged. These charismatic movements lead not to the future but instead to the past—in perverted form.

That is, fascism in Italy glorified the Roman Empire—the fascists were attempting to revive Roman power and military norms. In Spain, fascism harked back to the power and glory of the conquistadors, who conquered the New World—violence and military power were extolled, as in Italy.

In Germany, Nazism harked back to the Teutonic Knights and the Germanic tribes that conquered Rome and dominated feudal Europe. Again, violent and military norms were made central—along with racism against the Jews, which was not part of fascism.

In Russia, communism began as a vision—a blueprint—for a utopian future. However, Stalin destroyed this utopian vision and, instead, brought Russia back to its czarist past—Stalin was Ivan the Terrible all over again, only much more terrible.

And Mao Zedong? He was supposed to create a Marxian utopian future, but he ended up—with the "Great Leap Forward"—becoming the last emperor. Mao knew that he had betrayed the image of the future that he had sought. Thus, unlike Stalin, Mao stepped down and told Deng Xiaoping to take China on the capitalist road.

With China developing the fastest-growing capitalist economy in the world, the Western nations—and the rapidly growing Chinese middle class—expected the nation to move toward legal-rational authority and democracy, like Hong Kong, Singapore, and Taiwan.[3]

However, Xi Jinping betrayed this movement forward and, instead, led China backward toward an increasingly totalitarian dictatorship.

Recently in 2023, with the Chinese economy stagnating, Xi has come to San Francisco to the Asia Pacific Economic Conference to regenerate Chinese capitalism with American business capital. Will this lead to a slow liberalization? Time will tell.

19.6 Islamicism as the Newest Charismatic Movement Globally

The Muslim nations have always felt themselves in competition with the Western Christian nations. And Western colonialism, with its focus on oil, exacerbated this and led the Muslim nations to feel they were being dominated and exploited by the West and its religion.

The Islamicist movement has emerged from this colonialist, oil-based Western domination.

However, like most of these charismatic movements, it harks back to the past.

In this case, the Islamic radicals wanted to reestablish "the caliphate"—the traditional authority of the Muslim kings, who combined military power with Islamic religious authority. The caliph was the leader of both the army and the Muslim religion.

So the Islamicists have pledged to drive out Western colonialists, including the Israeli Jews, whom they link directly with the British and French colonial powers. And the Islamicists pledged to reestablish the caliphate and to strictly adhere to Koranic law—not the rational secular law of democratic constitutions but rather the Sharia Law of the Koran.

The Islamic State of Iraq and Syria (ISIS), Al-Qaeda, the Taliban, Hamas, and Hezbollah are all Islamicist groups caught up in the Islamicist movement that excites the Muslim world globally.

Unfortunately, the Islamicist movement, like fascism and Stalinism before it, leads to the past, not the future, and to violence and military dictatorship, not legal-rational authority and democracy.

So is there any hope in the Islamic world?

---

[3] Ronald M. Glassman, *China in Transition: Communism, Capitalism, Democracy*, NY, Praeger, 1990.

The United Arab Emirates and Qatar have been exhibiting a successful attempt at modernization—economically, politically, and socially.

In Abu Dhabi, there is an architectural installation called "the Abrahamic Family House." It consists of a mosque, a church, and a synagogue. All three are spectacular, and they symbolize the Abrahamic Accords, in which the Arab nations recognize the State of Israel.

If Israel—with the USA's help—can defend Hamas—Islamicist fanatics—and then establish a Palestinian state, then it is possible that Islamicism will be superseded by modernist policies. Such politics could lead to legal-rational authority in the future.

Then, of course, there is Iran, but Iran—though it is a theocracy and the ayatollahs and Persian guard rule dictatorially—is modernist in orientation. Iran has science—rational science—advanced enough to create an atomic bomb. Of course, this scares the world (and especially Israel). But Iran is not Islamicist, and its people have demonstrated—en masse—for legal-rational authority and democracy.

Led by the women of Iran and the college-educated middle class, Iran may make the transition to legal-rational authority.

19.7 Conclusions on the Global Political Transition

It was thought that the third wave would expand globally. And though it has not, optimism about the future persists.

Many nations are slow to develop economically and socially, and so they may be slow to make the transition to legal-rational authority.

The recent events in Poland, where the Polish people voted for democracy and legal-rational authority, are hopeful. And Ukraine, too, is moving in a legal-rational direction.

Xi's dependence on free market capitalism is good for the future of democracy.

So we must wait, and we must see, for the events in Venezuela serve as a warning that a regression to authoritarian domination is always a possibility. Look at how this possibility rears its head with Trump running again and pledging to drag this nation toward dictatorial domination.

Part VI
Technological Change Beyond Our Imagination, and Its Sociological Impact

Chapter 20
Technological Change and Its Sociological Impact

20.1 The Rapid Pace of Technological Change

Technological change is occurring at such a rapid pace that it is beyond our rational control and, sometimes, beyond our imagination. Artificial intelligence (AI), for instance, seems to be able to "think" and adapt to new situations beyond those for which it was programmed. We do not know what this think-capable technology will do—some of the things it will do will be good and some disastrous. Yet, at this moment, we have no clear process for controlling AI.

Aside from AI, there are other technological inventions that have already impacted our lives. I am referring here to the expanding Internet technology, which has allowed for all kinds of new economic, political, and social interactions that have already changed our lives. And these changes are occurring globally.

I am referring to buying online—Amazon, Alibaba, etc.—and how this is affecting stores, malls, department stores, and food stores; meeting on Zoom—business meetings, personal meetings, and academic classes; dating online—dating for marriage, dating for fun, and dating for sex; and, lastly, the political blogs and social media websites through which globalized humans join opinion groups, political groups, extremist groups, and silly fun groups such as those on TikTok. In this political category, Facebook, Twitter (X), and all the podcasts come to mind.

So given these dramatic and rapidly expanding technological changes, let us look at the socialized impact of what we have at this moment in time, realizing that tomorrow, a new change will occur that is beyond our ability to predict because a certain technology has not yet been innovated.

R. M. Glassman, *The Great Global Transformation*, Contributions to Political Science, https://doi.org/10.1007/978-3-031-90566-7_20

20.2 Some Economic Changes Linked to the New Technology

20.2.1 Buying Online

One can buy anything online now. Platforms like Amazon, Alibaba, and others facilitate online buying—it is easy to buy; it is easy to pay with PayPal, Zelle, and Apple Pay.

So since it is so easy to buy online, what happens to stores and malls?

Small boutique stores and mom-and-pop stores are having difficulty staying in business. They are going out of business in droves. But so, too, are many big chain stores.

It is simply easier to shop online than to drive to or walk to or subway to a store.

Everywhere one goes in the USA, stores are closing—whole shopping centers are abandoned.

The problem with buying online, however, is the return policy. So much of that which is bought online gets returned because you cannot try it on; you cannot really see what the product is until you actually see it in reality rather than on the computer or your phone.

However, most companies have a generous online return policy, so online buying is thriving.

So what is the problem? Who cares if stores close and shopping centers disappear? Well, online buying is solitary, while shopping at stores and shopping centers is social.

When individuals are solitary, they are more likely to become depressed and feel isolated. Even interacting with store clerks whom you do not know is psychologically more beneficial than existing alone in isolation.

Isolation tends to push individuals into their own limited perceptual consciousness—this is not good. Oftentimes, such an individual longing for human contact then goes back on the Internet and joins an Internet-generated social group. Unfortunately, these social media groups are too often extremist, paranoid, conspiratorial, or silly.

Isolated individuals make extremist groups powerful, and they make silly videos "go viral." So we see dangerous people emerge from extremist sites, and funny and silly individuals develop a huge following.

The faux social world of the Internet is definitely problematical.

In any case, in terms of the economic sphere, online buying, paying, banking, and stock speculation are creating new social configurations. Will stores survive? Will city centers become obsolete in terms of shopping? We do not know yet. Will suburban shopping centers survive? We do not know yet.

20.2.2 Banks, the Stock Market, and the Internet: New Forms of Money and Economic Transactions

First, there was barter: trading one commodity for something comparable but different. This went on for centuries.

Then, in Mesopotamia, among the Sumerians, money was invented. People had used shells and other decorative items as money—a medium of exchange—for eons. But when the Sumerians used metal bars—copper, silver, and gold—in standardized weights and measures, this caught on and spread rapidly throughout the Middle East, Europe, and Asia (2500 BCE).

Centuries later, around 400 BCE, the Lydians invented coined money. Coins stamped with the city or king's imprint and carefully weighted and measured for metallic purity replaced the metal bars: copper, silver, gold, and alloys of these metals still grounded the coins.

The Chinese invented paper money, but this did not really catch on until the nineteenth century in Europe and North America—and even then, it was backed up by hordes of gold and silver. Even today, Fort Knox, in the USA, and similar hordes in Switzerland back up paper money.

Then, in the twentieth century, checks issued by private and public banks began to replace paper money.

Then came the great credit card explosion, wherein plastic cards, not only acted to facilitate exchanges but also included bank loans—at high interest rates (if not paid off quickly—and most people did not pay them off quickly).

These credit cards have become digitized, such that they can stimulate computer-generated money transactions. And bank cards, linked to ATM machines, can now dispense money without any bank clerk necessary.

So plastic, digitized money and credit cards are now replacing paper money and checks.

But technology changes too quickly now. Hence, fully digitized transactions—requiring no credit or debit card—are now taking the place of the plastic currency.

This fully digitized money—Zelle, PayPal, and other computerized systems of money exchange—is occurring rapidly. Along with digitized plastic cards, this will be the new medium of exchange.

Of course, digitized money went to the next level with "cryptocurrency," like Bitcoin. However, this cryptocurrency, at the moment, has no backing, so it is not yet accepted as a medium of exchange but, instead, has become a commodity in itself that is traded like a stock with a variable value dependent on stock market dynamics rather than banking stability.

So the future of money—as a medium of exchange—is undoubtedly in the digital, computerized realm. But its exact form is not yet clear, and its backing—though not gold—must be stable and guaranteed by world governments.

Polanyi spoke of money as capital—money used to make more money. He called this kind of money a "false commodity." But, actually, money used to make more money is the basis of capitalism.

Here, however, we are discussing money not as capital but rather as a medium of exchange.

To conclude on this topic, banking, borrowing, purchasing, and all transactions related to money are now being dramatically altered by computer technology. We are just in the infancy of this dramatic change.

20.2.3 Computerized Stock Market Trading and Sports Betting

Stock market trading was once an esoteric phenomenon. A very small group of individuals—often with seats on the New York or London Stock Exchange—actively traded stocks and bonds. Occasionally, an unusual individual, such as George Soros or Warren Buffett, spent their time trading and, because they made huge fortunes, became Wall Street legends.

However, now in the twenty-first century, trading stocks online has been facilitated to a huge group of middle-class investors. Financial companies compete for this new market, offering all kinds of assistance to those who trade stocks on their platform.

This demonetarization of stock trading access is wonderful in principle. But, in actuality, it generates a casino mentality and acts as a high-class betting system.

Why? This is because these stock trading venues do not encourage stable, long-term investing strategies. Instead, they encourage speculation and the desire for a quick hit and a big win. The problem with this mentality is that the stock market is not predictable—analysts and traders get their predictions wrong as often as they get them right.

So a casino atmosphere ends up predominating, wherein some day traders make big bucks, while others lose. Warren Buffett is appalled by this new day-trading process, and he has encouraged investors not to do this kind of day-to-day trading. He encourages long-term, stable diversified investment strategies.

However, the new "demonetarized" trading platforms encourage speculation—day trading becomes an overwhelming mental absorption; it becomes gambling.

Thus, while it is good that stock market participation has been extended to vast numbers of the middle class, this process has produced two different phenomena: (1) the stable long-term investment of middle-class pension funds—401Ks, etc.—which has been good for the middle class, and (2) the day-trader phenomenon, which has led to a casino conception of the stock market, which can end up generating instability in the segment of the middle class engaging in risky stock trading.

And all of this can be accessed in one's own living room in one's own home with one's home computer.

As this day-to-day trading phenomenon became more popular, sports betting platforms emerged and gripped the working class sector of the population. Lacking the capital and skills for stock trading, the working class focused their betting on sports.

The working class knows sports—they have favorite teams and favorite players. They love to speculate on the outcomes of games. So sports betting companies created sports betting platforms for the working class—and for anyone and everyone who wants to bet on sports.

Sports betting is even bigger than day trading on the stock market. And like day trading, it encourages gambling, risk-taking, and the desire for an instant big hit.

Since a few people hit it big on sports apps—because they are set against the user and for the company—anger has increased among the working class. The more they gamble, the more they lose and the angrier they get. Already jealous of the college-educated middle class and already angry and confused by the social and cultural changes occurring, betting losses make the situation worse.

So to conclude here, the expansion of access to stock market trading is, in principle, a democratizing event. However, because winning at day trading is statistically difficult, a casino mentality is generated rather than a stable stock investment mentality.

This casino mentality is reinforced by the expansion of sports betting platforms by financial companies.

The result of both these factors is that the rich have gotten richer, while the middle class and the working class have not made any actual gains. This leads to class-based anger, which is generated not at the rich but rather at Blacks, women, gays, Jews, immigrants, and other minorities.

20.2.4 Business, Academic, and Social Meetings on Zoom

Meetings on Zoom, or any other computer platform, have created something wonderful and something terrible.

The wonderful part is that people from all over the world—in any country, city, or rural area—can meet with each other on their computers. They can see each other and talk to each other—amazing! But, of course, they are not with each other; they are actually isolated—alone with their computer screens. This is the terrible part.

The Wonderful Part of Zoom Meetings

It really is wonderful that an international corporation can hold meetings enabling their management teams in London, Paris, Hong Kong, Tokyo, New York, L.A., Toronto, and elsewhere to talk with each other.

They can see each other, interact with each other, and make joint decisions on policy and profit decisions, for instance.

Similarly, universities can offer classes emanating from their campuses to students all over the world. Professors and students can be anywhere in the world and meet together to learn.

The professor must be affiliated with a given university and vetted by it. But they can then teach the class from anywhere in the world. The students must be admitted to the university program and complete the assigned work, and they can be anywhere.

So a world academic community is being created, and even language differences can be overcome: in face-to-face Zoom classes, language skills are necessary, but in synchronous classes, language can be translated on screen to any language needed.

Further, social meetings—with friends or topical groups—can be done and are done online. This is wonderful as friendships can be maintained even when people move across the globe.

Of course, telephone contact has already allowed for such communication, but seeing friends on the computer screen raises the level of connection between individuals and groups.

Business, academic, and friendship meetings on the computer are truly wonderful. However, these are not actual meetings—they are real, but the individuals involved are isolated once the computer screen is turned off.

The joke that at a Zoom meeting one needs to be dressed only from the waist up shows the problem. The people and the meeting need to comply with only minimal social necessities. When the meeting is over, it is over. Groups cannot collect at the office coffeemaker, the student union, or the host's kitchen. The individuals are alone and isolated.

Isolation and aloneness are not good for humans. We are social animals—we emerged in our evolution in groups. Individuals who are isolated are more likely to become depressed, anxious, and paranoid.

Unfortunately, the latter mental stresses occur when individuals find themselves in isolation. The computer meetings on Zoom are not enough to stabilize human behavior.

So the new computerized meeting venues are wonderful—because they allow for global interaction—but terrible—because they contribute to individual isolation and loneliness.

Zoom Meetings and the Reorganization of Office Space and Urban Office Buildings

Is this the end of the era of great urban glass towers?

Think about it: the great glass towers are office buildings—but what if we do not need any offices anymore? All the prominent urban centers are business centers. Where once there were the palaces of kings and the churches of priests, now there are the skyscrapers of giant corporations.

Just as most of the palaces have become museums and many churches are tourist attractions, so, too, might giant office buildings become obsolete.

Why do we need giant office buildings if white-collar employees are going to be working from home on their computers?

Offices are becoming vacant all over the world. Companies like "We Work," which provided office space at rental prices, have gone out of business. Old office buildings are being abandoned and being turned into apartment dwellings. But this is not viable in many cases.

New office buildings are being reconfigured inside—the whole concept of an "office" is being reconfigured to fit computer meeting realities and computer transactional realities. Doing business and conducting meetings are all digitized now. So what should an office look like? Should there even be an office? Will the giant towers be abandoned like the kings' palaces?

If this happens, what is a city? If buying online kills stores and doing business online kills office buildings, will big cities be abandoned? Will suburban dwellings increase? Will the international movement of the middle class become normative if one can work from anywhere?

All these changes are occurring, but it is too soon to tell exactly what the new urban-suburban configuration will be. Also, it is too soon to tell where the global movement of the middle classes—who are in the business and academic world and the scientific world—will lead to.

20.3 Dating Online: Marriage, Fun, and Sexual Relationships

In modern mass-urban societies, it is difficult to meet people socially. People meet easily at high school and college, but as the average age of marriage has crept up to an incredible 30 years of age, it has become difficult for people to meet in the post-college world.

The workplace has young men and women in large numbers, but office etiquette has shifted: do not flirt with or date people you work with; it is too dangerous. You can be sued in court, you can be called before Human Resources, and you can be disciplined, so don't do it!

There are afterwork bars and restaurants, and those do facilitate social meetings. But in these settings, men and women are cautious and often put up defensive walls around themselves, preventing easy interactions between people who do not know each other.

Of course, friends and friendship groups facilitate introductions and allow for some vulnerability and openness. But even this process often falls short, leaving individuals lonely—lonely for love, sex, and companionship.

20.3.1 Enter Computer Dating Apps

Dating platforms can be divided into marriage sites, dating sites, and sex sites.

Marriage sites are fascinating in that in the USA, they are divided by religion, race, ethnicity, age, and more.

The most successful in the USA, at this moment, are religious marriage sites. So Christians look for Christians, Jews look for Jews, etc. And fundamentalist Christians look for each other, Orthodox Jews look for each other, and religious Catholics look for each other..

Religious marriage sites seem to be successful in hooking up like-minded individuals.

So, too, are age sites—especially over 60, senior citizen sites. We are living longer, and senior citizens who have lost a partner to death or divorce seem to want to try again. This occurs especially in senior sunbelt areas in America, but it occurs even in the big cities.

Seniors are very open to new marital or near-marital relationships, and they are finding them online.

The 20 or 30 somethings seem less able to commit and are more likely to use a dating app than a marriage app.

Dating apps do facilitate dating, but at the moment, such dating seems very unstable in that it is unlikely to lead to marriage but is likely to result in more dating.

The problem in this is that too much dating leads to cynicism—that is, a general mistrust of the opposite sex and a good deal of negative stereotyping about all men or all women or the girls today or the guys today—you fill it in; it has tended to be negative.

The older the 30 somethings become, the more the negativity sets in.

What of sex websites?

We are living in an open era of sexuality. There is still some stigma on women who "fool around" too much, but none on the men. The women still run the risk of being thought of as "sluts," while the men are "Don Juans." However, the negative stigma is not so strong as to prevent women from having sex with different guys they are dating.

So sex apps are popular, but they do not lead to permanent relationships in most cases. Therefore, though it can be fun if the vibes are right, in the long run, it is not satisfying to most individuals. And, of course, there are those sexual encounters wherein the vibes are not in sync at all, and the experience is unsatisfying in terms of sex itself, to say nothing of relationships.

Given the often isolating nature of modern urban societies and the late marriage pattern emerging globally among college-educated men and women, marriage, dating, and sex websites could become an integral part of modern social life, providing a way of finding one's love or one's life partner or just providing a way for a sex-hungry couple to "hook up."

As with so many of these technological changes, there are both positive and negative elements involved, and these changes are so new that we cannot yet fully evaluate their impact.

20.4 The Effect of Internet Technology on the Political Sphere

20.4.1 Fake News, Conspiracy Theories, and Foreign Interventions in Democratic Elections

In an earlier book entitled *Can Democracy Survive in the twenty-first Century?* (Springer, Heidelberg, 2020), I present a detailed analysis of the effect of these new Internet platforms on the political process. Here, in this book, which details the global transformations that are occurring, I wish to emphasize the enormous impact that these new alternative news sources have on the electoral process of modern democracy.

We should remember that prior to the Internet, with newspapers, radio, and microphones, violent movements with conspiratorial worldviews and scapegoated minority groups did emerge—they did not need the Internet to succeed.

Fascism and communism spread worldwide, and violent charismatic leaders, such as Mussolini, Hitler, and Mao, succeeded in creating totalitarian dictatorships that had an impact on their own countries and the global political landscape.

Thus, what is now occurring on Facebook, X (Twitter), TikTok, podcasts, and blogs is not new. Newspapers and radio produced their share of extremism—right-wing and left-wing political figures gained enormous followings, and they pushed people toward violent political acts.

What is worse now is that the reach of these Internet political platforms is wider than earlier media reach—every corner of the globe is absorbed into the mass communications networks that pervade our computers, tablets, and smartphones.

Also, the immediacy of news flashes is greater than ever—everyone knows everything about everybody almost instantly.

However, since the world political culture is very much aware of the earlier era of fascism, communism, totalitarianism, and violent dictatorial dominations, the present generation—especially the college-educated generation—is actively attempting to prevent a return to autocracy, violence, and genocidal behavior that occurred from the World War I era into the post-World War II era.

Because of this historical memory, we have today both the reemergence of extremism in the political sphere and a concerted effort to prevent this extremism from coming to fruition in new neo-fascist and neo-Stalinist movements.

Therefore, though Hungary's neo-fascism and Venezuela's neo-Stalinism have occurred, Western European and American democracies are trying to prevent their spread. Unfortunately, they could not prevent Putin from re-Stalinizing Russia or Xi from re-Mao-izing China. But the Western democracies are actively attempting to stop the spread of dictatorial government and to counteract the extremism found on Internet political platforms.

Unfortunately, pressing in the opposite direction, Russia, China, North Korea, and Iran are actively hacking into the Internet and attempting to undermine Western democracy in every nation in which elections are occurring.

It is a veritable Internet war—a war of words and images, fake news, and virulent conspiracy theories—images are falsified—faces attached to naked bodies in scandalous positions; words are falsified—the big lie—whatever it pertains to—is repeated over and over again until it is believed by a large portion of the population—such as the Trump election was stolen—he really defeated Biden; or, all the immigrants are murderers, rapists, drug dealers and infected with diseases—they will poison our blood—Trump got this from one of Hitler's speeches.

So these new technologies emerging on the Internet have generated extremist movements globally: "populism" in Europe, which is a reaction against immigration from the Middle East and Africa, and gay liberation movement and women's liberation. Also, Islamic terrorist movements in most of the Islamic countries, generated against the USA, Britain, and France who had been dominating the Arab nations and Iran; and against women's liberation and gay liberation as well.

Both populism and Islamicism have been spread and reinforced by Internet political platforms, and since everyone has a smartphone, these movements become personal and immediate to those who join in. Populist rallies and Islamicist attacks are easily coordinated through the use of smartphones—these minicomputers are ubiquitous globally.

20.4.2 The Good News About Political Platforms on the Internet

While extremism is definitely encouraged and energized on the Internet, so, too, is democratic participation.

Voting percentages are up in most of the world's democracies. Women and Blacks are participating fully in new democratic political processes.

More people, more women, more Blacks, and more minorities—such as the Indians and Pakistanis in the UK—are running for office and winning. Women have been prime ministers in Norway, Denmark, Germany, New Zealand, and the UK. Nikki Haley—a Sikh, the child of Indian immigrants, and a woman—is running for President of the United States.

Political awareness and political sophistication are as broad a phenomenon as political extremism.

So both the frightening increase of political extremism and fake news conspiracies and the wonderful increase in democratic sophistication have occurred through the new Internet mass media of communications.

All of this is very new in terms of its playing out on the Internet, but it is not new in the sense that it did occur before during the era of radio, newspapers, and microphones (for mass rallies).

At this moment in history—2024—the world's democracies are rallying against the world's dictatorships in a war of words and images playing out on the Internet.

We do not yet know who will win this Internet war—it is a new "Cold War" but with hot images and inflammatory words.

Charismatic right-wing and left-wing movements have been generated globally. Yet all of these right-wing movements—populism, Islamicism, "Putinism," and "Xi Jinpingism"—look to the past. Populism wants women and gays to go back in the closet and disappear or become subservient; Islamicism wants to recreate the caliphate, the Islamic theocratic kingship of the Middle Ages; Putin wants to recreate the lost Soviet Union; and Xi Jinping wants to recreate Mao's China.

All these extremist movements want to return to the past, and all are violent.

The democratic movement wants to lead the world to a future of nonviolent, rational-legal politics with social justice for women, gays, Blacks, and other minorities and with a humanistic ethic that asserts that every human life is meaningful and must be cared for.

This rational, humanistic, and democratic set of political ideals has been just as successful as the violent autocratic political ethos, wherein human life is counted as worthless and mass murder and martyrdom are accepted as part of the political process.

20.5 Conclusions on the New Technology and Its Impact on the Political Sphere

New Internet platforms—social media platforms, podcasts, blogs, and videos—can be used to enhance democracy: constituencies become better informed, and political participation has been increasing, both in voting and in running for office.

But the Internet can also be used as part of enhanced surveillance in order to create an even more total version of totalitarianism than existed under Nazism or Stalinism. Xi Jinping is moving China in this direction.

The competition between democracy and dictatorship is occurring globally, and we shall see where the "Big Blue Marble" spins us. Here, we are on the brink of space travel, and nothing on Earth has been resolved.

Technological changes and innovations are coming on fast and furiously. They are changing everything. They are altering the workplace, the shopping malls, the shape of cities, our workspace relationships, and our personal relationships—every aspect of modern life is being impacted and changed by this technological explosion that has occurred in the twenty-first century.

We cannot live without our cell phones and computers, and we want them and everything that comes with them.

So we will have to deal with both the good and the bad effects that they have on our social existence.

We are *Homo sapiens*; we are the species that has consciousness and can create an ever-advancing technology. This technology will take us to the stars—if we do not destroy ourselves with it first.

But even if we survive and we go to the stars, we still must study and try to understand the effect that the new technology is having on our social lives.

Humans, given our ability to be aware of our own death and our own life, will never be fully "happy." Therefore, we must study what it is that makes us anxious, depressed, unstable, and disturbed. We also need to study what makes us feel secure, hopeful, stable, and optimistic.

We humans evolve—not only in terms of technological improvements but also in terms of scientific knowledge and ethics.

Thus, the Aztecs did not have the wheel—but they also lacked a humanistic ethic as they indulged in human sacrifice on a mass scale. And, oh yes, they did not know the cause of the diseases that would almost annihilate them.

This is not meant to denigrate the Aztecs. Cortez said that Mexico City was larger and more beautiful than Madrid. This is said to remind us that we humans—*Homo sapiens*—evolve: technologically, scientifically, and morally.

Part VII
Our Place in the Universe

Chapter 21
The Universe and Our Place in it

21.1 Human Beings Create a Scientific Stock of Knowledge

As human beings, we have been able, through our intelligence and our ability to create a growing stock of knowledge[1]—especially rational-scientific knowledge—to create the Webb telescope.

Humans have been looking at the sky and mapping it, and wondering about it, for millennia.

21.1.1 The Ancient Priesthood's Map of the Sky

The ancient priesthoods of Samaria, Babylonia, Egypt, India, China, and the Maya—given leisure time by the agricultural abundance—brilliantly mapped out what they could see with the naked eye. They created calendars and were able to predict the movements of the sun and the moon, to herald eclipses, and to describe the movements of the stars in the night sky. Without the aid of a telescope, they were able to amass an amazing amount of knowledge.

Of course, they had no idea why the universe they were mapping exists—and neither do we. So along with their great skill at calendar making, predictions, and tracking the movements of objects in the sky, ancient priesthoods put forth theological explanations for the creation of the universe and its functioning.

The ancient priesthoods in Sumer, Babylonia, and China also created astrology. This was an attempt to link human behavior and personality to the constellation of stars under which an individual was born.

---

[1] Peter Berger and Luckmann, *The Social Construction of Reality*, NY, Random House, 1970.

R. M. Glassman, *The Great Global Transformation*, Contributions to Political Science, https://doi.org/10.1007/978-3-031-90566-7_21

The astrological "signs" are a rational attempt to predict human behavior as linked to the careful mapping of the stars and planets. The concurrent constellation of the stars was supposed to predict happenings in human lives.

Though rational, this is not a successful avenue of collective human wisdom. Astronomy, psychology, sociology, and other social sciences would replace astrology in the modern rational-scientific worldview.

Further, as magnificent as the descriptive and predictive knowledge created by the ancient priesthoods was, the theological explanations are disappointing. All the explanations are simply projections from our own human experiences.

The first theologies were very primitive: the universe is created from an egg by the great Cackler, a female goddess; the universe is masturbated into existence by a male god; a male and female godly couple copulated the universe into existence; or the Sky God, a male, and the Earth Goddess, a female, together brought forth the universe in sexual union.

Then various forms of the father god were projected to have created the universe and to watch over it, controlling all human and nonhuman actions and occurrences.

Freud[2] has it right: lacking the understanding of why the universe—and why we human beings—exist, the ancient priesthoods and the people under their control projected that father gods and mother goddesses controlled the universe. Superhuman humanoid gods and goddesses controlled all the actions in the universe.

Now, as unhelpful as these explanations are, we must understand that in ancient civilizations, the priesthood generated codes of humanistic ethics. That is, codes for ethical human behavior were developed in Sumer, Babylonia,[3] Egypt, India, China,[4] and other ancient civilizations so that even though the explanations for the creation of the universe were projections, the moral codes produced led to the improvement of human relationships in large-scale human societies.

I have already discussed the development of humanistic ethics, which reached its ancient zenith with the Ten Commandments and the Jewish biblical insistence on the sacredness of human life—every human life.[5]

For now, let us continue our discussion of the description of the universe produced in the ancient world.

As highlighted, pre-Socratic Greek philosophers collected information on the universe from Babylon and Egypt.

---

[2] Sigmund Freud, *Moses and Monotheism*, New York: Vintage Books, 1961.

[3] The Code of Hammurabi.

[4] Confucius, *The Analects*, NY, Amazon, 2000.

[5] Jewish Bible, Genesis, Ten Commandments.

21.1.2 The Pre-Socratic Greek Philosophers Create Science

From Thales to Anaximander to Heraclitus to Pythagoras and then to Aristotle and beyond and to Aristarchus and Ptolemy, the Greeks developed a rational-scientific and mathematical description—and a predictive system—for understanding the universe.[6]

The Greeks still had no telescope, but they improved the mathematization of the predictive process. And their descriptions became more accurate in terms of the movements of the planets and the moon.

By the Hellenistic period, in Alexandria, the Greek scientists were even creating moving models of the solar system. Of course, Ptolemies' models had the earth at the center and the sun and the planets revolving around earth. The Aristarchus model had the sun at the center and all the planets, including earth, moving around the sun.

The Hellenistic mathematics became so sophisticated that the predictability of the Greek astronomers was greatly improved over the previous priestly calculations.

The Greeks viewed the solar system as a beautiful phenomenon—that is, the planets and the moon moved in aesthetically lovely circles or eclipses, and their movements were regular, smooth, and predictable. Pythagoras called it "the music of the spheres"—the planets, as perfect spheres,[7] moving in rhythm like human music and dancing. Pythagoras had discovered the mathematics of the chords—chords of music that produced a harmonious sound. He projected the harmony of human music into the movement of the planets—hence "the music of the spheres."

Aristotle reiterated the view that the universe could be understood through improved observation and mathematization and that it was our job as thinking human beings to increase our knowledge of the universe. And to Aristotle, the universe was a beautiful thing, and the movement of the planets was so regular and perfect that he referred to such movements as "the music of the spheres"—reiterating Pythagoras' motion of the "the music of the spheres."

So to the Greek philosophers, the universe was beautiful and the movements regular—the planets and the stars appeared as a rhapsody of mathematically regulated splendor.

But, of course, the ancients had no telescopes.

To the naked eye, the night sky is exciting and beautiful, and the occasional shooting star is exhilarating.

But Greek science, which brought the knowledge of the entire ancient world to its fruition, was shut off by the rise of Christianity. The death of Hypatia in the hands of the bishop of North Africa signaled the end of the Hellenistic astronomy

---

[6] John Burnet, in Early Greek Philosophy, Google Books, 2000.

[7] Ibid., on Pythagoras.

school—as well as the death of the mini women's liberation movement, which had some impact in ancient Greece, with Plato being its greatest advocate.[8]

21.1.3 *The Arabic Golden Age and the Revival of Greek Science*

It was not until the Arabic Golden Age, 600 years later, that astronomy, mathematics, and science in general was revived and extolled.

With Avicenna[9] and Averroes,[10] science was revived. The writings of the Greeks were translated into Arabic and, even Spanish Jews, such as Maimonides,[11] read the Greek treatises and expanded upon them.

Though the Arabic-speaking scientists (and the Persian-speaking scientists) made great gains in mathematics and physiology, it was not until the Italian Renaissance that the real breakthroughs in astronomy would occur.

21.1.4 *Galileo[12] and Renaissance Science*

The telescope was invented and perfected in Italy and the Netherlands, allowing for a better view of the solar system.

Enter Copernicus[13] and Galileo. Copernicus used advanced mathematics to prove that the earth rotated around the sun—he proved what Aristarchus had already theorized but which Ptolemy had rejected. Copernicus was clever enough to publish his theory posthumously so that the Church in Rome would not condemn him.

Galileo had a telescope—he did not invent it, but he did improve it. With the telescope, he saw the planets and the moon more closely than ever before. His findings were spectacular—even seeing the rings of Saturn for the first time.

Of course, Galileo did get into trouble with the Roman Catholic Church, but his notebooks—including his sketches of the solar system—went North to France, the Netherlands, Germany, Scandinavia, and England.

---

[8] Plato, *The Republic*, London, Penguin Classes, 1950. Women were to be fully liberated in Plato's ideal republic.

[9] Ibn Sina (Avicenna), Philosophy in the Arabic Golden Age, NY, Amazon, 2013.

[10] Ibn Rushd (Averroes), Philosophy in the Arabic Golden Age, NY, Amazon, 2013.

[11] Moses Maimonides, *The Guide for the Perplexed*, NY, Amazon, 2014.

[12] Galileo, *Notebooks*, NY, Amazon, 2010.

[13] Copernicus, Sun Centered System, *The Motion of the Sphere*, expanded from Aristarchus of Ancient Greece.

From that time onward, astronomy, utilizing ever-improved telescopes and mathematics, mapped out the solar system, then the Milky Way Galaxy, and, finally, all nearby galaxies.[14]

But it was not until the building of the Hubble telescope, and then the Webb telescope, that astronomers gained a view of the entire visible universe.

21.2 The View from the Hubble and Webb Telescopes and Our Modern Conception of the Universe

The ancients were able to map the night sky and locate all the visible stars and planets. All the ancient priesthoods—the Babylonians, the Egyptians, the Chinese, the Maya, and the Hindu Brahmins—created calendars that were accurate. They also attempted to link the movements of the stars to human activities. Astrology was put forth in the Middle East, India, and China. Astrology, however, has little potential for predicting human behavior.

As mentioned, the Greeks created the rational and mathematical approach to understanding the universe. Astronomy replaced astrology as the Greek approach to understanding the universe, and it was astronomy that was improved during the Arabic Golden Age (900–1300 CE) and the European Renaissance (1200–1800 CE).

Astronomy took off (pardon the pun) as a full-fledged science from the Enlightenment to the present.

Now, with the Webb telescope, we have entered a new phase of astronomy, simply because we are seeing so much more of the universe than ever before.

21.2.1 An Infinite Universe in Constant Turmoil

What we see from the Webb telescope is a seemingly infinite number of galaxies in every direction we point it to. Billions of galaxies housing billions of stars are visible in every direction. And the farther the telescope picks up images, the more galaxies it finds.

Now, since in every direction we see a seeming infinity of galaxies, the earth, from our perspective, is at the center of the universe!

Of course, there is no center to an infinite universe, but for all practical purposes, we—human beings—are at the center of the universe. No, we are not at the center of the solar system. The sun, obviously, is at the center of the solar system. However, the solar system is in the Milky Way Galaxy, which is one of an infinite number of galaxies in a seemingly infinite universe of space—or dark matter; astronomers do not yet know whether dark matter and dark energy actually exist.

[14] Tycho Brahe and others.

Given the infinity, the earth is our center of the universe, unless some other kind of coordinates prove more useful.

21.2.2 Are We the Only Beings in the Universe Who Know We Are in the Universe?

There are billions of life forms on earth, but human beings—*Homo sapiens*—are the only life form on earth that has consciousness of ourselves in the universe.

Given the infinite nature of the universe, it would seem likely that other conscious beings exist somewhere. However, at the moment, no other conscious beings have been found. Of course, we have not gone out of our solar system, so we actually do not know. But the Hubble and Webb telescopes have shown us a barren universe—so far—with no life forms visible. And remember that of the billions of life forms on earth, none have enough consciousness to know that they exist and that they exist in a seemingly infinite universe. Mammals, like elephants, dolphins, and dogs, have consciousness and can be interacted with intelligently. But they do not have enough consciousness to be self-conscious of themselves in the universe.

21.3 What Are We Seeing Through the Lens of the Webb Telescope?

We are seeing galaxies of stars swirling around black holes—which we can identify because their event horizon is lit up even though they are dark.

The galaxies are all moving rapidly. And galaxies do sometimes collide, causing gigantic explosions and the destruction of stars and planets and solar systems.

But in the galaxies are gases, and from these gases, new stars are formed and new planets as well. So there is destruction, and there is regeneration. And these are processes that astronomers can understand and describe—both chemically and mathematically.

21.3.1 Everything Is Moving: Heraclitus[15] Got it Right

Heraclitus, a pre-Socratic philosopher in ancient Greece, said that everything is in flux; everything is always changing—"the sane man cannot step into the same river twice, because it is neither the same man nor the same river."

---

[15] John Burnet, in Early Greek Philosophy (Heraclitus), Google Books, 2000.

And, of course, the man gets older, and the river flows—it is not the same man on the same water.

So, too, the universe—everything is in flux, everything is moving, and everything is changing.

Think about this: we feel like we are sitting quietly in a library while we are writing this treatise. But actually, the earth is rotating on its axis, the earth is rotating around the sun, the solar system is moving rapidly in the Milky Way Galaxy, the Milky Way Galaxy is rotating around a giant black hole, the whole galaxy is moving in space or dark matter, and all the galaxies are moving rapidly—moving away from each other. Is the universe expanding? Or are the galaxies moving more randomly? They do crash into one another.

In any case, everything is moving and everything is in flux—always changing.

21.3.2 Is the Big Bang Theory a Theory of Creation?

Astronomers, physicists, mathematicians, and other cosmologists have produced the most wonderful theory about the origin of the universe. They have described the movement of creation as "the Big Bang," and they have then described every nanosecond after the Big Bang and what occurred in that time slot.[16]

The Big Bang theory and the description of its aftermath are a magnificent set of theories of descriptions and mathematical formulas. This is magnificent physics because it gives scientists an incredible understanding of how the universe works. And using mathematical formulas, astronomers can predict and understand events that have been beyond our comprehension.

At the atomic level, the subatomic level, and the microatomic level—from the tiniest particle—the quark?—to the most gigantic black hole, modern astronomers have produced a profound understanding of the universe. They will get us to Mars and beyond, and they could blow us off the face of the earth with hydrogen bombs. But is the Big Bang theory a theory of the creation of the universe?

Follow this description presented most familiarly by Hawking in his book *A Brief History of Time*.[17]

In the beginning, the entire universe—all the energy and all the matter—existed as a "singularity," a tiny point containing all the energy in the universe and all matter of the entire universe. Then the pressure was so great that the singularity exploded. The Big Bang occurred, and space and time occurred with it. Before the Big Bang, the singularity existed in no space and no time.

As we have acknowledged from the first nanosecond onward, the Big Bang theory is magnificent.

However, let us go back to the "singularity."

---

[16] Stephen Hawking on the *Big Bang Theory*, *A Brief History of Time*, 1988.

[17] Ibid.

How did the singularity get where it was? How was it created? Stephen Hawking does not know, and he falls back on … maybe it was God?

Since the Big Bang theory depends on the already-existing "singularity," it is not a theory of creation. Who created the singularity, how did it get there, where did it exist if there was no space, and where did it exist if there was no time?

21.3.3 Is There a Creator God?

Xenophanes,[18] another pre-Socratic Greek philosopher, said that if Ethiopians had a god, they would have dark skin and curly hair, and the lions would create a lion-god. So we Greeks have invented Greek-looking gods—none of whom exist.

Freud theorized that we project a father god or a mother god from our unconscious desire to be parented and protected.[19]

There is no humanoid god; Sartre[20] is correct—"god is dead, we are alone in the universe."

Looking through the lens of the Webb telescope, tell me what kind of a god would create the universe that we are seeing?

We are seeing billions of galaxies with billions of stars, black holes, comets, asteroids, space rocks, explosions, and generations of stars, all moving in a rapid and spectacular fashion.

But there is no music in these spheres! Unlike Pythagoras and Aristotle, who thought that the planets revolve smoothly around the sun and that the universe is beautiful—almost musical—in its movements, and unlike Greek philosophers, we see a chaotic universe whose movements are understandable but frightening—frightening because there is so much destruction in it; black holes swallow everything that moves near, galaxies collide, stars explode in supernovas; and other stars are newly formed.

Some of the images we see are beautiful—gloriously colored galaxies and star systems. Some are grey and frigid like the rocks on Jupiter's moons.

And the very size of it all is daunting.

What kind of anthropomorphic god would create this?

Democritus said that the gods and goddesses do not exist, and the human soul dies with the body. So all we have is the here and now, and we must learn to enjoy our life—for it is short.[21] Democritus did *not* say go for all the pleasure you can. He, like most Greek philosophers, believed that all things must be done in *moderation*. Any good done in excess becomes evil.

---

[18] John Burnet, in Early Greek Philosophy (Xenophanes), Google Books, 2000.

[19] Sigmund Freud, Moses and Monotheism, New York: Vintage Books, 1961.

[20] Jean Paul Sartre, *Being and Nothingness*, NY, Amazon 2012.

[21] Democritus formulated the atomic theory with Leucippus and advocated for democracy and rational Philosophy.

So pleasure, yes, but in moderation.[22]

In the Renaissance, German philosophers—after the Protestant Reformation—said god created the universe, and like a clockmaker, once the universe was created, he stepped back from it and just let it tick.

The clockmaker philosophers, however, still envisioned the universe as regular and beautiful—the movement of the clock was like the music of the spheres.

The Webb telescope does not show us any music or anything like a smooth-running clock. We are seeing chaos in infinite, changing, swirling confusion.

No humanoid god could create chaos—gods are supposed to create *order* from chaos. But we are seeing chaos. However, our scientists can understand it. They understand it on every level—from the subatomic to the enormously large.

The question is, does this universe that the Webb telescope is showing us have any *meaning*?

The answer is no, there is no meaning—that is, no human meaning and, therefore, no humanoid godly meaning.

So we are alone in a meaningless universe.

Jean-Paul Sartre believed that this was wonderful. Free of all moral and cultural constraints, we humans could now determine our own destiny. *Existentialism* was born. We humans can choose our own destiny.[23]

Yes, but can we do anything we want, or are there ethical constraints on our behavior?

I will assert that there should be humanistic ethics constraining our existential freedom, such that we are free to maximize our life chances, but we are not free to hurt other human beings in doing so.

I will come back to a discussion of humanistic ethics, but, first, a few more comments about the universe as seen through the lens of the Webb telescope.

Aristotle said that he did not know how the universe was created, but we must study it as if it has always been here and always will be here.

So we do not know whether the universe burst forth from a singularity with a Big Bang.

We do know that the universe is here. And with the help of better and better telescopes, we can see more and more of it.

The universe has no human meaning, and we do not know why we are here or why we are the ones who have the consciousness of being here. All we can do is try to regulate human life in a humanistic way.

---

[22] Epicurus on pleasure. Epicurus believed that the soul died with the body (contra Plato), so enjoy life now. Seek pleasure in *moderation* and avoid pain. The Stoics believed that the soul lived on and people should withhold pleasure and live a moral life.

[23] Jean-Paul Sartre, *No Exit*.

So far, though we have consciousness, we have not been able to overcome our animal heritage of aggression, territoriality, violence, and irrationality. We still invade, we still kill, and we still live with tribal-like identities and hate the "other."

Can we overcome our animal heritage[24] and become fully human? Or are we cursed to be aware of ourselves destroying each other and the planet?

---

[24] Conrad Lorenze, *On Aggression*, NY, Amazon, 2012.

Chapter 22
Can Humanistic Ethics Predominate on the Big Blue Marble?

22.1 Human Beings as Both Animal and Human

Humans emerged as an animal species, with all the instincts and drives that animals exhibit. Then at some point in hominoid evolution, our level of consciousness reached a new level. Yuval Noah Harari[1] calls this "moment" the "cognitive revolution."

At the moment of the cognitive revolution, our consciousness of ourselves, others, and the world around us reached a new level. Mammals, like elephants and dolphins, have consciousness—they can recognize themselves in the mirror; they care for others like themselves; and they become upset when one of their own kind dies.

However, they do not have enough consciousness, and they do not have language, so they cannot communicate at our level, and they cannot build up a stock of knowledge based on experience. Therefore, their level of consciousness does not increase, whereas the human level of consciousness does increase as we build upon our growing stock of knowledge.

It is not that our level of consciousness increases; it is that our knowledge of ourselves and the world increases. We humans—throughout our history—have learned more about ourselves and our world. We are seeing more and more of the universe, and we are learning more and more about our physiology and our psychology.

Hegel, though his work is often opaque, obscure, and proto-fascist, had the intensity to take on the development of human self-consciousness. In his *Lectures on the Philosophy of History*,[2] Hegel describes the stages of human history in terms of the

[1] Yuval Noah Harari, *Sapiens: A Brief History of Humankind*, 2011.

[2] George Hegel, *The Philosophy of History*, NY Amazon, 2011.

R. M. Glassman, *The Great Global Transformation*, Contributions to Political Science, https://doi.org/10.1007/978-3-031-90566-7_22

development of increasing the consciousness of self. Each stage of history has its own worldview, or Zeitgeist, in which human development progressively improved.

Let us look at Hagel's stages of history.

22.2 Hegel's Stages of History and the Progressive Improvement of Human Self-Consciousness

Harari, in his book *Sapiens*, makes it appear that once humans gained cognitive superiority over other living creatures, our domination of the globe was guaranteed. However, it is not that simple, for, along with the superior intelligence that the cognitive revolution gave human beings, came an increasing awareness of death, suffering, and injustices. Awareness of the future brought with it knowledge of our own imminent death, while awareness of the past brought remembrances of those who had already died.

So the cognitive revolution brought with it fear and anxiety, along with heightened intelligence and superior planning ability.

The existential anxiety about our own death generated fear of nature and religious explanations surrounding the fear of nature.

In Hegel's view, this first stage of human existence, the stage he called "primitive religion," revolved around our fear of all the forces of nature: the fear of storms, diseases, volcanoes, floods, and more.

The "naked apes," or early hominoids and *Homo sapiens*, could do little in the face of nature's fury. So humans projected spiritual powers upon the natural world—the spirits of nature, with wills of their own, as well as good spirits and bad spirits—spirits that helped us and spirits that destroyed us. These were projected onto nature. And these spirits were all out of our control and, as yet, beyond our understanding.

According to Hegel, humans felt insignificant as compared to nature and the world of spirits. Therefore, human self-worth was at a low level, and human self-consciousness brought as much fear and anxiety for humans as it did survival benefits.

It was not until the agricultural revolution and the emergence of what Hegel called "Oriental empires" that human self-consciousness gained self-confidence.

Now, Harari, in *Sapiens,* thinks that the agricultural revolution was the worst trick ever played on humans because 90 percent of humans were subjugated, while 10 percent—the aristocracy and priesthood—gained all the benefits—all the luxury goods, all the power, and all the prestige.[3]

Harari, of course, is correct. However, he misses Hegel's point, which is that with the agricultural revolution and the Oriental empires, humans gained a good deal of control over nature.

---

[3]Yuval Noah Harari, *Sapiens: A Brief History of Humankind*, 2011.

With a surplus of food generated from grain production and storage and the subsequent domestication of animals, generating a whole new source of meat and dairy products, the sheer number of *Homo sapiens* went from thousands to millions, and even though those millions were oppressed and exploited, they no longer lived in fear of the natural world.

The world of spirits became anthropomorphized—the good and bad spirits became humanoid gods and goddesses.

So now it was the sky god copulating with the earth goddess or the sun god bringing warmth to life or the moon goddess bringing fertility to women.

The gods and goddesses embodied nature but were now seen as more playful and more human, if still destructive and often malevolent.

Thus, human self-consciousness improved. Humans lived in nature but could control nature to some extent. Humans could create irrigation and control river flooding—even though they were still afraid of great floods. Humans could dominate other animals and put them to work—even though they were still afraid of diseases. And humans lived longer, and more of their children survived.

So Harari is correct that 90 percent of the population was subjugated and denigrated. But they were surviving by the millions and becoming the dominant species on earth.

Still, according to Hegel—and Harari—any given human life was not worth much. Human life was cheap and expendable.

However, the emerging belief that the human "soul" lives on beyond the body helped alleviate the existential fear of death, which the cognitive revolution had ushered in along with our heightened intelligence.

Therefore, "Oriental religion"—as exhibited in Egypt, Babylon, India, and Taoist China, improved the human conception of the self. Human self-consciousness was raised to a higher level than it was during the primitive religion stage.

The next stage, according to Hegel, is dual development: that is, (1) there is the emergence of the Jewish humanistic ethos, emerging from Judaic monotheism and its Ten Commandments, and (2) there was the rise of rational-scientific thought in ancient Greece.

Let us look at these separately.

22.3 Jewish Monotheism and the Humanistic Ethics of the Ten Commandments and the Talmud

It says in the Talmud—and this is quoted over and over again by Jewish Rabbis—"To save one life, to save of mankind."

Every life is important because every life is sacred because humans are made in God's image; male and female—they are made in God's image.[4]

[4] Jewish Bible, Creation.

Since humans are godlike, every life is sacred.

This is very different from Oriental religions wherein it was believed that the soul lives on beyond the body, so "this life" is not important. In Judaism—and Hegel recognized this—it is "this life," not the afterlife, that is important.

According to Hegel, human self-consciousness reaches a new level with Judaism because every life is sacred and every individual is important. Human self-worth is reinforced because of this new belief.

Thus, ethical humanism is born with Judaism, and it is carried by Judaism all through the diaspora period and into the modern world.

We shall have more to say about this, but, first, let us look at other portions of the new Zeitgeist: Greek rational science.

22.4 The Pre-Socratic Philosophers and the Creation of the Rational-Scientific Worldview

Hegel was discussing what appeared to be the stages of religious development—primitive religion," "Oriental religion," and then monotheistic, moralistic Judaism.

But, Hegel was really trying to understand the stages of human consciousness of self, beginning with very little self-worth and a terrifying fear of the forces of nature and a huge human population expansion, but with any given individual human life expendable, and finally, to Judaism wherein each individual life was held at sacred, and the human consciousness of self was greatly improved.

But what were these terrifying forces of nature—the world of frightening spirits? During the Oriental religious period and the Judaic period that emerged from it, the forces of nature were partially controlled, and human beings flourished as never before—as mentioned, *Homo sapiens'* numbers went from thousands to millions.

The forces of nature, though better controlled, were not really understood.

So Hegel was correct to jump over to the Greek world, wherein pre-Socratic philosophers were attempting to understand the basic elements of the natural world and wherein they were attempting to predict the movements of natural objects through mathematical formulations.

This is not the place for a history of science—we have presented that. I just wish to reiterate Hegel's notion that the Greeks created a new Zeitgeist—a new worldview: the rational-scientific worldview.

From Thales—who is credited with pioneering the scientific schools of thought—the quest for the basic elemental substance from which all other substances are made began.

Thales took the works of Egyptian, Babylonian, and Persian priests, who posited that "fire, air, earth, and water" are the potential basic elements.

This school of thought culminated with the words of Leucippus and Democritus, both of whom posited that an unknown substance—a tiny particle, the smallest uncuttable particle—the atom—is the basic substance from which all other substances are made.

Thales founded something else as well. He urged his students to disagree and to develop different theories as to what made nature tick. He encouraged them to propose different hypotheses and to seek empirical proof to sustain them.

This eventuated in the scientific method: observation, experimentation, and mathematization.

As to mathematization, we are coming to Pythagoras, of course.

The Pythagorean theory relating to triangles had been known for thousands of years before Pythagoras' era. In Babylon, it was used to make more precise buildings. The Egyptians also used geometry to create nearly perfect pyramids and palaces.

Pythagoras, however, used mathematics—beginning with geometry—to understand the distances and movements of the planets and other objects in the universe.

Thales had already brought Egyptian geometry to Miletus and was already teaching it to his disciples. But Pythagoras took it to the next level, believing that numbers were the key to understanding the universe and all the movements within it.

Pythagoreans figured out how to measure everything—the circumference of the earth, its distance to the moon, and more. They created formulas for predicting the movements of the planets and the moon.

To sum up, the scientific method of observation, experimentation, and mathematization was developed, along with the idea of hypotheses and theories, which could and should be challenged and changed depending on new findings or improved mathematics.

According to Hegel, this rational-scientific worldview gave human beings a new self-confidence, for, then, humans were learning how the universe works and were even predicting its movements.

Putting together the Judaic celebration of every individual life with Greek rational-science, Hegel declared that human beings had reached a higher stage of self-consciousness and self-confidence.

Hegel then jumped over the Arabic Golden Age and the Italian Renaissance and went directly to German Protestant Christianity and contemporary science.

He asserted correctly that in German Protestant Christianity, the individual is even more emphasized than in Judaism because Luther had asserted that every Christian—male and female—had to be educated enough to read scripture and to interpret scripture on their own. No Pope, no cardinals, no bishops, no priests, and, of course, no rabbis could interpret scripture for the Protestant Christian.

Individualism became heightened with Protestantism. So the individual was not only valued, as in Judaism, but the individual was encouraged to *excel* in all their endeavors as well.

I will come back to modern science and its role in the twenty-first-century Zeitgeist. First, I wish to show that Hegel's emphasis on Protestant individualism was well taken, for it eventually led to twentieth-century existentialism and to Maslow's idea of self-actualization.

22.5 From Hegel to Sartre and Maslow

22.5.1 Protestant Individualism

Individualism was made central in Luther's Protestant Christianity. According to Luther, every individual Christian—male or female—had to be educated enough to read the Bible on their own. No priest, no bishop, no cardinal, or no Pope could interpret scripture—the individual Christian had to interpret the Bible on their own.

Hegel is correct that this encouraged individual self-consciousness, and it made every individual important.

Max Weber expanded this notion when he insisted that the "Protestant ethic" engendered the "spirit of capitalism,"[5] for capitalism—which emerged in the Protestant countries of England, Scotland, and the Netherlands—encouraged individualism. However, capitalism encourages selfish individualism—that is, every individual is supposed to compete with every other individual, and the winning businessman takes all the profit for himself (or herself). No sharing of wealth is tolerated in pure capitalism. The whole system is based on competition between individuals, and the winner takes all. It is a Darwinian "survival of the fittest" mentality. Therefore, I am calling this "selfish" individualism.

And, of course, though it is a selfish system, modern capitalism produced the most productive, creative, and dynamic economy the world has ever seen. Still, vast class differences in wealth has left modern capitalist societies with terrible tensions, including a very high crime rate and a good deal of social disorder.

But modern high-tech capitalism does encourage individualism and self-development.

22.5.2 Democracy and Rational Individualism

If capitalism encourages selfish individualism, democracy encourages a more rational individualism. That is, in a democracy—ancient or modern—each individual gets to vote on policy matters. Of course, the debates are emotional, and demagogues play to the irrational elements of the human personality. However, once the vote is taken, the winning policy is established through rational, lawful, and constitutional institutions.

So even though there is a mix of irrational-emotional factors and rational policy factors, the final process demands rational lawful implementation. Every individual is expected to vote, and every individual is expected to understand the implications of the new policy that will be implemented.

This democratic individualism—the individualism of the citizen—is not fully rational, as mentioned, but it is not selfish and is, rather, community oriented. What

[5] Max Weber, *The Protestant Ethic and The Spirit of Capitalism*, NY, Random House, 1953.

is best for my city-state; what is best for my nation-state? These are community decisions—not communist, not socialist, but still community oriented.

Individualism is fully reinforced by the one-person-one-vote system of democracy. But it is not a selfish "Darwinian" individualism; it is a patriotic community-oriented individualism. Of course, if there is no consensus, such debates can tear a community apart. However, democracies can and do remain stable if the rational implementation of policies through lawful means is maintained.

22.5.3 Capitalism and Selfish Individualism in the High-Tech Industrial Economy

In nations that exhibit modern high-tech industrial capitalism and possess democratic governments, individualism is encouraged through excellent educational opportunities, career training, citizenship, and humanistic psychology.

So this brings us beyond Hegel and to Sartre and Maslow.

22.5.4 Sartre's Existentialism

Jean-Paul Sartre asserts that "God is dead, we are alone in the universe." Therefore, we, human beings, are free—free to develop our own ethics and our own life path.

Sartre focuses on the latter—the life path. He encourages every individual to develop themselves (Sne de Beauvoir was his life philosophical companion and lover).

Sartre insists that there are no cultural and psychological barriers that cannot be overcome if the individual persists in their quest for succeeding at their life goals.

Existentialism encourages self-development and demands self-fulfillment. It assumes that the individual can achieve what they see as their life goals, as long as they do not allow social, psychological, or political barriers to inhibit them.

Of course, this assumes a free and democratic society—and Sartre risked his life fighting the Nazis in France. But even in a country like Putin's Russia—before the Ukrainian War—an individual could pursue their personal and professional goals so long as they stayed out of politics.

In a free society—perhaps even in the capitalist sector of Chinese society—existentialism is an important encouraging philosophy for individual self-fulfillment.

22.5.5 Maslow Adds to Sartre's Existentialism—Self-Actualization[6]

In the USA, where psychology is emphasized more so than in Europe, Maslow developed the notion of "self-actualization."

Maslow states in advance that this cannot occur without political freedom, economic abundance, and educational opportunity. So Maslow is assuming that this self-actualization can only occur in a modern democratic capitalist society.

Maslow presents an elaborate "hierarchy of needs," which must be fulfilled before self-actualization can be undertaken.[7]

Like Marx, with his "species being,"[8] Maslow establishes that one's physical needs—food, water, and shelter—must be fulfilled and one's economic needs—good job and career—must be fulfilled, and political freedom must be in existence.

Then an individual can attempt to actualize their personal desire for some sort of creative achievement.

In this modern high-tech capitalist world, in which workaholic career demands can be overwhelming, individuals have been able to achieve some modicum of self-actualization.

That is, 50,000 people ran the New York City Marathon; thousands of would-be novelists are self-publishing and circulating their books on Amazon and Barnes & Noble. Individuals belong to poetry groups and artist communes in which their productions are circulated and judged for prizes.

So it is under modern high-tech capitalization, not utopian socialism, that self-actualization—species being—is being achieved.

Thus, as the entire globe goes through a convulsive and disruptive transformation, the hope is that as the great global transformation takes hold and alters the nations of the earth, self-actualization will become increasingly possible.

What Maslow emphasizes that goes beyond Sartre is that personal psychological barriers may exist that inhibit an individual's attempt to actualize their self-development. Various forms of modern psychology are therefore indirected by Maslow to free the individual from their psychological blocks so that self-actualization can occur.

Maslow's self-actualization goes beyond Sartre's focus on cultural and social blockages to individual development and focuses on psychological factors. Added to existentialism, the notion of psychological self-actualization adds the possibility of freedom from anxiety, depression, self-deprecation, and other psychological maladies that inhibit self-development.

To conclude, this modern individualism, within the context of a free, democratic, and high-tech capitalist society can reach a new level, as Hegel would call it. That is, individual self-consciousness is raised to a new, even higher level, such that every

---

[6] Maslow, Self-Actualization, in *The Hierarchy of Needs*, American Journal of Psychology, 1946.

[7] -

[8] -

individual may achieve some level of self-actualization and psychological "happiness."

It is the quest—the attempt—that is critical. One may not actually achieve one's life goals, but Sartre and Maslow want us to try. And Hegel asserts that the modern individual is conscious enough of his or her "self" that trying to achieve life goals is very likely, even if success is elusive.

22.6 Rational Science Is Amoral, So Humanistic Ethics Must Be Added to It

The rational-scientific worldview gives us an increased knowledge of the universe and everything in it—including ourselves—*Homo sapiens*.

But science is about knowledge; it contains no ethics. Scientists will discover cures for diseases, and they will make atomic bombs. The individual scientist will have ethical imperatives, but the science itself has no ethics in it.

So, as we explore the universe, we must add humanistic ethics to the scientific Zeitgeist: secular humanism or religious humanism—either, as long as humanistic ethics are made central.

The Chinese are attempting to put a moon station into existence on their own—this is just what we humans need to avoid. We do not want the militarization of space.

Space is so dangerous—so difficult for the human species to survive, in that cooperation will hopefully be forced upon all nations, including the Chinese. We shall see.

The manufacturer's authorised representative in the EU is Springer
Nature Customer Service Centre GmbH, Europaplatz 3, 69115 Heidelberg,
Germany. If you have any concerns regarding our products, please
contact ProductSafety@springernature.com

Printed and bound by CPI Group (UK) Ltd, Croydon, CR0 4YY
01/10/2026
02225953-0018